EFFECTIVE DATABASE MANAGEMENT

Alexander Gaydasch, Jr.

Prentice Hall, Englewood Cliffs, NJ 07632

Library of Congress Cataloging-in-Publication Data

GAYDASCH, ALEXANDER.
    Effective database systems.

    Bibliography: p.
    Includes index.
    1. Data base management. I. Title.
QA76.9.D3G39 1988   005.74   87-19364
ISBN 0-13-241472-4

Editorial/production supervision
and interior design: *Susan Fisher*
Cover design: *George Cornell*
Manufacturing buyer: *Barbara Kittle*

Printed in the United States of America

10 9 8 7 6 5 4 3 2 1

ISBN 0-13-241472-4

Prentice-Hall International (UK) Limited, *London*
Prentice-Hall of Australia Pty. Limited, *Sydney*
Prentice-Hall Canada Inc., *Toronto*
Prentice-Hall Hispanoamericana, S.A., *Mexico*
Prentice-Hall of India Private Limited, *New Delhi*
Prentice-Hall of Japan, Inc., *Tokyo*
Simon & Schuster Asia Pte. Ltd., *Singapore*
Editora Prentice-Hall do Brasil, Ltda., *Rio de Janeiro*

To Claire, for her patience and support.

CONTENTS

Implement   All Significant Corporate Data Can Be Maintained
in One Large Database   A Well Designed Database will
Contain No Redundancy   The DBMS ''model'' (Hierarchical,
Network or Relational) is a Key Selection Criterion   Logical
and Physical Design are Completely Independent   The DBA
or DRM is (or should be) the ''Czar'' of Information
Stewardship   A Database Reflects all Relationships between
Data   ''Data-Driven Design'' will Make the Analysis of
Processes almost Trivial   DBMS and ''Fourth Generation''
(4GL) Technology will make Application Programmers Extinct

PREFACE

Database Management Systems, commonly known by the acronym DBMS, are a hot item. The past decade has seen an extraordinary increase in their availability and use. About half of all data processing installations run at least some of their applications under a DBMS and a DBMS is available for practically every computer—from a micro to the largest mainframe.

Unfortunately, the popularity of DBMS software has also spawned more than its share of hype and unfulfilled expectations. Almost every new software product that reads and writes records is now called a Database Manager or Database Management System. Even the lowly filing cabinet is cheerfully referred to as "our database" by the clerk who files employee records in the personnel department. In fact, success has eluded many DBMS installations. The technology has been oversold, is not easy to master, and requires a substantial investment of human and financial resources.

Effective Database Management is an attempt to present database technology in a real world context, warts and all. In addition to the usual descriptive material, the reader is offered pragmatic insights generally missing from more theoretical texts. This orientation reflects knowledge gained almost entirely through actual implementations rather than through academic work.

The products we are primarily interested in are capable of:

- Processing thousands of update and query transactions per day
- Maintaining databases that range into the tens of millions of records
- Operating concurrently with other, non-DBMS applications

- Accommodating dozens of terminal users at the same time
- Maintaining a high degree of data integrity, backup and recovery

The emphasis of this book is, therefore, on mainframe products, not on DBMSs for personal computers. Although extremely useful, micro-based DBMSs are not currently designed for large scale, multi-user, multiprocessing applications. Of course, as personal computers become more powerful (more memory, faster speeds, higher volume peripherals, multi-user operating systems, etc.), the differences between PC-based products and their mainframe cousins will narrow.

This book is intended primarily for students wishing to supplement theoretical material with a more anecdotal, informal view of the technology. It may also be useful to practitioners who wish to develop a broader understanding of the subject. It is a practical guide to the selection, implementation and use of Database Management Systems.

Alexander Gaydasch, Jr.

1

WHAT IS
A DATABASE MANAGEMENT
SYSTEM?

PROLOGUE: A NOTE ON TERMINOLOGY

DBMS technology is replete with terms that often mean different things depending on context and on specific DBMS software. There is no standardized terminology, and this makes the job of teaching and the job of learning DBMS concepts more difficult than it should be.

The following guidelines are intended to help the reader understand the way terms are used in this book.

Field, Data Item, Data Element, Attribute

These are essentially interchangeable terms that describe the smallest unit of data of interest to us and to the DBMS. Customer Name, Invoice Number, Order Date, and Part Number are examples.

Entity, Record, Record Type

An *entity* refers to a person, place or thing of interest to our application. A Customer, an Order and a Part are entities. A popular way of starting the database design process is to think about entities and the processes in which they are involved.

Once entities are translated into something a computer can deal with, they become *records*. Thus, our flesh-and-blood Customer, who we initially thought of as an entity, becomes a Customer record containing fields such as Customer Number, Customer Address, Telephone Number, Credit Rating, and so on.

At first glance, this distinction may seem artificial. However, keep the following concept in mind: entities do not always become computer records and records do not always correspond exactly to entities. For example, a Customer Address may start life as an entity but may ultimately become part of the Customer record. The chapters on database development give a detailed account of how we derive records from entities.

Record type refers to the kind of record we are speaking of—Customer record, Order record, Part record, etc. It is really the name of the record and denotes its function. I will use the term "record" whenever I am not specifically referring to an entity.

Data Structure

A *data structure* is a diagrammatic representation of a database; it shows the record types used and the relationships between them. Data structures help us understand the application and aid us in the design of the database.

Occurrence and Instance

An *occurrence* is real data for one record of a specific record type. Thus, Jones Manufacturing Company is an occurrence of the Customer record and Small Clip is an occurrence of the Part record. When we refer to a specific occurrence, we usually say "the record for Jones Manufacturing Company." When we are speaking generically, we say "an occurrence of the Customer record."

An *instance* is real data contained in one or more records spanning different record types that are related. Order 1246 for the Jones Manufacturing Company, which consists of 1,000 Small Clips, 150 ⅛" Nuts, and 10,000 1" Bolts, is a single instance of the Customer, Order and Part records. In functional terms, it represents a complete Order for a specific Customer.

Data Model

A *data model* can refer either to a specific database design or to one of the theoretical models along which the major DBMS products that are in use today have evolved. These models include: *hierarchical*, which postulates that data relates in a superior/subordinate fashion; *network*, which advocates a structure that allows any record to relate to any other record; and *relational*, which rejects structure entirely in favor of two-dimensional tables. Each of these data models will be described in separate chapters.

CHARACTERISTICS OF A DATABASE MANAGEMENT SYSTEM

In a generic sense, a database—or data base (two words)—is a collection of interrelated data that can be accessed by an individual using a computer. Ideally, a database contains useful information that is shared by many people for a variety of purposes. In our context, however, a database is not a database unless it is under the control of a *Database Management System* (DBMS).

This rather complicated software product provides a comprehensive mechanism for defining a database and for storing, updating and accessing data in it. A database system differs from conventional systems in some important respects.

Conventional file systems are generally comprised of *flat* files or variations thereof. A flat file is a two-dimensional array of data items. That is, all records in a flat file are of the same record type. Thus, a Customer file contains Customer records, an Order file contains Orders, a Parts file contains Part records, and so on.

There are no connections between record types. A Customer record will not bring us to the Order records for that Customer; nor will an Order record provide us with Part records that describe what was ordered.

There are, of course, non-DBMS systems that use more complex variations of the flat file. However, they are rarely as full featured as a DBMS and they lack other characteristics that make DBMS products unique. A true DBMS must enable and support:

- Data independence
- Complex data relationships
- Control of redundancy
- Applications generality
- Ease of use

These concepts are central to our understanding of how databases work.

Data Independence

This is perhaps the most important difference between a DBMS and other software. In order to understand data independence we must understand the difference between the *logical* and *physical* aspects of data.

The term "logical" refers to the way data appears to the person accessing it. This could be a programmer, a customer service representative, a factory foreman, or a university registration clerk. Invoices that belong to customers, parts comprised of sub-parts, classes that are filled with students, are examples of the logical aspect of data. It is the business, or functional, dimension.

The physical dimension, on the other hand, is of interest mainly to technicians. It refers to the way the computer actually stores and manipulates data and data relationships. Naturally, the physical dimension must accommodate the logical dimension. Otherwise, the system won't work.

In older systems, if we wished to add a new field to a record, all programs using that record—regardless of whether or not they were actually using the new field—would need to be changed and recompiled. This is because the logical representation of the data in a file was identical to its physical representation.

The data independence that characterizes DBMS products enables us to change some definitions of data, and relationships between data, without the need for massive changes in application programs. This is called *logical independence*. Data independence also enables us to change many of the physical storage characteristics of data without altering its logical relationships. This is called *physical independence*.

Logical and physical independence isolates application programs from the data they use and enables relationships between data to be defined without dictating physical storage characteristics. This has profound implications for the design and maintenance of application systems:

- Programs accessing a database can be written without direct knowledge of its storage characteristics.
- Different programs and applications can have different *views* of data. Thus, a program needs to access only those parts of a database relevant to the work it is doing.
- Data element definitions can be changed without the need to modify programs that do not use those data elements.
- Physical storage characteristics can be changed for optimum efficiency, often without affecting the logical definitions of data.

Complex Data Relationships and Control of Application Data Redundancy

A DBMS provides an orderly method of representing complex data relationships without an excess of duplicated data that must be maintained by the application. In Figure 1.1, if we wish to relate students to classes to instructors using traditional files in a college registration system, we must maintain redundant fields in each record. The student's ID must be in both the student record and the class record. The instructor's ID must appear in the class record as well as the instructor record. Without the presence of these common values, students, classes and teachers cannot ''find'' one another. Furthermore, programs that update these records must not allow students to be mistakenly enrolled in a class twice, must check to be sure that a student enrolling for a course is properly registered, and so on.

A DBMS provides the mechanism for bringing related records together and automatically performs many of these functions. Figure 1.2 illustrates how a database structure might accomplish this.

Figure 1.1   Three Record Types in a "Flat File" Student Registration System

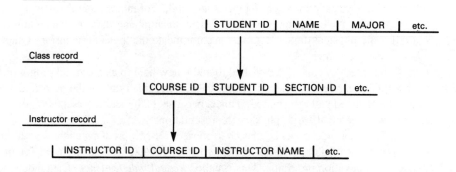

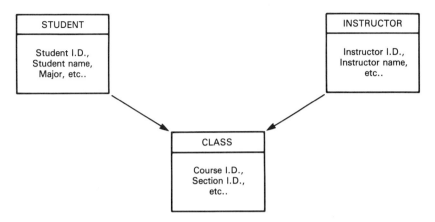

Figure 1.2   Three Record Types in a Database Student Registration

As we shall see later, a DBMS does not always reduce redundancy. In fact, it may even duplicate data. But a DBMS does reduce the possibility of error inherent in relying upon either an update program or an entry clerk to maintain the proper relationships between data. The DBMS software does this work.

The registration system example is relatively simple. A more true-to-life database is illustrated in Figure 1.3. Related records are connected by arrows. It would be extremely difficult to develop a traditional file system that would accurately capture the relationships between the twenty-two record types in this database.

Application Generality

A true DBMS can be used to support inventory, accounting, marketing, production, educational and other applications for a diverse clientele. If a product is capable only of supporting, say, bill-of-materials processing, it is not really a DBMS. Though useful for a specific purpose, it does not meet the criteria of generality.

Ease of Use

This is an elusive, subjective quality. In our context, ease of use means the presence of features that make the DBMS convenient for programmers, systems analysts and end-users—the people who develop the applications and the people who use the final product.

Programmers should be able to use conventional languages such as Cobol and Assembler to access data; analysts should be able to develop and maintain data and other system definitions without resorting to excessive paper documentation; and end-users should have flexible access and reporting capabilities that enable them to analyze data in new and different ways with minimum reliance on technicians.

The ease-of-use criterion is very relative. Some DBMS products are very complex and difficult to master for database designers and programmers. However, the alternative—developing applications with complex data structures using traditional file

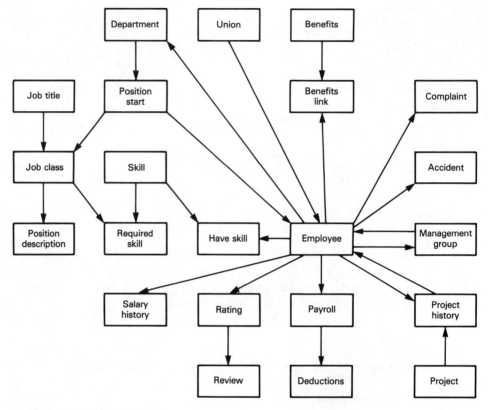

Figure 1.3 A Personnel Database

methods—may prove to be even more complex and will not enjoy the other advantages a DBMS offers.

What a DBMS Is Not

A DBMS is not simply a way to access data. Nor is it a storage technique. It is a comprehensive method for defining and using data. To mistake a DBMS for an access method or a storage technique would be like mistaking a house for its plumbing. The plumbing is important but a house consists of much more than water pipes.

A DBMS does not control a huge corporate database that is a comprehensive repository of all information needed by an organization.* No one can really identify all the data an organization uses. Even if this information could be defined, the physical limitations of today's hardware and software would make updating and access intolerably slow and cumbersome. In addition, an army of clerks would be required to keep the data accurate.

*This is not to say that a DBMS cannot control a database (or databases) containing data crucial to the operation of a business. There are many such databases.

A DBMS is not a "management information system" or a "data bank" or an "application." It is a software product that can be used to implement and control management information systems, data banks and other applications.

At the present time, a DBMS does not eliminate the need for traditional systems.* There are several reasons for this. First, a DBMS is highly computer-resource intensive. It would be wasteful to use it for applications that did not significantly benefit from its advantages. Second, if a firm uses packaged application systems (and most firms do), the probability that all of their packages will run on one DBMS is remote.

Finally, every data-processing installation, except the very newest or the very smallest, runs a wide mixture of application systems developed at different times and based on different technologies. It is neither necessary nor possible to rewrite every application to suit a specific DBMS.

A DBMS does not entirely eliminate data redundancy, the need for program changes when data is redefined, or other evils associated with traditional systems. It merely reduces these problems. As we shall see in later chapters, there are always trade-offs between taking maximum advantage of DBMS features, the need for high performance and a rational use of computer resources.

RELATIONSHIP TO OTHER COMPONENTS

How does a DBMS interact with the operating system, application programs and other parts of the computing environment? Figure 1.4 illustrates these relationships.

The operating system loads and begins executing an application program. The program requests access to a database by issuing *calls* to the DBMS. The DBMS translates these calls into information that enables the access method to find the desired data. The data then makes its way back to the application program, where it is processed. All of this is happening under the overall control of the operating system, a big, smart traffic cop.

The key difference between this arrangement and events in a traditional system (illustrated in Figure 1.5) is the interposition of the DBMS between application programs and the access software. It is this middle-man role that makes data independence and the other features of a DBMS possible.

Note the elements of a DBMS environment:

- An operating system
- Access software
- Computer hardware
- Application programs
- People
- The DBMS

An understanding of the relationships between these components is important. A DBMS

*DBMS and DBMS-like products are replacing traditional file systems. However, the process will probably take another decade to complete. Until then, DBMS and conventional systems must coexist.

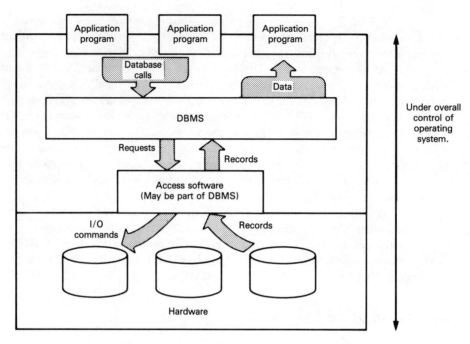

Figure 1.4 Interaction Between a Database Application and Other Components

must be compatible with the operating system, access software, and the hardware with which they operate. The hardware/software environment must also have adequate power. Compatibility and computing power, which includes disk storage and all other hardware capacity, is a critical part of the selection criteria for a DBMS.

Figure 1.5 Interaction Between a Traditional Application and Other Components

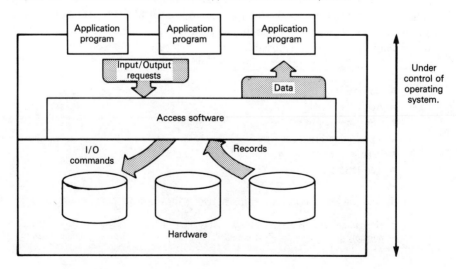

Application programs can be written in a language that is "native" to the DBMS or can be written in standard computer languages (e.g., Cobol, PL1, BAL). Because not all DBMS products support the major languages, this is another selection factor that must be considered.

A DBMS environment cannot exist without people who are familiar with the technology. This is part of the Database Administration (DBA) function and is discussed in the chapter on organizing the database environment.

THE CONSTITUENT PARTS OF A DBMS

The Database Manager

This is the heart of a DBMS, without which nothing else in the system can work. The Database Manager provides the ability to store, update and retrieve data. It also provides the ability to design the database and to change its design as needed.

The Database Manager works with the host operating system and the access methods native to the environment. The ability to use one or more languages with the DBMS may also be part of the Manager. However, because of the importance of this feature and because some DBMS vendors include one language with the Database Manager and additional language capabilities as options, we will treat this language facility separately.

Data Definition Language (DDL)

The Data Definition Language provides us with the means to describe our data to the DBMS, including data elements, records and the relationships between records. The use of the DDL results in the creation of a *schema*, which is a complete picture of our database and the rules by which it is to be accessed and updated.

Data Manipulation Language (DML)

The DML provides us with syntax that can be used in a Cobol, Assembler, PL1 or other standard programming language to navigate the database and find the record, or records, we are looking for.

If we wish to retrieve all the Part records for a customer's latest Order, for example, we must first find the desired Customer record, search his Order records until the latest Order is found, and then read all the Part records for that Order. DML gives us the facility to do this.

Host Language Interface

This component enables programs written in standard computer programming languages such as Cobol to access and manipulate data in the database. Instructions that are part of the Data Manipulation Language are coded into the program and are translated by the host language interface into chunks of code. This establishes a link between the application program and the DBMS.

The importance of the host language interface is threefold:

- Programmers do not need to learn a special language (other than the DML) in order to develop DBMS applications.
- Programs can generally be written in the language that is already in use at the installation.
- The most appropriate language for the task at hand can be used: assembly language when program execution speed is critical, Fortran for scientific applications, Cobol when ease of maintenance is important, etc.

PC-based DBMS products, as well as some mainframe DBMS's, may lack a host language interface. Instead, they rely on the power and capabilities of the "native" language developed by the vendor specifically for that DBMS.

Query Language

This is an English-language-like facility that enables people with minimum computer knowledge to access data and display it on a terminal quickly and easily. No programming in the traditional sense is required. Instead, a (generally) simple "DISPLAY CUSTO-MER-NAME, CUSTOMER-ADDRESS IF LAST-BUY-DATE = 850630" type of syntax might be used. Or, the query language might be in a tabular format. In this case, the user keys the values he wishes to select (e.g., all customers who bought after 06/30/85) into the appropriate column on the screen. All data meeting the desired criteria is then displayed.

The reason a query language is an important part of the DBMS is that most data processing installations experience difficulty in quickly responding to user demands for new ways of examining and manipulating data. A query language enables some of the work to be done by end users, thus freeing up computer people for more technical tasks. A DBMS without a query language is like a Cadillac without air conditioning: if you're going to spend that much money, you might as well get all the conveniences!

Report Writer

This is a close relative of the query language. Whereas a query language provides data to a computer terminal, a report writer produces paper reports.

Report writers generally provide English-like programming languages. These vary from the complex, which are almost full-function computer languages intended for computer programmers, to the very simple, which can do only basic calculations and formatting. In either case, report writers save time and money—for the end user and for the programming staff.

Screen Formatter

This is a facility that aids programmers in constructing screen formats ("painting a screen") without the laborious process of specifying the multitude of complex control characters required by the hardware and the operating system. This is an important DBMS feature because many database applications make extensive use of display terminals.

Utilities

A DBMS environment requires the extensive use of support software, including:

- *Load programs* to build new databases or reorganize the physical storage of existing databases after extensive use has caused storage inefficiencies.
- *Unload programs* to extract data from databases for use in other systems, for database reorganizations, and for making certain kinds of definitional changes.
- *Purge programs* to remove unwanted records.
- *Validity checking programs* to ensure that related records can find each other successfully.
- *Database dumps* that enable programmers and database technicians to view data in its raw form (i.e., in its physical rather than logical dimension).
- *Backup and recovery facilities* to ensure that important data is saved until an update cycle has been successfully completed and, in case of failure, to restore the damaged portion of the database.

The Data Dictionary (DD)

This is an important feature of any DBMS. It is a facility that enables programmers, systems analysts and end-users to document an application and its supporting databases and to control changes to same. Use of a DD can vastly simplify the paperwork involved in designing application systems.

In its basic form, a DD documents data definitions, relationships between records and between data elements, report formats, ''views'' that various programs have of the database, and other information that describes the database and the application system.

A more sophisticated DD generates the actual definitions needed by the DBMS to create and use the database. It may show the effect proposed definitional changes will have on various system components, and may even prevent the implementation of adverse changes—the removal of a data element needed by several programs, for example.

Many DDs can also document information about nondatabase files. Therefore, the same mechanism can be used for both traditional and DBMS applications.

The absence of a DD makes application development more difficult and defeats one of the major advantages of a DBMS—the imposition of a more orderly approach on the design process.

The above components are all necessary for a fully functional mainframe DBMS. However, they may not all be available from the same vendor. Although the database manager, the host language interface, and the utilities are usually packaged together, some of the other components may need to be purchased from other sources. As we shall see in the chapter on selecting a DBMS, a major criterion is the availability of these products—from either the DBMS vendor or from other sources.

In addition to the components we have discussed, other software may be included as part of the DBMS. Some products provide their own high-level programming language in lieu of, or in addition to, the host language interface, the query language and the report writer. Development aids such as program generators, which produce Cobol (or other) code based on English-like instructions, may also be included.

RELATED TECHNOLOGIES

Unlike hot dogs or peanut butter, software is not covered by truth-in-advertising laws. An overabundance of rodent hairs in hot dogs, or a scarcity of peanuts in peanut butter can result in the removal of the offending brand from grocery stores. Not so with software. Anyone can call anything by any name. At present, there are no official standards—no prescribed conventions or definitions.* In this climate, some software manufacturers make up the rules as they go along.

This causes confusion for people attempting to sift through the competing claims of many different products. In this chapter, I have tried to provide a workable definition of DBMS and a description of DBMS components. However, other software has DBMS-like features that are useful for people who do not need all the features a DBMS offers. Two types of related products are described below.

Data Management Systems (DMS)

The main purpose of DMS software is to automate certain repetitive data maintenance and retrieval tasks. DMS languages are designed to provide maximum results with minimum programming effort.

The most popular DMS product is probably MARK V, which offers a powerful report writer/query language and some file maintenance capabilities. Other products include Quikjob, CULPRIT, Easytrieve, Data Analyzer, and RAMIS II.

A key difference between these products and a DBMS is their emphasis on access to existing files, rather than the creation and use of new data structures.** When new files are built, they do not usually have the range of structural options—both logical and physical—offered by a DBMS.

DMS software does not usually provide as much data independence or redundancy control. In addition, it usually lacks the comprehensive backup and recovery features normally included in a DBMS. DMS products are oriented toward a single application, rather than toward the integration of multiple applications using a common database.

Although most DMS products are general purpose, some are designed for a specific function. An example is the Statistical Analysis System (SAS), which generates statistics from data files, as well as providing some other data manipulation capabilities.

An important footnote to any discussion of DMS and DBMS products is the in-

---

*The National Bureau of Standards and various data processing organizations have made attempts to implement industrywide standards. For a variety of reasons, mainly having to do with the Wild West nature of the marketplace, official standards have not been workable. The closest thing we have are the de facto standards created by vendors such as IBM through their power in the marketplace.

**There are exceptions. Some DMS products are compatible with, and can even create, DBMS files.

creasingly blurred distinction between product types. As data manipulation software grows more powerful and becomes an integral part of many applications, the important question is "what features do we need?" not "what label does the product carry?"

Fourth-Generation, User-Friendly Development Tools

DBMS packages first came into popular use during the third generation of computer hardware—that is, in the 1970's.

Fourth-generation software was so dubbed not only because its introduction coincided with fourth generation hardware, but because it was supposed to usher in a golden age of easy-to-use technology for building application systems quickly. Since every software vendor wants its products to have an up-to-date image, the term "fourth-generation" has been sorely abused.

The better fourth-generation products seem to have one or more of the following characteristics:

- At least some usability by people with little or no data-processing expertise
- A friendly report writer/query language
- Automated documentation facilities, such as flowcharting software and data dictionaries
- Prototyping facilities that allow interactive screen design and data manipulation
- Interactive program development
- The ability to generate Cobol or other standard language codes from simple instructions

Many products that predate fourth-generation terminology have some of these characteristics. In the sense that a DBMS provides a data dictionary, a report writer/query language, and other components that help the application developer, it can be said to be a fourth-generation development tool. But the main thrust of DBMS software is not the provision of tools as such; it is the capability to define, manage and use complex data structures.

A SUMMARY OF BASIC CONCEPTS

This summary of DBMS concepts is intended to aid the reader in understanding the chapters that follow. It is not a substitute for the more detailed descriptions found in the chapters that describe major data models, normalization and the steps of database development.

A database and the DBMS software by which it is controlled can be examined from two perspectives: the external, or *logical*, representation of data and processes; and the internal, or *physical*, representation. We have already touched on this dichotomy in our earlier description of how a database differs from conventional files.

The following concepts are primarily logical. They deal with how the programmer, systems analyst and end-user see and describe data.

- Structures and tables
- Sets

- Relationships
- Keys
- Normalization

Other important concepts are associated with the physical aspects of data—the way data is actually recorded on the hardware medium. Although they influence the logical world, they are of greatest interest to database technical specialists. Physical concepts include:

- Addressing
- Pointers
- Physical layouts

Here, then, is a quick explanation of both physical and logical concepts. Understanding them will make the rest of the book easier to follow.

Structures and Tables

In a database context, a *structure* is nothing more than a diagrammatic representation that helps us think clearly about data. Two commonly used structures are the *tree*, or *hierarchy*, and the *plex*, or *network* structure.

Tree and plex structures are illustrated in Figure 1.6. The difference between

Figure 1.6 Data Structures

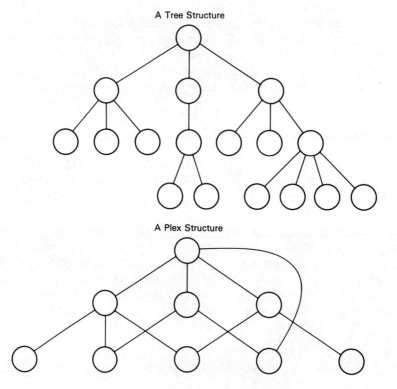

A Tree Structure

A Plex Structure

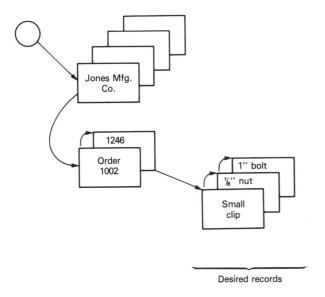

Desired records

Navigation steps;
Find Jones Mfg. Co. customer record.
Read order records untl last (latest) is read.
Read all parts records for that order.

Figure 1.7 Navigating a Database

them is in the rules they follow: trees are strictly hierarchical; networks are "free-for-all"—any point in the structure can be connected to any other point. The chapters on hierarchical and network data models describe tree and plex structures in detail.

We *navigate* a database structure when we wish to find a specific record or records. Suppose we wish to access all the Parts records for the last order placed by the Jones Manufacturing Company. First we find the Customer record. Then we search the Order records for Jones Manufacturing until we find the most recent one. Finally, we read all the Parts records for that Order. This is illustrated in Figure 1.7.

Tables provide a nonstructural alternative for analyzing data and designing databases. They are two-dimensional, flat files consisting of *rows*, which are analogous to records, and *columns*, which represent record attributes. Tables are generally used when designing relational databases and are described in detail in the chapter on the relational data model. A sample table is shown in Figure 1.8.

Invoice number	Order date	Customer number	Sales person	Terms	Order amount
1246	4-14-85	0127	122	C	$22,575.00
0761	6-17-85	0254	003	N30	1,200.00
1002	5-21-85	0127	122	C	95.00
0845	1-13-86	0307	400	N30	12,640.00
0998	12-12-86	5652	400	C	50.00
1001	12-12-86	0914	921	C	2,850.00
0004	3-01-86	5652	003	N60	1,070.00

Figure 1.8 A Table

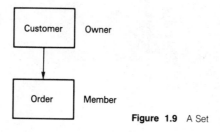

Figure 1.9 A Set

Sets

A *set* is a two-level structure consisting of one *owner* record and one or more *member* records. Figure 1.9 illustrates a set in a Customer Order database. Set definitions are used primarily in designing network databases and have an important influence on the ultimate physical layout of data. Hence, the concept of sets is almost as much a physical as a logical phenomenon. See the chapter on the network data model for more information.

Relationships

Relationships between data give us perhaps the most important information we need to design a database. There are two generic types of relationships: *one-to-many* and *many-to-many*.

One-to-many relationships are hierarchical. The relationship between a Customer and an Order, illustrated at the top of Figure 1.10, is an example of a one-to-many relationship.

Many-to-many relationships are not hierarchical and can only be represented by a network structure. The relationship between Parts and Orders in a Customer Order database is an example of a many-to-many relationship: an Order consists of many Parts, and a Part can appear on many Orders. This is illustrated at the bottom of Figure 1.10.

One-to-many and many-to-many relationships, as well as several special cases, are described in detail in Chapter 5, The Hierarchical Model, and Chapter 10, The Steps of Database Development.

Keys

A *key* is an attribute that uniquely identifies a record. Customer Number is an example of a key. Keys are described in Chapter 8, Normalization.

Normalization

Normalization is a formal process of organizing data into records and fields with as little redundancy as possible. It is a technique usually associated with relational databases but can, in fact, also be used with other data models.

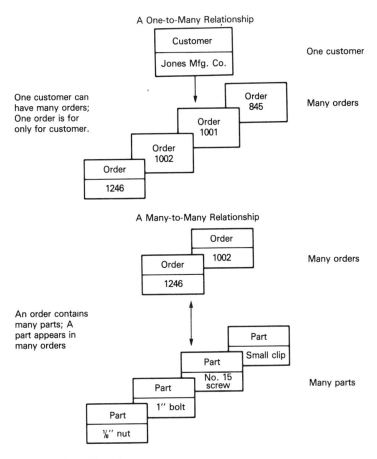

A One-to-Many Relationship

One customer

One customer can
have many orders;
One order is for
only for customer.

Many orders

A Many-to-Many Relationship

Many orders

An order contains
many parts; A
part appears in
many orders

Many parts

Figure 1.10 Relationships

The process of normalizing data consists of analyzing how the values of some data attributes fix or determine the values of other attributes. The creation of tables then proceeds based on this analysis.

The degree to which we have succeeded in eliminating redundancies is reflected in the state to which we have normalized our tables: *first normal form, second normal form* and *third normal form* are progressively higher stages of normalization.

Addressing

Just as navigation deals with the logical dimension of finding records in a database, *addressing* deals with the physical dimension.

The simplest way of finding a record is to search sequentially through a group of physically contiguous records until the desired record is found. This can be done by reading each record in sequence, as in Figure 1.11. However, if our records have a key and are stored in sequence by that key, we can do a *binary* search, which often brings us to the

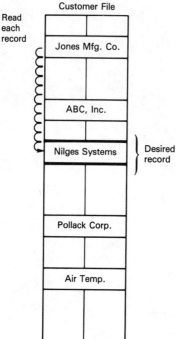

Figure 1.11 A Sequential Search

desired record with fewer read operations. An example of a binary search is illustrated in Figure 1.12.

The first read operation in a binary search goes to the middle of the file. If the key of the record read is higher than the key of the record we are looking for, we travelled too far. We cut our distance in half and read down the file. If the new record found has a lower key than the desired record, we have gone too far down. We must proceed to go up the file by half the previous number of records. This process continues until we find the desired record.

We can also use an *index* to find records. An index works in conjunction with a "main file" that contains most of the data for a particular record type or types. As Figure 1.13 shows, each entry in the index file contains the locations of records with specific values. Thus, we confine most of our searching to a comparatively small file, the index, in lieu of laborious searching larger files.

Direct access addressing techniques involve converting a key into a unique positional indicator or hardware address that is used to find desired records without the need to perform multiple read operations. The most common techniques for doing this are:

- Using the key itself as a relative positional indicator (e.g., Customer Number 1246 is the 1,246th record in the file).
- Using a *hashing algorithm* to convert a key to a unique (or almost unique) positional indicator.

Product-specific addressing techniques are described in the chapters on data models.

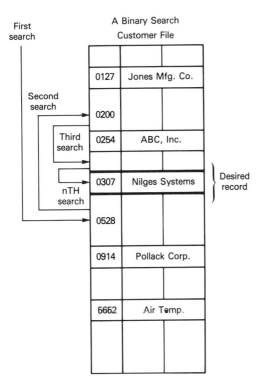

Figure 1.12 A Binary Search

Pointers

Pointers are covered extensively in the chapters on the hierarchical and network data models. They are fields within a record that contain the addresses of related records. Pointers can point to other occurrences of the same record type, to the first (or last) occurrence of the subordinate record type, or back to the owner record. Pointers are illustrated in Figure 1.14.

Figure 1.13 Indexes

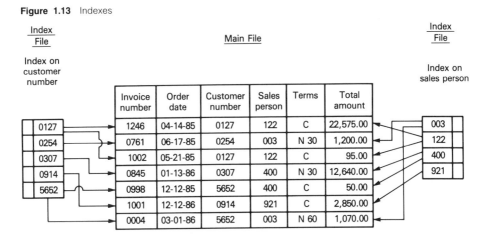

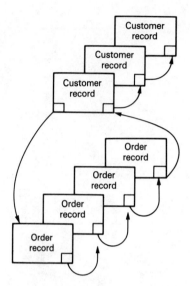

Figure 1.14 Pointers

Physical Layouts

The records that constitute a database can be arranged on the hardware storage device in a variety of ways. Groups of related records are placed in specific *areas* that function more or less independently—despite the fact that they are all part of the same database and are governed by the same software. Related records within each area can be contiguous or can be widely separated but connected by pointers. Figure 1.15 illustrates the use of areas.

Free space consists of empty spots strategically located throughout the database

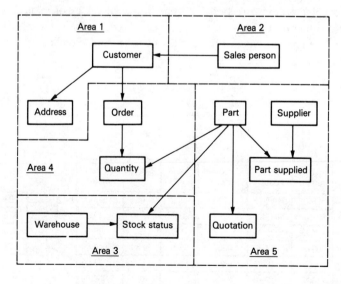

Figure 1.15 Areas

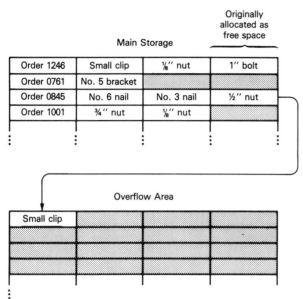

Main Storage			Originally allocated as free space
Order 1246	Small clip	⅛″ nut	1″ bolt
Order 0761	No. 5 bracket		
Order 0845	No. 6 nail	No. 3 nail	½″ nut
Order 1001	¾″ nut	⅛″ nut	

Overflow Area

Small clip			

Figure 1.16   Free Space and Overflow

that are reserved for the insertion of new records. *Overflow* is a special part of disk storage, often at the end of each cylinder, that accommodates records that do not "fit" into the prime storage area. Overflow is used when the free space scattered throughout the main area of the file becomes filled or when "collisions" occur—that is, when a hashing algorithm produces the same address for records with different keys. Figure 1.16 illustrates free space and overflow concepts.

Physical layout concepts are covered in greater detail in the chapters on data models.

DISCUSSION QUESTIONS

Name and describe the five characteristics that make a DBMS unique.

Does installation of a DBMS eliminate the usefulness of traditional file systems? Why or why not?

Describe how a DBMS plays a middleman role between application programs and data.

Name four of the major components of a DBMS.

What is the difference between a DBMS and a Data Management System?

2

WHO NEEDS
A DATABASE MANAGEMENT
SYSTEM AND WHY?

INTRODUCTION

Now that we know what a DBMS consists of and what makes it unique, let us look at the benefits it offers, its drawbacks, and the conditions under which its acquisition is appropriate. Contrary to some database gurus, DBMS software vendors, and other enthusiasts, the use of a DBMS is not universally appropriate. In this chapter we will examine the pros and cons of DBMS technology and discuss the business and organizational factors that should influence the DBMS decision. An important part of that decision is costs—how do we identify DBMS-related costs and isolate them from the normal costs of running a conventional file environment?

You may wish to revisit this chapter after you have read the more technical sections of the book.

ADVANTAGES OF A DBMS

Some DBMS benefits reflect the features that make it different from other products; other benefits are not necessarily limited to a DBMS environment but are more difficult to achieve in non-DBMS installations.

An Ordered, Consistent File Design Methodology

In contrast to conventional file systems, a DBMS offers not only greater flexibility for structuring data, but a greater opportunity for design discipline. Several important things tend to happen:

- The designer is forced into careful, extensive analysis when defining data and relationships because the DBMS cannot function without this information.
- The complexity of the design process often prompts the DBMS vendor to provide lessons in data analysis and design techniques. This is extremely helpful and is the only time many analysts receive formal training of this sort.
- The ability of databases to serve multiple applications encourages a broader, less parochial view of data. This contributes to better integration between systems.
- The use of a data dictionary, which is rarely found outside a DBMS environment, helps standardize the data design process and documents the resulting data structure.

Some DBMS advocates believe that DBMS applications can be developed faster than traditional applications. The discipline of an ordered file design methodology, the presence of a data dictionary, the availability of query languages and report generators, etc., are mentioned in support of this contention.

However, real-life experience shows that this is not always true. Even after the initial, expensive learning period, the complexities of DBMS systems and the organizational and technical interactions required to implement them may negate development advantages.

**Complex Data Relationships and Control
of Application Data Redundancy**

This allows the design of databases with very complex structures. Without this unique capability, an awkward amount of data redundancy would be required and some applications would not be feasible.

Easier System Changes

Because of data independence, some changes to data definitions can take place without reprogramming. This is a great advantage. System maintenance becomes easier and the system becomes more responsive to changing user needs.

Increased Data Integrity

A DBMS supports data integrity in the following ways.

Control of Redundancy   The amount of data redundancy is often lower in a DBMS-based system than in a traditional system. The reason for this is the ability of the DBMS to support complex data structures. This encourages the development of databases that are more comprehensive than conventional files. It results in fewer data elements that need repetition in different files to satisfy different applications.

The significance of reduced redundancy is not so much in the saving of storage space—although this can be important, especially for large databases—but, rather, in the reduction of update errors and in the elimination of inconsistencies.

If a data element exists in three files, all designed at different times for different purposes, its meaning may vary from system to system. Even if the definition is the same, the value of the element may differ depending on the time of the month or the point in the business process at which it is updated.

Identifiers that tie related records together must generally be repeated in flat file systems. Their accurate updating depends on the quality of the application program that performs the update. With DBMS, this updating can be done automatically.

Automated Enforcement of Relationships between Records The enforcement of desired relationships, such as the need for a Customer record before an Order record is added—and, conversely, the need to keep a Customer record until all of the orders are fulfilled—can be done automatically with a DBMS.* In a traditional system, such enforcement must be done in the application program—a potentially complex, error-prone procedure.

Security Provisions Security and "need-to-know" considerations may require the ability to keep prying eyes away from certain data. A DBMS has the ability to restrict user access to certain parts of the database. Depending on the sophistication of the DBMS, unauthorized parties may be locked out of part of a database (e.g., the payroll portion), selected types of records (e.g., salary records), or selected record values (e.g., payroll records for people outside the specific user's department).

Control of Overlapping Updates and Queries This is one of the most complicated technical issues in data management. It is of critical importance when more than one person will be accessing and/or updating a database at the same time. The following example illustrates the significance of this issue.

In an on-line customer order system, stock availability information must be absolutely accurate. Each order clerk's withdrawal of stock from inventory to satisfy a customer order must immediately be reflected by the system. This way, another customer placing an order at the same time will not be misinformed about the availability of an item.

If one person is updating and another is examining the same record at exactly the same time, misinformation could occur. Suppose one red plaid shirt is in stock. Mary, one of our order clerks, receives an order for a red plaid shirt. Before Mary finishes processing the order, Bob, another clerk, gets an order for the same shirt. He accesses the "red plaid shirt" record (as yet unmodified by Mary's order) and finds that a shirt is still available.

---

* Not all DBMS products are capable of enforcing this kind of relationship. See the chapters on DBMS models.

By the time his customer has given Bob all the information necessary to place the order, Mary finishes recording her order, which triggers a subtraction of one red plaid shirt from stock. Bob's customer has already hung up the phone and is happily anticipating the delivery of his shirt, which will never arrive.

A good DBMS can prevent this kind of problem through the use of lockout procedures. In our example, Bob would have received a "record in use" message until Mary finished placing the order. The shirt record would then have indicated an out-of-stock condition.

Restart and Recovery   Hardware, software and people are imperfect. Therefore, computer systems must have provisions for minimizing the damage that can result from feeding last month's data into the computer by mistake, experiencing a hardware failure, encountering a previously undetected program bug, and other problems.

A DBMS provides a number of restart and recovery facilities. One such facility is a provision for restarting jobs at predetermined checkpoints instead of always returning to the beginning of a jobstep. Another facility is the ability to store before-and-after images—that is, the contents of records immediately before and after they are updated—on a special journal file. This is useful when part of a database must be restored. It enables restoration of the database to its original condition if bad data was applied (roll back) or to its changed condition if the updated portions were destroyed (roll-forward).

More Extensive Use of Common Data Between Applications

One of the most important bottom-line goals of a DBMS is to enable different applications to share data. For example, management has traditionally complained that their accounts payable system wasn't very well integrated with the inventory systems, which, in turn, didn't link very well to the general ledger system. If a manager wanted a report combining data from all three systems—say, a match between orders, receipts and payment—a fairly complex process of extraction, sorting, matching and even manual checking had to take place. It was complicated and took a substantial amount of time to complete.

A DBMS helps solve this sort of problem. Relationships between data can be defined with greater ease. Each application has its own view of data and does not, therefore, carry the extra baggage represented by unneeded data. Complex relationships—inevitable when structuring data to satisfy multiple applications—are easier to implement than with traditional file arrangements.

Unfortunately, many DBMS installations have not made much progress in achieving systems integration. The main reason is that identifying data relationships for a single application is difficult enough; it is even more difficult, given time constraints, to forge understandings with other departments on how their data is to be represented in a specific database or databases.

Thus, each system still tends to be built with a single user in mind. When related systems are developed, it is often easier to build more databases than to retrofit. Major structural changes, though easier with a DBMS than with conventional systems, are still troublesome and disruptive.

Improved Accessibility of Data

Data accessibility really means four things: the data must be there to begin with—that is, it must be on machine-readable media; it must be structured in such a way that logical connections between related elements can be made; software must exist for retrieving the data; and, lastly, this software must be flexible enough to allow selection based on a variety of data values and conditions.

In conventional systems, logically related data cannot always be accessed because it is scattered over multiple incompatible files. A straightforward connecting mechanism such as a common identifier may not exist; and, even if it does exist, the programming needed to pull data out of files with different file structures can be very time-consuming.

Data tends to be more accessible in database systems because it is more likely to be under the control of the same DBMS. Logically related data can be brought together more easily. Query languages, report writers and other data access aids that are normally part of the DBMS software can also help make the process easier.

The Practical Ability to Develop Sophisticated Applications

Some data structures and business requirements are so complex as to defy conventional solutions. Although in theory almost any application can be built using the older file structures, in practice it can be very clumsy and time-consuming—and the resulting system may be very inflexible and difficult to maintain. A DBMS may be the only realistic solution.

Figure 2.1 illustrates DBMS benefits by contrasting a DBMS environment against its traditional counterpart.

DISADVANTAGES OF A DBMS

Mainframe DBMS products are complex, expensive, and use a large amount of computing power. Here are their major disadvantages.

High Start-Up Costs

The cost of selecting, acquiring, and installing DBMS software can be high. In addition, developing the first application is almost always a frustrating experience that costs far more than using conventional files. If hiring new staff and using consultants proves necessary, the process becomes even more expensive. Expensive birth pains accompany every installation. Major DBMS costs will be discussed later in this chapter.

TRADITIONAL ENVIRONMENT	DBMS ENVIRONMENT	BENEFITS
Each application has its own master file with some overlapping data.	Data can be used for multiple applications; data is stored only once.	Control of redundancy.
Each file is updated separately. This is often done at different times by different systems, resulting in discrepancies.	One program updates data in one (or a few) shared databases.	Increased data integration.
Changes in data definitions or record sizes must be reflected in every program accessing the file.	Data descriptions are separate from application programs. Only programs using changed data may need modification.	Easier system changes.
Usually one or few access paths are defined. Additional retrieval must be custom-built.	Can automatically maintain many access paths, giving more ad hoc flexibility.	Improved data accessibility.
Programmers supply their own data definitions and names—often without regard for the needs of other applications.	Programmer must use data names and definitions approved by DBA. These are usually maintained in a data dictionary.	Consistent design methodology.
Data security must be implemented by the programmer.	DBMS software controls data access.	Increased data integrity.
Automatic recovery is not provided, or is provided in limited form by the operating system. Standard recovery is difficult to define and implement.	Recoverability can be automatic. Transactions against the database are logged and restoration can be done to the last intact record.	Increased data integrity and security.

Figure 2.1 The Benefits of a DBMS Environment

Technical Complexity A DBMS requires substantial experience and knowledge. The rules for defining logical relationships and the many options usually available for physical storage and access are not mastered in a day. Very large differences in performance can result from seemingly minor design changes.

Much of this work is done by database experts. However, applications analysts must also have a solid understanding of how physical storage, retrieval and updating takes place under various design alternatives. They must understand backup and recovery procedures, how and when concurrent processing is permissible, and other complex technical subjects.

Programmers must learn how to use the programming tools available with the DBMS. These include the Data Management Language (DML) used in conjunction with Cobol, Fortran and other conventional languages; ad hoc query languages; report writers; screen formatters; and various support utilities.

Need for Increased Staff

A DBMS installation cannot function without database experts. These usually include a database administrator (DBA) and various technicians. Although in-house staff can be trained in these roles, most companies hire at least one person from the outside to organize the environment, help train people and direct the implementation of the first DBMS application.

In the long run, overall staff requirements may return to pre-DBMS levels, if use of the DBMS simplifies and speeds up the creation of reports, queries and less complex applications. The "applications backlog" is invariably cluttered with many requests that could easily be handled by user-friendly DBMS tools—if the data were available in convenient form.

Inefficient Resource Usage

A DBMS is designed to operate with reasonable efficiency for a wide variety of data structures and applications. In a sense, it is meant to be all things to all people. Therefore, it usually cannot match the efficiency of a well-designed conventional file system that is targeted specifically for one application.

Because of its generalized nature, a DBMS contains a vast amount of software overhead. DBMS application programs must traverse more layers of software than their conventional counterparts before any useful work is accomplished. In addition, DBMS data retrieval and storage technology, which must satisfy a wide variety of potential needs, is frequently not as efficient as custom solutions.

Difficulty Handling Large Transaction Volumes

The resource problem described above precludes the use of most commercially available DBMS's for very high transaction volume systems, or those which use exceptionally large databases (i.e., hundreds of millions of records). Such applications are poor candidates for a DBMS solution. A customized application developed by absolutely top notch talent is required.

The following sections identify factors that must be considered when deciding if acquisition of a DBMS is appropriate. They describe application needs and organizational characteristics that justify the use of a DBMS, including the need for integrating major applications, the presence of complex data relationships, the need for system flexibility, and the willingness to invest in major new development efforts.

Major factors that should be considered are functional and organizational. Functional factors are application and data-oriented. They address the characteristics of key applications likely to run under the DBMS and the data these applications will use. Organizational factors address the ability and willingness of the company to pay for the DBMS—both in terms of dollars and in terms of organizational change.

FACTORS THAT FAVOR A DBMS

Factors that tend to favor the acquisition of a DBMS are described below.

Complex Data Relationships

Perhaps the single most important justification is the presence of complex data relationships between significant data. The stress is on "significant." Since even the smallest organizations have some inherently complex data relationships, the importance, usability and volume of data represented by those relationships must be significant to justify a DBMS. Systems in which the relationships between data are relatively simple do not require a DBMS.

Suppose that we are in the software business and offer a variety of products that run on a wide variety of computers and operating systems. Let's further suppose that we offer several different purchase and lease plans depending on the buyer's status (e.g., an educational institution) and geographic location. (We have special agents that take care of customers in faraway places.) For this application we need to establish some complicated relationships between data.

The salesperson must be aware of the specific version of the product appropriate for a particular customer—there are about 150 choices—in order to quote the correct price, refer the customer to the proper service agency and prepare the right contract.

The order entry person must verify that the correct computer/operating system combination has been keyed. Otherwise, the wrong version of the product will be sent. Finally, customers that share the same version must be sent correct new releases and must be put in touch with people in the company who can answer their questions.

This requires a complex maze of data relationships. If we had used conventional file structures, we would be hard pressed to make the system answer very basic questions without extensive effort and redundancy. Specific questions, such as "How many of our customers use the basic version of the system on a Dec 20 running under the TOPS20 operating system?" and "How many of these customers are behind on their maintenance payments?" would be difficult to answer.

The Need for Systems Integration

Systems integration is needed when data relationships cross application boundaries or when the same information is carried in multiple files.

A system such as payroll may not need to be integrated into many other systems. Its only relationships may be with the general ledger system to record payroll expenses and with the personnel system to update job classifications. (In fact, both of these functions can probably be done in ''batch'' mode, which makes system integration even less critical from a timing and control standpoint.)

An order entry system for a company selling sophisticated industrial machinery, however, is a different story. The accounts receivable system must be checked to see if the customer owes on any previous purchases; the credit system (or a credit service bureau) must be queried to verify creditworthiness; the product master file or catalog system must be checked to verify the availability of the technical features being ordered; and the inventory file must be checked to see if the item is in stock.

At this point, we have done only our preliminary work—now we can write up the order! This brings additional systems into the picture: the production control system, if we are going to build the item; the billing system to prepare an invoice; the customer service system to prepare a ''welcome'' letter if this is a new customer; the sales commission system to pay the salesperson, and so on.

The Need for Ad Hoc Reporting and Data Access

Ad hoc means ''for the particular end or purpose at hand and without reference to wider application.'' In a computing context, this means the ability to get data in ways that were not anticipated when the application was developed.

Although many software packages allow relatively easy and flexible access into traditional as well as DBMS files, the value of such software is enhanced in a DBMS environment. The presence of all (or most) of the information needed for an application in one place provides us with data that is more consistent and meaningful.

High Level of System Changes

Because of the independence of data from programs in a DBMS environment, some changes to data definitions and relationships can be made without reprogramming. Therefore, a system that may require many changes over time is a good candidate for use with a DBMS.

Systems that are most prone to extensive changes are those without a well-defined manual or automated predecessor. Systems which automate procedures that have been in place for a long time tend to change less.

Extensive Decision Support vs. Transaction Processing Requirements

A transaction processing system is an application designed primarily to produce tangible products, such as customer bills or payroll checks. Information needs for such a system are fairly predictable because the system repeats the same series of processes week after week and month after month. Ad hoc data retrieval requirements are minimal.

A decision support system (DSS) or a management information system (MIS),* on the other hand, are applications designed primarily to provide information for decision making. The type of information that will be needed and the way it must be accessed is more difficult to predict than for a transaction processing system. Therefore, the data structuring, integration and presentation mechanisms that are part of every DBMS may be needed.

In practice, most transaction processing systems have some DSS/MIS capabilities. Conversely, even the most information-oriented systems often provide a tangible product.

Progressive, Experimental Attitude

Some organizations nurture and encourage progressive thinking. Their "corporate culture" fosters an adventurous attitude toward new ways of serving their markets, more advanced ways of building their products, and more effective ways of motivating their employees. Companies that possess such an attitude are more likely to try new data processing techniques. More importantly, they have the patience required to make the new techniques work.

Successful Long-Range Planning

An important benefit of using a DBMS is that it can provide a useful mechanism for building future application systems that are integrated.

However, this building-block approach cannot effectively be utilized unless the firm takes long-range business planning seriously. Without such planning at the corporate level, EDP management cannot effectively prioritize and plan future applications. Systems continue to be developed in a haphazard manner, even with the presence of a DBMS.

Willingness to Defer Benefits

Some firms pay serious attention to the long term as well as the short term. New ways of doing things need not always be justified on the basis of next quarter's or next year's bottom line.

A DBMS is a long-term investment. Unlike some types of software, a DBMS will not immediately begin to yield benefits. In fact, costs will increase until the first application has been implemented and has begun to reflect the advantages of the new tech-

---

* Although DSS and MIS are not really the same, their differences are irrelevant for our purposes. DSS consists primarily of "what if?" and other modelling capabilities applied to historical information derived from data files. Its orientation is to help people make decisions now. MIS, on the other hand, is more generic, covering any aggregate or individual information that is of interest to management. Presumably, it, too, will be used for decision making but its impact is more subtle and less immediate. Potential product pricing alternatives based on various labor and materials combinations is an example of DSS. Monthly sales reports provide an example of MIS.

nology. This may take several years—a fact data-processing managers are well advised to make clear to management.

Willingness to Recognize Intangible Benefits

Even after several DBMS applications have been implemented, specific dollar benefits are difficult to attribute directly to the DBMS. The data processing budget will probably continue to rise; systems will still be expensive to develop; and some of the more subtle benefits of DBMS processing may not be obvious except to old-timers who remember doing things the old way. Therefore, management must be willing to recognize some improvements that cannot be measured in dollars and cents.

Management Commitment

This is an essential element of any DBMS acquisition. Management must understand the difficulty of learning the new technology and the length of time it will take for benefits to become visible. Continuing commitment from top management will encourage both users and computer people to persevere.

Ability to Staff the Database Administration (DBA) Function

The use of a DBMS requires a support organization that helps systems analysts and programmers design and implement databases. This DBA organization coordinates data definitions and provides other services needed in a DBMS environment.

   Hiring and training EDP staff to design DBMS-based applications is difficult enough; acquiring even a small staff of real experts can be overwhelming. Small companies and firms that do not pay competitive salaries may have difficulty maintaining the DBA function.

FACTORS THAT MITIGATE AGAINST A DBMS

Although there can be many good reasons to acquire a DBMS, some factors make such an acquisition questionable. Here are the most important such factors.

Very High Transaction or File Volumes

A DBMS is designed to be useful to the greatest number of customers. Flexibility, ease of use, and the ability to represent a large variety of data structures inevitably conflict with efficiency in handling very large volumes of data for specific applications.

Adequacy of Present Systems

Usually, new products are not acquired unless old ones become unsatisfactory. However, managers sometimes rush into a new technology for the same reason Hillary climbed Mt.

Everest: because it's there. This may be a noble goal in sports but not a very rational way to run a business. If present conventional file systems are doing an adequate job—even if major modifications are sometimes required—it is probably unnecessary to convert to a DBMS.

Substantial Conversion Costs

Selecting, implementing and using a DBMS is expensive. One of these expenses may be the cost of converting old data files to the new DBMS environment. This conversion process can include:

- Developing programs that will "clean," rearrange, and otherwise prepare data for loading into a database.
- Manually analyzing data that cannot be adequately manipulated by the computer. This can be an extremely lengthy, labor-intensive process.
- Comparing the results of the new DBMS-based system against results from the old system. Parallel tests can go on for months before the system is made to work properly.
- Rewriting existing systems to make them compatible with the new DBMS applications. If introduction of a DBMS will require massive changes to other systems, costs may outweigh benefits.

COST CONSIDERATIONS

Few organizations attempt a thorough assessment of costs when selecting a DBMS. They assume that state-of-the-art software always represents progress. Unfortunately, the adoration of new technology is not always a good business practice. An attempt must be made to ensure that the acquisition and use of a DBMS is justified—even though extensive guesswork about costs and benefits may be required.

Significant expenditures of time, energy and money that will accompany the acquisition and use of a DBMS should be examined. One convenient way to do this is by looking at the cost picture from a number of perspectives covered in the following sections. A checklist of major cost groupings is found in Figure 2.2.

Fixed vs. Variable

Fixed costs are almost entirely use-independent. That is, they remain relatively stable regardless of how many DBMS-based applications are developed.

Fixed costs come in two categories: the cost of buying, installing, and maintaining the DBMS; and the cost of learning the product, as reflected in the mistakes, false starts and longer-than-normal development associated with the first application. These fixed costs will be incurred whether the DBMS is used for many applications over the years or if it is abandoned after the first one.

Variable costs are those associated with use—that is, with the development of each DBMS application. The significant learning component of the first application doesn't count—it is a fixed cost. Neither do costs that would be incurred regardless of the technology used (requirements definition, program specifications, etc.).

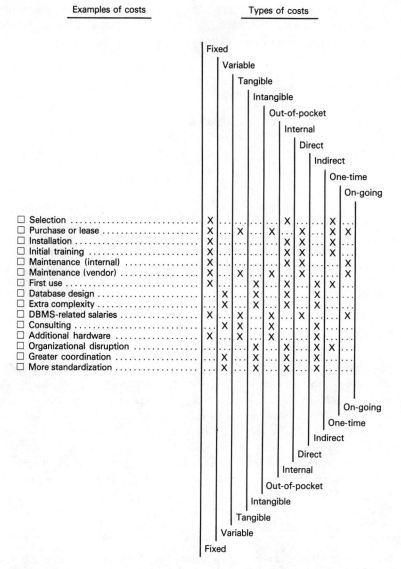

Figure 2.2 Summary Checklist of Costs

Tangible vs. Intangible

Tangible costs are palpable and concrete. They should always be assigned a dollar value. Examples are:

- The cost of purchasing or leasing the DBMS

- Salary costs for a Database Administrator and other DBMS experts
- Consulting costs
- The cost of additional hardware

Intangible costs are those that cannot be defined or calculated with any reasonable degree of precision. They include:

- Organizational disruption caused by the new technology
- The need for greater coordination between data processing groups
- The need for more standardization and more bureaucratic rules and procedures

Intangible cost estimates may be attempted or may be described without assigning dollar figures. If intangible costs are estimated, the basis of calculation should be clearly stated. For example: each programmer/analyst will spend approximately one hour per working week in various coordination tasks resulting from the presence of the DBMS. At an average benefit-inclusive rate of $40 per hour for 50 programmers, this will result in an annual cost of about $104,000.

Because a dollar value can ultimately be assigned to any "cost," there is really no clear distinction between tangible and intangible. It is largely a matter of perception and accuracy. Tangible costs tend to be attributable to specific individuals, jobs, and hardware/software components. Intangible costs tend to be less attributable to specific people or machines, and are more difficult to estimate.

Out-of-pocket vs. Internal

Out-of-pocket costs represent payments to an outside party. They are "real" in the sense that a financial obligation is incurred.

Internal costs represent "payments" that groups within a company make to each other (e.g., the accounting department "buys" time from the corporate computer center). Internal costs may result in a shift of priorities, a substitution of one type of activity for another; but they do not directly result in extra expenditures.

Incidentally, great care must be taken—especially in large organizations—to sort out politics from reality in the establishment of internal costs. A data-processing organization may, for example, decide to encourage greater use of a specific computer or operating system by setting artificially low rates. If these low rates do not reflect the out-of-pocket costs of leasing and maintaining the equipment, we end up with an unrealistically favorable cost/benefit formula. If, on the other hand, prices for use of a crowded machine are inflated, we may be discouraged from pursuing an otherwise reasonable alternative.

Out-of-pocket costs consist of payments a company makes to vendors, suppliers, employees and other parties. These are more immediately felt than internal expenses and are considerably more straightforward: they are set by the marketplace and are not influenced by internal company politics.

The immediacy of out-of-pocket expenses generally makes them more difficult to justify than internal expenses, which result in budget manipulations rather than direct expenditures of cash. A firm may be willing to rearrange its data processing priorities and internal budgets to accommodate a DBMS, thus sacrificing less important activities or applications—but may be unwilling to spend more money.

Here are some examples of out-of-pocket costs:

- The cost of DBMS software
- The cost of extra hardware that must be acquired to run DBMS-based applications

Examples of internal costs are:

- The time spent evaluating DBMS packages
- The time needed for maintaining complex DBMS software

Direct and Indirect

Direct costs are those that can be specifically and entirely attributed to the DBMS. They include:

- DBMS software
- DBMS support staff
- Maintenance payments to the DBMS vendor

Indirect costs are those that can only be partially attributed to the presence of the DBMS. They should, therefore, be estimated on a pro-rata basis. Indirect costs may include:

- A hardware upgrade needed to support a more powerful version of the operating system—which, in turn, significantly enhances the capabilities of the DBMS.
- Development of new standards, which may be needed in any case, but which are given a higher priority with the introduction of the DBMS.

One-time vs. On-going

One-time costs are fixed costs that are incurred only at the beginning of the DBMS project or at significant future junctures —major hardware upgrades, for example. One-time costs include:

- DBMS selection and installation
- A hardware upgrade to accommodate the DBMS
- Education and training at start-up time

On-going costs are fixed costs that continue as long as the DBMS is in use. They include:

- The salary of the Database Administrator (DBA) and other DBMS support staff
- DBMS maintenance fees to the vendor

The Significance of Cost Categories

Fixed, variable, tangible, direct and out-of-pocket costs can give us a fairly accurate indication of the ''real'' costs involved in the DBMS decision. Projections of intangible, indirect and internal costs are usually less accurate but help expose hidden costs. A distinction between one-time and on-going costs is also useful. It is needed in order to plan cash outlays and to realistically amortize DBMS costs.

Most costs fit into more than one category: for example, DBMS maintenance fees are fixed, tangible, out-of-pocket, direct and on-going. Hardware costs can be both fixed, in that they don't change with each application, and variable, in that the hardware in many installations is upgraded every few years.

In the following sections, DBMS costs are described in the context of the major "events" that comprise the life of the DBMS: selection, start-up, development of the first application, and continued use.

DBMS Selection Costs

DBMS selection is extremely important and is described in the next chapter. Costs associated with the selection process are both internal and out-of-pocket. Expect the selection process to continue for at least three months and involve a variety of people on at least a part time basis. One or more people will frequently be assigned full-time.

The major activities that take place during selection are:

- Requirements definition
- Development of evaluation criteria
- Preparation of a Request for Proposal (RFP)
- Identification of, and contact with, potential vendors
- Product evaluation
- Final selection

These activities involve a considerable amount of work—three-to-ten, or more, person months, depending on company requirements. Perhaps more importantly, they drain resources from other projects.

Implementation and Start-up Costs

Following is a description of the costs associated with introducing a DBMS into the company.

The DBMS Package and Supporting Components   The cost of the DBMS and supporting software represents the most obvious out-of-pocket expense incurred by the company. Costs can vary widely depending on features, hardware size and the vendor's eagerness to gain new customers.

A DBMS for mini and mainframe computers can cost as little as ten thousand dollars or as much as several hundred thousand. DBMS products for personal computers are priced in the mid hundreds to low thousands. Minicomputer versions of a DBMS are usually less expensive than their mainframe cousins. In addition, a product's popularity and reputation add to the price. Newer systems from start-up firms tend to be less expensive than established products.

It should also be noted that software is often sold without some of the components we discussed in Chapter 1. The query language, report writer, and other components that make the DBMS convenient and useful may be extra-cost options.

Additional Hardware and Software   Software vendors tend to overstate the performance of their products for a specific machine configuration. More often than not, an upgrade is needed soon after installation. The original operating system may also be inadequate, necessitating a move to more advanced software.

Training   The level of free training provided by the DBMS vendor is usually sufficient to enable database design to begin. However, the in-depth education needed by the DBMS support staff and technically inclined analysts often costs extra. Travel and lodging expenses may also be incurred for less-frequently taught out-of-town courses.

Database Standards   Although database standards developed at the time the DBMS is implemented are usually not very good, a preliminary version should be written. (Standards developed after a DBMS has been in use will be more accurate and realistic.) Implementation of a data dictionary is also recommended. Standards and a data dictionary will encourage an orderly approach and will lessen the inefficiencies resulting from lack of experience.

Costs of the First Application

Unless the first application is very modest, its development costs will probably be two or three times higher than the cost of comparable future applications. No matter how much education and training is provided, lack of hands-on experience slows down development and makes it more expensive.

The following are some extra costs that frequently accompany the first application.

Design Mistakes   The design of any DBMS application must eventually take into account the physical storage and retrieval activities that lurk behind the scenes. However, documentation and courses cannot cover all the nuances of such a complex product. There is no substitute for hands-on experience. As more applications are developed, fewer design mistakes are made and less rework is needed. Each succeeding application becomes less expensive to develop.

Package Inadequacies   Unfortunately, new software products—as well as new versions of mature products—are sometimes brought to market before they are fully tested. An attractive feature may prove difficult to use, very resource-consuming—or, it simply may not work. Even mature products have bugs and misleading documentation. In either case, the first application will unearth inadequacies that cannot be learned in class or from manuals.

Need for Outside Help   Often, it is impossible to fully staff the first DBMS project internally. Lack of experience makes for unacceptably long development schedules that can only be shortened through the use of consultants. This is obviously a more expensive proposition than doing the entire job in-house.

Need for Backup and Recovery   Although specific backup and recovery requirements must be identified for each application, the DBMS features that support these requirements, once learned, are not difficult to clone. Making sure that backup and recovery are successful the first time is the hard part.

Confusion over Roles and Methods   The responsibilities of various groups in a DBMS environment will depend to some extent on people's unique personalities and skills. For example, in a company where systems designers are highly technical, the DBA may play a lesser role than in a shop where designers have more of a business, or functional, orientation.

Since practical organizational arrangements must be established through actual experience with the DBMS, time may initially be lost through disputes, misunderstandings and lack of direction. By the second or third system, the development process becomes more smooth.

The absence of tried-and-true design techniques also hampers the first application. No database development methodology—including the one discussed in this book—can be effective until it is customized to its specific environment. Even then, it must be used extensively before people feel comfortable with it. In fact, the most common situation is that the first application is developed without the use of *any* recognizable methods or standards. An appropriate methodology—and the discipline to use it—often does not enter the picture until the second, third, or even fourth application.

On-going Costs

The following categories represent costs that will continue for as long as the DBMS is in use.

The DBMS Package and Supporting Components   If the DBMS is leased rather than purchased, its out-of-pocket cost is on-going. (Incidentally, the penalty for leasing is generally high: the lease/buy break even point arrives in one to three years). If the DBMS is purchased, it may be amortized over a period of three, five, or more years depending on tax provisions and other financial considerations.

Standards Maintenance   The use of sophisticated software requires increased attention to standards. The development and maintenance of DBMS-naming conventions, preparation of guidelines for the use of various product features, and the establishment of other standards require time on the part of both development and DBMS support staff. Although standards development often takes place in spurts, it should be continuous.

Support Staff Salaries   Even a small DBMS installation usually has a database administrator—perhaps a current employee that performs data administration activities on a part-time basis. Medium-size shops may have as few as one person, or as many as half-a-dozen people, supporting DBMS activities. A data administration staff of ten or more is not unusual for larger installations.

Increased Control and Coordination   Interaction between people costs money. Approvals, discussions, meetings, and company politics can be time-consuming. A DBMS environment requires more, not less, interaction. This is an intangible cost that must be borne by all DBMS users.

Learning Curve for New Personnel   As the use of database technology becomes more widespread—over 50 percent of all minicomputer and mainframe installations already use some form of DBMS software—the cost of training new people will diminish: more and more programmers and analysts will come equipped with DBMS skills. For the forseeable future, however, demand for people with DBMS experience will continue to outstrip supply. This situation forces companies to incur training costs.

Software Maintenance   Software requires maintenance. In addition to the fees charged by the DBMS vendor, about ten percent to fifteen percent of the purchase price annually, "fixes" must usually be applied by company personnel on company time. This ties up computing resources, requires work by technical support personnel, and may even necessitate some application program changes.

In addition to deliberate, planned fixes and enhancements, bugs will inevitably appear. This happens with all products, but in complex DBMS software each bug is likely to be costlier. It will be more difficult to find and more time-consuming to fix.

Database Maintenance   Databases must occasionally be unloaded and reloaded to optimize their physical distribution on mass storage devices. This is especially true for large databases with a high rate of change. Although similar reorganizations are performed against flat files, their greater simplicity and inherent limitations make the process less frequent and less costly.

A NOTE ON MICROCOMPUTER-BASED DBMS

Both the advantages and disadvantages of using DBMS products designed for personal computers will be somewhat different than for their mainframe cousins:

- The complexity of data structures successfully handled by micro-based DBMS products is limited.
- Security, backup, and recovery procedures can also be meager. This is not a positive attribute, considering the fact that a one-thousand-record customer database for a small liquor store is just as important (relatively speaking) as a ten-million-record customer database for a large auto-parts distributor using a mainframe DBMS.
- Since PC-based DBMS applications are normally used by one individual at a time, many PC products do not offer the lockout and other concurrency features common to mainframe products.

- The time, commitment and hardware/software investment in a PC-based DBMS is not great. Therefore, start-up and operating costs are minimal.
- Organizational considerations are largely irrelevant. There are no special data-processing skills required to develop applications using PC DBMS products.
- Whereas mainframe DBMS products have difficulty handling *very* large volumes (e.g., tens of millions of records), many PC products may have difficulty handling even modest amounts of data (e.g., thousands of records).
- Virtually all sophisticated data-management products for personal computers use DBMS (or DBMS-like) technology—and most of those are based on the relational data model. So there is really not much of a choice between DBMS and conventional file systems for the PC unless you insist on building applications from scratch. Barring very unusual requirements, the data management software you use on your PC will be a DBMS and will be relational.

DISCUSSION QUESTIONS

Name and describe three advantages of a DBMS. Name three disadvantages.

Describe four factors that favor acquisition of a DBMS. Identify two factors that mitigate against a DBMS.

What is the difference between tangible and intangible costs? Direct and indirect costs?

Describe two important start-up costs.

Identify two differences between mainframe and micro-based DBMSs.

3

CHOOSING
A DATABASE MANAGEMENT
SYSTEM

INTRODUCTION

The selection of an appropriate DBMS (or DBMS's)* is extremely important to an organization. In many ways, it is more significant than selecting any other major software component. First, the impact of a DBMS will be felt throughout the entire company—not just in one or two functional areas. Second, a DBMS can consume computing resources at a startling rate, often necessitating significant hardware upgrades. Finally, this decision affects the most people. Unlike an application package, which usually needs only to be implemented and then maintained, or a system software component, which is likely to chug away in the background, a DBMS requires across-the-board support from installation through maintenance by almost every group in the data processing department.

The steps that must be taken in selecting a DBMS, however, are similar to the process of selecting other software. The selection process is organized and the selection team chosen; requirements are defined; evaluation criteria are developed; a request for proposal (RFP) is prepared (this is optional); potential products are identified and product information is gathered; products and vendors are evaluated based on the selection criteria; and the DBMS is selected. These steps are illustrated in Figure 3.1 and described in the following sections.

*Many organizations now have, or are in the process of acquiring, their second DBMS. In most cases, one of the older hierarchical or network models was installed in the 1970's for high-volume "bread and butter" applications. This was followed by the need for a more flexible relational or relational-like product in the 1980's. The older systems act as feeders to the relational DBMS.

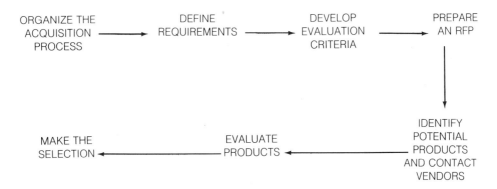

Figure 3.1 The DBMS Selection Process

ORGANIZING THE ACQUISITION PROCESS

The purpose of this step is to define how the selection and acquisition process will take place. It consists of planning the process and assembling a team of people to carry it out. The plan contains a list of tasks that must be completed in order to make the selection, a completion schedule for each task, and a list of task responsibilities.

The selection process should be managed with the same care reserved for important systems development and maintenance projects. Since a large measure of subjective judgement must be involved, it is tempting to continue the process indefinitely, thus postponing a decision. This should not be allowed to happen. Selecting a DBMS is not open-ended and the selection team must understand that the decision can never be risk-free.

The Selection Plan

Create a GANNT chart such as the one illustrated in Figure 3.2. It should contain specific task assignments, milestones, completion dates and, if desired, approximate person hours that will be required.

The GANNT can be at a high or low level of abstraction, depending on the magnitude of the effort and the importance placed on detailed planning in your organization. At minimum, it should contain the seven major tasks described in this chapter. Further detail may be added by subdividing each major task into subtasks of several days to one week in duration.

There is a great deal of overlap between tasks. For example, we can begin identifying potential products and contacting vendors for information almost immediately. Detailed requirements need not be known to begin the search. Likewise, we can begin filtering out obviously unacceptable products before our evaluation criteria are completed.

The GANNT should be updated each time a formal status meeting is held. Bi-

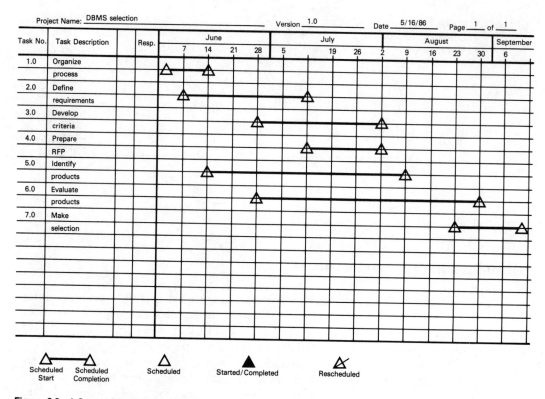

Figure 3.2   A Sample DBMS Selection Project Schedule

weekly or monthly updates are usually sufficient. Hopefully, your installation has an automated project control system that will save you from preparing the GANNT (or similar representation) manually.

The Selection Team

This selection team should consist of individuals who represent different vantage points and possess a variety of skills. The composition of an ideal team is as follows.

Team Leader   This individual is responsible for leading and coordinating the selection process. The team leader is the ranking member of the team and should have superior analytical and writing skills; substantial EDP experience in programming, systems analysis and project management; and should be a person who is respected by members of management.

Database experience is not essential and may, in fact, be counterproductive if it results in bias toward a specific product.

Software Specialist   A significant factor in the success or failure of a DBMS is system performance. Other indicators are the success with which current operating software can absorb the products under consideration and the extent to which changes to the environment must be made.

Since the software specialist knows the "bits and bytes," he or she can advise the team on these matters. Database design and tuning experience is highly desireable.

Systems Analyst or Programmer/Analyst   This should be a person with significant recent experience in programming and other technical activities—preferably in a database environment. This team member helps evaluate the systems development and programming facilities offered by candidate DBMS products.

Knowledgeable User   If the DBMS is being acquired primarily for a specific functional area of the company, a knowledgeable representative from that area should be on the team. He or she helps evaluate the "user friendliness" of query and ad hoc reporting facilities and, to a lesser extent, assesses the ability of each product to meet data structure requirements.

The opinions of an end-user can be extremely important because data processing people tend to ignore the importance of end-user facilities. This can result in excessive attention to technical elegance at the expense of user-oriented features.

Incidentally, the selection team need not literally consist of one person for each of the above roles. Multiple roles can be combined in a single individual. For example, the team leader can also be the software specialist.

DEFINING REQUIREMENTS

After the selection process has been organized, the team can begin to define its requirements. The decision to acquire a DBMS is usually prompted by the need to develop a major new application; it may also be prompted by the need to integrate several existing applications in order to provide better data in a faster, simpler, more timely fashion. Whatever the major impetus, requirements definition must consider the following:

- The most important (or first) application that will be developed under the DBMS
- Likely future DBMS applications
- Companywide data needs
- EDP goals
- Constraints

The driving force behind requirements definition is the first, or major, DBMS application. Although this flies in the face of currently fashionable theory regarding the importance of corporate data, it is the only workable approach in most situations. Only a tangible application can provide the specificity, immediacy, realism, and organizational support needed to build a comprehensive requirements definition.

A DBMS should not be selected exclusively or primarily in support of the *corporate data model*. If such a model exists—and there are very good reasons for developing one—it should be taken into consideration along with the other factors described in this chapter.

Each factor in the requirements definition is described below.

Application Requirements

Application requirements that influence DBMS selection are the characteristics of data for the application and the way that data will be processed. Requirements analysis tasks should include modelling application data, determining data volumes, estimating data volatility, identifying the types of processing that will be done, and defining necessary controls.

Modelling   The structure of application data must be determined first.

Ideally, the data model should be entirely independent of the specific DBMS that is ultimately selected. In other words, it should provide us with a picture of how data appears to a person rather than how it is stored by a specific DBMS. The model should be detailed enough to give us a notion of key data and relationships we wish to include in the first application, as well as major future applications. (See the chapters on database development for information on how much database design should be attempted prior to the selection of a specific product.)

Later, during the product evaluation phase of the selection process, the model may be transformed into data structures specific to the products being evaluated. These data structures can then be evaluated according to our selection criteria.

Database and Transaction Volumes   Knowledge about database and transaction volumes enables us to judge the relative importance of DBMS features that facilitate fast, high-volume processing. The volume of various record types that comprise the database is estimated as part of database design. Transaction volumes must also be estimated. This is done by examining the amount of business that impacts the major application, or applications, that will be built under the DBMS.

Transaction volume estimates may include:

- Average daily volumes
- Peak daily volumes for high and low seasons (e.g., December vs. February in the retail trade)
- Peak processing times (e.g., lunchtime telephone orders)

These specific volume categories are not always relevant and, for some application systems, volume is not terribly important. For example, as long as disk storage space is available and we can spare the extra off-shift processing time, a batch payroll system can pay ten thousand employees as efficiently as it can pay two thousand.

Data Volatility   Data volatility is the degree to which a database changes during the course of a single day or other time period.

Data volatility goes hand in hand with database and transaction volumes. If a large proportion of a database changes each day or hour or week, the DBMS must have a good set of data reorganization utilities. Otherwise, performance will soon take a nosedive.

Data volatility must be stated in terms of the number and percentage of records that are changed, added, and deleted daily. Changes to existing database records are of interest because they reflect the intensity with which accessing takes place. This impacts system performance. The addition of records is even more significant.

To accommodate the new data, space must be found on the section of the storage device allocated to the database. This may result in the shifting of existing records and a less-than-optimum placement of new records. (The most efficient placement of records is always achieved when the database is initially loaded. From then on, performance degrades until the database is ''reorganized,'' or reloaded. There will be further discussion of this topic in later chapters.)

The significance of all this is that volatile data requires a DBMS with a reputation for high performance—even if other features must be sacrificed.

Type of Processing   The way data is accessed and manipulated is closely related to data structure and volume analysis. Neither is meaningful without the other. Processing factors that must be considered are:

- The need for *real time* processing—that is, the ability to update records when changes are keyed into the computer, rather than periodically, as in batch processing.
- The extent of *on-line* query processing vs. on-line (or real-time) update processing. On-line processing means that updates are keyed in at a terminal but not necessarily applied immediately; real time update processing requires instant update as well as entry.
- The number of people who will access and/or update data simultaneously.
- The degree to which predefined vs. ad hoc queries and reports are needed.

Processing factors will influence the relative importance of efficient on-line work, the ability to handle many concurrent users, and the power and friendliness of query and reporting languages. Since there are always trade-offs between these features, the type of processing is an important determinant in the selection process.

Control Requirements   This includes security, backup and audit controls. Specific needs that must be considered are:

- Data sensitivity (i.e., the importance of protection against unauthorized access to data)
- The cost of recreating lost or destroyed update transactions
- The cost of recreating a database
- The importance of audit trails

The features available for protecting data and providing audit trails vary widely between DBMS's. That is why a definition of control requirements is important.

Corporate Data Needs

If it is used to its full potential, a DBMS should provide access to important data across applications. Therefore, we should not limit the requirements definition to the specific needs of the application for which the DBMS is being acquired. This means taking an educated guess as to the needs of future applications as well as the needs expressed in the corporate data model.

Some organizations choose a DBMS specifically for the purpose of storing information derived from a variety of sources and then facilitating its presentation in a fast, flexible manner. In this situation, the processing of data is left up to individual systems, such as inventory control or accounts payable, which then feed the "access only" application.

Selection of a DBMS for this purpose is still subject to the same rules that apply to products purchased for transaction-oriented applications.

The Needs of the Computer Department

In selecting a DBMS, the data processing department must pursue its own needs as well as fulfilling the needs of its clients. Data processing needs include the following:

- Compliance with installation language standards
- Ease of use for programmers
- Quality software support
- Comprehensive technical documentation
- The ability to change data definitions without massive reprogramming
- An acceptable level of computer resource usage
- Maintainability by internal technical staff

No matter how successful a DBMS is at fulfilling end-user requirements, it must still operate in harmony with other computing resources.

Constraints

A needs definition must contain selection constraints. These usually include:

- Maximum staffing levels that can realistically be marshalled in support of the DBMS. Budget limitations, as well as the availability of people, must be considered.
- Skills. This is the degree of sophistication current staff is able to achieve in order to work effectively with the DBMS.
- Hardware at the installation, including permissible upgrades.
- Operating and other types of software with which the selected DBMS must be used.
- Programming languages of choice.
- Application development schedules; some DBMS packages can be implemented more quickly than others.

The final activity in the requirements definition step of the selection process is the summarization of requisite features. The concise requirements list will be used in the next step to determine the relative importance of the selection criteria we will develop.

The sample needs summaries towards the end of this chapter illustrate the requirements for a large health-care library abstract system and an order entry system. Note the virtues of brevity and good organization in defining requirements.

This concludes the requirements definition step of the selection process. We will now develop evaluation criteria.

DEVELOPING EVALUATION CRITERIA

After requirements have been identified and a summary list has been prepared, evaluation criteria are developed. This is done by creating a list of potential considerations to be used in selecting the DBMS and determining the relative importance of each consideration for a specific set of circumstances. A comprehensive list of evaluation criteria and an abbreviated checklist are found in the last two sections of this chapter.

As these sections show, evaluation criteria can be rather technical. Don't be put off by this. As you examine DBMS products and learn more about database technology, your criteria will become less general and more technically specific. Here, then, are the tasks involved in developing evaluation criteria.

Create a List of Potential Considerations

Unlike requirements definition, which can proceed with little direct knowledge of database technology, the development of evaluation criteria requires an understanding of DBMS capabilities and features.

For example, in some applications, it is very expensive to rekey transactions when system failure occurs. This translates into the need for comprehensive journaling facilities. The awareness that such a technical feature exists—and may be more effective in some products than in others—provides a specific focus that would be impossible without an understanding of DBMS technology. Such understanding is gained by reading books and articles about databases, attending seminars and classes, and by reviewing product literature.

However, it is important to avoid interaction with vendors in the early stages of this process. Evaluation criteria are best developed without the prompting of salespeople, who are likely to prejudice the list toward their product. (As we shall see later, our evaluation criteria will, in fact, change and become more specific as we study individual products; nevertheless, the first cut should be as comprehensive and as nonproduct-specific as possible.)

Determine Relative Importance

The most common method of indicating importance is to assign numerical weights of 10-100 to each criterion, depending on its significance. Increments of ten are probably the most useful. Zero should not be used because if a consideration is of no importance it should not appear on the list. In addition to numerical weights, we must identify mandatory DBMS features. This is necessary in order to weed out unsuitable products early in product evaluation. Here are some hints on how to determine importance:

- The ability to process transaction and database volumes with reasonable efficiency is absolutely critical. If volumes are low, this criterion is easily met and, therefore, becomes relatively unimportant. If volumes are high, it becomes the single most important consideration.
- When file volatility is high and substantial on-line updating must be performed, the ability of the DBMS to efficiently move data around on the storage medium is of great importance.
- The ability of the DBMS to represent data relationships in a reasonably "natural" way is important because this may impact access efficiency and ease-of-use. Tortured, roundabout techniques to overcome inherent product limitations often prove unsatisfactory.
- Good utilities and development tools, such as a data dictionary, are also important. These features will tip the scales in favor of a product that contains them.
- Structural integrity features that will prevent the addition of incomplete data—for example, an invoice record without a customer record or a customer record without an address field—are important. This is expecially critical for customer service or financial applications.
- Record lockouts and other concurrency controls are needed if many people will be using the system at the same time.
- Journalling facilities are important if data is difficult or expensive to recreate.
- Good query and report languages are also important— particularly when the applications are supposed to provide extensive ad hoc query or report capabilities to end-users.

Application characteristics that place the greatest demands on a DBMS are:

- High on-line transaction volumes
- High data volatility
- Extensive on-line vs. batch processing
- Complex data relationships
- Extensive backup and recovery needs
- Extensive ad hoc vs. standard queries and reports

The determination of relative importance should culminate in the assignment of numerical weights to each evaluation criterion. This is an iterative process. We must experiment with the assignments to be sure that key considerations are not lost through disproportionate weighing of less important features.

For example, if we use fifty criteria and ten of them relate to highly important characteristics, we must be sure that the numerical gap between important and less important criteria is significant. This will provide a clear "win" for a product that meets important criteria but rates poorly in less critical areas.

PREPARING A REQUEST FOR PROPOSAL (RFP)

Preparation of an RFP is usually optional but it is a highly recommended step in the selection process. The RFP is a document given to selected vendors before the evaluation step begins. It contains requirements specifications, instructions on how and when the vendor is to reply to the RFP and, of course, the basis on which the vendor's products will be judged—the evaluation criteria.

RFPs are useful for these reasons:

- Specifications developed only for internal consumption tend to be less comprehensive and specific than a document sent to vendors.
- The formality of the RFP process encourages objectivity, which is sometimes lacking in a less formal approach. This translates into a stronger justification for the selection that is finally made.
- Because the RFP forces a consistent, organized approach, it saves time in the long run—even though time must be spent developing the RFP.
- A formal RFP forces everybody to do their homework. After all, the quality of the vendors' responses will reflect the quality of information provided to them.
- The RFP is the most effective way to organize competitive bidding. It is, in fact, required by law for many governmental organizations.

The requirements specifications section is the key element of the RFP. Unless the language and concepts are clear, an intelligent response will not be possible. It is particularly important to remember that the vendor may not be familiar with application- or industry-specific terminology; therefore, its use should be avoided whenever possible.

Instructions to vendors are also important. These guidelines explain the mechanics of the bidding process and the contractual arrangements that will be required. More importantly, in a DBMS selection, vendors may be asked to design a database from information on the data model developed during the requirements definition step. If this is inadequate, a vendor cannot demonstrate a meaningful database design.

Vendor instructions should consist of the following:

- Contract provisions that must be included in order to be responsive to the RFP.
- Dates by which proposals are due.
- The required format for the proposal. This is important because much time can be wasted comparing proposals done in different formats.
- The names, business addresses, and telephone numbers of selection team members that can answer vendor questions.
- Expected proposal contents—that is, information that must be included in the proposal. This will probably include background information on the vendor, as well as the detailed solutions the vendor proposes in response to the requirements definition.

The evaluation procedures section of the RFP describes the method that will be used to evaluate vendor proposals. This is where our evaluation criteria, complete with weighing factors, comes in. Also included are planned agendas for meetings and presentations that will take place during the selection process.

The steps needed to select a DBMS are very similar, with or without the use of an RFP. The key difference is in degree of formality. After potential vendors have been identified (see next step), the RFP is sent to them. A preproposal meeting is usually held to explain the RFP in greater detail and to answer questions. Formal proposals are then expected.

IDENTIFYING POTENTIAL PRODUCTS AND CONTACTING VENDORS

Datapro, the *ICP Software Directory*, Auerbach journals, and similar publications are excellent sources of information on DBMS products. So are trade journals such as *Computerworld*. Colleagues at other companies are also a helpful resource.

Based on a careful review of these sources, an initial product list is compiled. However, a neat division does not always exist between DBMS's and related products, such as data management systems. Therefore, care must be taken to search multiple categories for candidates.

The following minimum standards should be met before a DBMS is included in the initial product list:

- *Age*. Unless it is commonly known that a DBMS has gone through substantial revisions (e.g., IBM's IMS), avoid products that are more than ten or fifteen years old. Remember, some of the products listed in *Datapro*-type publications are dinosaurs that are no longer actively marketed.
- *Hardware*. Exclude products that are unavailable for your line of computers.
- *Programming languages*. The DBMS should be compatible with at least one language used in your installation.
- *Specialization*. Some products are intensely application specific (e.g., a bill-of-material processor for manufacturing companies). Avoid them if you are looking for a general purpose product.
- *Major deficiencies*. Exclude products that appear to lack important features such as the ability to accommodate multiple database users simultaneously.
- *Customer base*. Unless you have very esoteric needs, stick with products that are widely used (i.e., at least fifty installations).* A word of caution: number-of-users figures in reference publications can be extremely inaccurate. Frequently, they fail to reflect recent sales and, conversely, product abandonment.
- *Cost*. If the price of the DBMS is clearly out of line with your budget, it makes no sense to consider it.

There are exceptions to these guidelines. Therefore, if in doubt, include a product in the first-cut list; it can always be removed from consideration later.

The initial product list normally consists of five-to-ten products, about which each vendor is asked to send information. After a careful reading of product literature, judicious questioning of vendor technical and sales personnel, and some telephone calls to DBMS users, it is usually possible to cut the initial list in half. Factors that were not visible at first glance now become apparent.

EVALUATING PRODUCTS

We now have everything we need to begin a detailed evaluation of DBMS products: requirements, weighed evaluation criteria, DBMS information, and a manageable number

---

*A large customer base encourages continued vendor support. Also, in case of vendor financial problems, it increases the chances that a buyer will be found who will take responsibility for the vendor's customers and will continue to provide support.

of candidate products. Our job is to learn as much as we can about each DBMS and its vendor, and to assign points based on our evaluation criteria. This process consists of the following steps and techniques.

Vendor Technical Presentations and Demonstrations

Technical presentations usually consist of an audio-visual portion followed by workshops and working sessions with potential system users. The scenario usually begins with a glossy sales pitch describing the wonders of the product. Vendor technical personnel then instruct programmers, systems analysts and end-users on how to develop reports and on-line queries, use the data manipulation language, and design databases.

Presentations, demos and the less formal meetings with vendors that go on throughout the evaluation phase, are the most important source of information. However, care must be taken to remember the following:

- Demonstrations always present the product's strong points—never its weaknesses. In addition, they are run in a controlled environment that does not reflect actual operating conditions in your installation.
- Conversely, there is an old saw in data processing: demos never seem to work right when important people are viewing them. If a demo fails, don't necessarily fault the product.
- Features seen for the first time may appear miraculous. Delay your judgement. The same features may be available with all or most of the other products you are evaluating.
- Don't necessarily assume that the (hopefully) competent technical people you are dealing with during the DBMS evaluation typify the vendor's staff. Frequently, the best people participate in presales activities; trainees are assigned to postsales installations.
- Be sure that the marvelous things seen in demos are available for your specific configuration. New features are not usually available for all versions of the DBMS at the same time. Some features may never make it to your machine.

Customer Visits

In addition to vendor presentations, site visits to several customers who use the DBMS should be made. Customer visits should be approached with caution and a degree of skepticism, since vendors tend to recommend only happy customers. Calls should be made to obtain a cross-section of opinion about the product. Customers selected for site visits should be asked candid questions, preferably outside the presence of the vendor's representatives.

However, care must be taken to filter out comments not relevant to your specific situation. For example, dissatisfaction with vendor support from a remote Idaho customer may not be relevant in New York city.

The following lines of questioning are of particular value.

- How large, in terms of both database volumes and the number of transactions processed, is your biggest DBMS application?
- Is data volatility high?
- How complex are the data structures?
- What kinds of processing problems have you experienced?

- What DBMS components do you use and how happy are you with them?
- Has vendor support been adequate?
- Has it been difficult to hire people skilled in the use of this DBMS?

This is, of course, only a partial list; however, it does cover some important questions.

Although the experience of specific customers cannot always be extrapolated to another situation, certain key elements should be carefully evaluated. Lack of vendor responsiveness, inadequate product documentation, an abnormally high incidence of system failures, inexperienced or unavailable vendor personnel, and difficult installation procedures may be common, pervasive problems.

Vendor products and services may improve with time. This is why recent experience is the best guide. But sometimes problems are endemic, and a vendor's assurance that a particular problem no longer exists (or has never existed) should be carefully verified.

Preparing a Prototype

This is the process of taking our application data requirements and producing a prototype database using the candidate DBMS. The prototype can then be compiled, loaded with sample data and tested.

This gives us a preview (but only a preview) of what the DBMS can provide. We can determine if the product is capable of supporting our data relationships and the ease with which this can be accomplished. Access paths to needed data can be tested and, given an adequate amount of test data, we can even perform some preliminary timings.

Preparing a trial database is done primarily by vendor personnel from information provided in the requirements definition.

As with simulation, benchmarking, demos and other predictors of system behavior, the results of experimenting with our trial database should not be taken as gospel. It is only one (albeit important) consideration in selecting the DBMS.

Simulation

Simulation is the process of approximating run times for specific computer jobs. This is done by feeding simulation programs data on the characteristics of the environment and the application being simulated.

Environmental characteristics include internal (CPU) speeds, the input-output channel configuration, the speed of the peripherals, and instruction execution speed. Application characteristics for database systems include the logical and physical design of the database, data volumes, and program-specific data such as the number and types of instructions in the program.

Simulations can be notoriously inaccurate. They are only as good as the principles on which the calculations are based and on the accuracy of the data that is fed in. Since computer performance is frequently nonlinear, we cannot say, "Our volume estimates were off by 20 percent; therefore, run time will take 20 percent longer than the simulation indicated." Run time can, in fact, take twice as long.

Benchmarking

A benchmark is a comparison test. It pits a portion of a current application system against a version converted to run under the candidate DBMS. A series of actual production jobs, including on-line processing if applicable, are run under both systems and run times are compared.

Accurate benchmarks are very difficult to perform—especially for DBMS applications. Benchmarking results should be tempered with a good understanding of what is happening behind the scenes: unrelated programs running at the same time, the accuracy of the data model, the degree to which a benchmarked code includes important system features, etc.

Team Reviews

Team reviews are intended to expose candidate products to careful scrutiny—not only by the evaluation team but by other interested parties. Reviews should be held at appropriate checkpoints throughout the selection process.

Of obvious importance are reviews after each major step: requirements definition, the development of evaluation criteria, preparation of the RFP, identification of vendors, product evaluation, and product selection. Less obvious is the need to pause and think about our assumptions and findings.

Unless carefully planned meetings with specific discussion agendas are held, we may lose perspective and veer off on the wrong tangent. This is particularly dangerous during the product evaluation stage.

We will be bombarded with truths, half truths, features, phantom features, and an assortment of seductive sales pitches. We will have second thoughts about some of our evaluation criteria. And the features, strengths and weaknesses of various products will begin to run together.

It is, therefore, essential to take stock periodically. Recent findings should be methodically examined, open issues discussed, incomplete information identified, and a list of things remaining to be done should be prepared. In addition, people outside the evaluation team should have an opportunity to review the quality and soundness of the approach being taken. This injects an additional dose of objectivity into the selection process.

Product Scoring

The first step in product scoring is to verify that each candidate DBMS will, in fact, meet requirements. This is done by comparing DBMS features with the mandatory evaluation criteria we identified earlier.

The next step is to score the products. This is perhaps the most agonizing part of the entire selection process. At best, it is an honest attempt to be objective. At worst it is tyranny by numbers.

We must candidly recognize that, no matter how comprehensive our criteria and how much care has been taken to be objective, the scoring of products will be imprecise. Therefore, the risk of choosing the wrong product cannot be avoided.

In the course of the evaluation process we will learn a great deal about DBMS products. Consequently, some of our criteria will change. Features we once thought were of critical importance turn out to be unimportant. Conversely, seemingly minor features may loom larger than we originally expected. Other criteria may be dropped because none of the candidate systems are capable of fulfilling them.

Despite all this uncertainty, we must not allow bias toward a specific DBMS to seduce us into removing or downgrading a needed feature. Changes in our thinking must be directed towards constructive accommodation with reality—not toward accommodation to a specific product.

Vendor Analysis

The long-run effectiveness of a DBMS depends to a large extent on the maintenance and enhancements provided after the system is acquired. Therefore, evaluation of the vendor is almost as important as evaluation of the product itself.

Vendor evaluation should concentrate on the vendor's professionalism, financial stability, and support capability. Specific questions that should be asked are included in the Sample Evaluation Criteria section.

MAKING THE SELECTION

After the field has been narrowed to two or three candidates, the final selection is made. Sometimes the decision clearly favors one product. More likely, the selection will be close.

One vendor may offer a good DBMS used by many customers, a large support force and the resources of a large corporation. Another vendor may be small and of questionable stability but may offer a superior, reasonably priced product. Yet another may have the best DBMS, excellent supporting products and a fine reputation but may price his product substantially higher than the competition.

To a large extent, close calls are settled instinctively, no matter what our points totals tell us. Such a decision may be based on important factors that are difficult to quantify—although if we have done a thorough job in developing our selection criteria these nonquantifiables will be few. They may include intangible factors such as the rapport established with the vendor, a perception of the vendor as responsive and eager, or the impression of competence.

The final step of the selection process is to settle the details of the DBMS acquisition. Major contractual and financial questions should already have been discussed during the evaluation process. However, a residue of unresolved issues may remain. Specific financial terms, delivery schedules, performance guarantees, and other factors that are usually not major evaluation criteria may be considered at this time.

One other important point should be noted. It is always a good policy to pursue at least two alternatives until the very end of the selection process. Vendors are usually more experienced in the negotiation of terms and conditions than buyers. Therefore, it is not to the buyer's advantage to become locked into a specific vendor before all negotiations have been completed. If bridges have been burned, the vendor, rather than the buyer, will participate in the final negotiations from a position of strength.

Some of the terms used in the following three sections—the Requirements Definition samples, the Evaluation Criteria samples, and the Features Checklist—are technical and have not yet been defined. The reader may wish to return for a more careful examination after reading Chapters 5 through 10.

SAMPLES OF A REQUIREMENTS DEFINITION

A Health-Care Library Abstract System

This is a summary requirements definition for a service bureau that provides a reference service for physicians. Books and articles on a large variety of medical topics are abstracted and extensively cross-referenced by author, title, publisher, publication date, source, key words, and subject. Subscribers across the U.S. use their personal computers to dial in to locate medical information. They can then contact the source of the information (e.g., a university library) to acquire the complete article or book. This service is available twenty-four hours a day, seven days a week.

Application Requirements

- Data Structure* (see Figure 3.3)
  — moderately complex
  — primarily one-to-many relationships, some many-to-many
  — access is by one key or a combination of keys
  — only Library of Congress Number (if available)
    and internal ID are unique
- File and Transaction Volumes
  — very large database
  — low update transaction volumes with no seasonal or other variations
    (less than fifty changes to the database per day)
  — moderately high volume on-line processing
    (one thousand queries per day)
- Data Volatility
  — low (less than 1 percent of file changed each update run)
- Type of Processing
  — all inquiry processing is remote
  — multiple access paths (multiple keys and concatenated keys)
  — on-line processing is inquiry only

*"1" and "M" on the diagram indicate relationships between entities:

   1:M means one-to-many (e.g., author may have published more than one article).

   1:1 means one-to-one (e.g., an article or book has a unique Library of Congress Number).

   M:M means many-to-many (e.g., an article can be identified by more than one key word and a key word represents many articles).

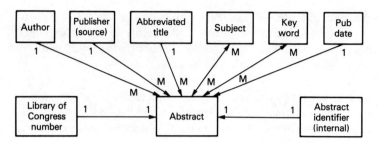

Figure 3.3 Data Structure for a Library Abstract Database

— all updating is batch (on-line updating is not needed)
— no ad hoc queries or reports (all are predefined)
- Control Requirements
  — access control is very important to discourage hackers (the company's product is an expensive service that we do not wish to give away)
  — no journaling or audit trails are required for updates
  — tracking is needed for all queries (customers are charged by query)
  — database backup and security are very important
  — very high up-time is required (this is a competitive service)

Corporate Data Needs

- May require distribution of a database outside the U.S. to facilitate international service
- A record of customer inquiries is sent to the billing system, which will probably not be converted to a DBMS application in the near future

Computer Department Needs

- Limited application changes will be made after the system is installed
- Software support must be very good and very fast because of limited staff and low allowable downtime

Constraints

- Must run on IBM 3081 multiple CPUs under MVS/XA and CICS
- Must be a widely used DBMS because development will be done by outside consultants due to desirability of maintaining low staff levels.

An Order Entry System

This is a summary requirements definition for a medium-sized mail order company that sells auto parts at retail and prides itself on product availability and fast delivery. Most customers are local and orders may be placed during normal working hours. The system is available for batch processing between 6:00 P.M. and 8:00 A.M.

There are no plans to change computer vendors although hardware and software upgrades are acceptable. All major systems will eventually run under the DBMS. However, order entry is the major application for which the DBMS is being selected.

Application Requirements

— Data structure (see Figure 3.4)
— complex data structure (Figure 3.4 is a simplified version)
— both one-to-many and many-to-many relationships
■ File and transaction volumes—medium-sized customer database (ten thousand customers)
— high transaction volumes (two thousand per day)
— large seasonal variations (pre-Christmas processing is four times the volume of January/February processing)
— transaction processing varies by 50 percent during an average day, with the greatest number of transactions during lunchtime
■ Data volatility
— high volatility for order records
— moderate volatility for customer records
■ Type of processing
— all processing is on-line, real-time
— batch processing is for report generation only
— some on-line query processing
— all data entry is in local mode, performed by telephone order clerks located adjacent to computer room
— customer access is by name or number only
— extensive ad hoc queries
— limited need for ad hoc reports
— some predefined queries
— extensive predefined reports
■ Control requirements
— authorization and log-on controls are minimum because all processing takes place in a small, easily controlled area
— transaction logging is very important (most orders are taken over the telephone with no backup hard copy)
— database backup is important
— security is important due to the valuable customer list

Corporate Data Needs

■ Extensive interaction is required with other systems (e.g., inventory, accounts receivable, accounts payable)
■ Other systems will gradually be rewritten using the DBMS

Figure 3.4   Data Structure for an Order Entry Database

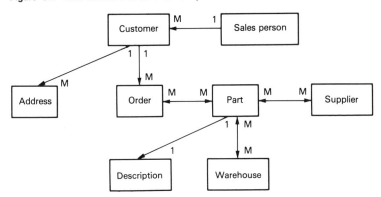

Computer Department Needs

- Extensive system change flexibility is needed because this is the company's first on-line order entry system and many changes are expected
- Little vendor software support is needed (the company has traditionally been very self-sufficient)
- Technical documentation must be very good because of almost complete reliance on in-house staff
- Due to its location in the center of a very large urban area with many computer installations, the selected DBMS need not be a widely used product

Constraints

- DBMS must operate on a Digital Equipment Corporation (DEC) computer, currently a VAX, which is a large "supermini."

SAMPLE DBMS EVALUATION CRITERIA

Technical and Functional Criteria

General System Capabilities and Characteristics

- Is the DBMS capable of handling large master file volumes (over one million records)? Large transaction volumes (over ten thousand transactions per day)?
- What is the largest application running on this DBMS in terms of:
  — database size (number of records and size of records)
  — on-line transactions processed daily (both updates and queries)
  — batch update transactions processed daily
  — number of users simultaneously accessing the database
- Does it handle on-line processing more (or less) efficiently than batch?
- How "tuneable" is the system for efficient storage and retrieval?
- How many people can use the system simultaneously?

Data Handling

- Are many-to-many, as well as one-to-many, relationships supported in a reasonably natural fashion?
- Can variable as well as fixed-length records be used?
- Is data compression available? How much space does it save?
- Is the DBMS primarily hierarchical, network or relational?
- Are data relationships predefined (i.e., fixed at compile time) or does "binding" occur at execute time?
- Are duplicate records allowed and, if so, can we select between "first" and "last" duplicate?
- Is multikey access provided? Is indexing available? Does random accessing provide for large keys? Can customized hashing (randomizing) routines be used?
- Does database navigation provide facilities for forward searches? Backward searches? Direct return to owner?
- What is the maximum number of record or segment types allowed? Search fields per record? Occurrences of a repeating group?

Control

- Is structural validation (referential integrity) provided? Is it mandatory or optional?
- Are separate "user views" (subschemas) available?
- Is concurrent processing available for: multiple queries? multiple updates?
- At which levels is concurrency available: record level? file level? Are lockouts optional or mandatory?
- Does the DBMS have deadlock prevention?
- Is transaction journaling available for on-line processing? Before-and-after-imaging of database records?
- Are both roll forward and roll back recovery available? Is checkpointing? How effective is restart/recovery processing?
- Are data encoding/decoding facilities available?
- How extensive are password and other authorization processing?
- Is the DBMS sufficiently modular to allow processing if one part of the system is down? Which parts can so function?

Change Flexibility

- How difficult is it to redefine data elements? Add new data elements? Delete data elements?
- How difficult are changes to relationships between records (i.e., structural changes)?
- How much data independence does the data dictionary support—that is, under what circumstances must programs be recompiled? Data unloaded and reloaded?

Integration with Other Types of Systems

- Is the DBMS compatible with other system software in use at the installation?
- Is physical implementation based on standard file organizations for the computer of choice? Or are the files that are created special and not externally readable?
- Can conventional files be used as input? Can they be created as output? What types of conventional files are supported?
- Can the DBMS be used with a variety of teleprocessing monitors? Or are we locked into a single monitor?
- Does the system monitor readily interface with other communications protocols?
- Is the DBMS available for other hardware?

Documentation

- How comprehensive is system documentation?
- Is it well organized? Cross referenced? Easy to understand?
- Is documentation available on-line or in manuals only? How often is documentation updated by the vendor?

Utilities

- Are file conversion aids available?
- Loads and unloads? Reorganization programs?
- Performance monitoring programs?
- Data integrity checking and "patch" programs?
- Test data generators and trace routines?

- Are utilities comprehensively documented?
- Are all utilities available in their full-feature form for your specific computing environment?

Data Description Language (DDL)

- How easy is the DDL to learn and use?
- Is the syntax in clear English?
- How good is DDL documentation?

Data Manipulation Language (DML)

- Does it support Cobol? BAL? PL1? Fortran? Other languages?
- Is it easy to use?

Query Language

- Is one available from the DBMS vendor? From other vendors?
- Is it easy to use? Is its syntax flexible? Is documentation well written and comprehensive?
- Does it have extensive Boolean (also referred to as "and/or") selection capabilities?
- Is it compilable or interpretive?
- Does it have "what if" (modelling) capabilities?

Report Language?

- Is it easy to use? How good is the documentation?
- Does it have extensive calculation and roll up, as well as formatting, capabilities?
- How efficient is it?

Data Dictionary (DD)

- Is a DD available only from the DBMS vendor or are other DDs available from other vendors?
- Is it easy to use? Is it well documented?
- What data redundancy control tools does it offer? Or is redundancy controlled manually by reading data dictionary reports?
- Can the DD store and manipulate information about conventional, non-DBMS systems?
- How "active" is it—that is, does it directly participate in database design activities or is it strictly a passive documentation tool? How easily can it be circumvented?
- Does it produce schemas and subschemas?
- Are data dictionary reports readable and comprehensive?
- Does it provide extensive "where-used" and other cross-referencing capabilities?

Physical Storage and Access Characteristics

- Is there a choice of physical storage and access techniques?
- Which of the following are available?
  — random storage based on a hashing algorithm
  — indexing
  — sequential storage (by physical proximity)
  — combinations of the above
- Are page sizes user defined or are they fixed?

Operational and Software Characteristics

- Is a "central copy" of the DBMS used? Or must there be separate copies for each user?
- Are resources dynamically allocated?
- If part of the DBMS is down will other parts continue to operate?

Hardware and Software Requirements

- How much memory is needed: minimum? maximum? How much is recommended?
- Can the current operating system be used or must it be changed or upgraded?
- Will a hardware upgrade be required? CPU? Mass storage devices? Other hardware?

Vendor-Related Criteria

Vendor Characteristics

- How long has the DBMS vendor been in the software business? How long has the company been developing and selling DBMS products?
- What are the vendor's annual gross sales? How large is the staff?
- Is the vendor profitable? If so, for how long? Have profits been erratic or steady?
- Is software the vendor's only business? Or does it exist primarily to support hardware sales?
- How many customers does the vendor have? How many customers use the DBMS version that runs on your specific configuration? Are there many customers in your geographical area?
- How strong is the company financially? Is it undercapitalized? Can it afford continued development of new products?
- How committed is the vendor to providing continuing enhancements for the DBMS version that runs on your specific hardware and software?
- Does a well-organized, active user's group represent the vendor's customers?
- Does the vendor have any attractive supporting products in addition to the components normally available with a DBMS?

Training

- How much training is offered at no cost: number of courses? Number of people that can attend?
- What types of courses are available? How comprehensive are they?
- Are they taught frequently in a wide variety of locations? Or are they taught only at the vendor's regional offices or headquarters?

System Maintenance

- Are the vendor's people well trained? Is turnover high? What is the average level of experience?
- How good is service quality? Availability in your area?
- Is there a "hotline"? Is there a guaranteed response time in case of system problems?
- How large is the local support staff in relation to the number of customers that must be serviced?
- What types of services and problem resolution does the local vs. regional or national office provide?

- Is consulting support available from the vendor? Are there other consulting firms that specialize in developing applications under this DBMS?
- How much vendor support is provided at no charge for installation? For training?
- How often are fixes provided and how are they applied—by the customer or by the vendor? Are they applied by the vendor via dial-up to the customer's system? Or by sending a new set of object programs to be installed by the customer?

Cost

- Is there a choice between lease or purchase?
- What is the initial purchase price? Which components and features are included in the base price and which are priced separately?
- What are annual maintenance charges?
- What are the licensing provisions and costs with respect to multiple sites? Multiple copies at the same site?
- How much installation and training are provided free of charge? How expensive are classes?
- Are consulting services available? At what rates?

Contractual Arrangements

- Does the vendor always use a standard contract? Or can the contract be custom tailored to the needs of the client?
- What financial or other liabilities is the vendor willing to assume in case the DBMS does not work properly in your environment?
- Can the DBMS be used on a trial basis? If so, for how long?
- Does the customer receive source- as well as executable code?
- To what extent do customer-made changes to the DBMS software invalidate vendor support?

CHECKLIST OF DBMS FEATURES

Data Characteristics

- Basic unit of data
  — character
  — data element (field)
  — group
  — record
- Record type
  — fixed
  — variable
- Relationships supported
  — 1:1
  — 1:M
  — M:M
- Structure
  — hierarchical
  — network
  — relational

- Duplicate records
  - — supported?
  - — choice of order
  - — no choice of order
- Referential integrity
  - = nonexistent
  - — mandatory
  - — optional
- User views (subschemas)
  - — supported
  - — not supported
- Data compression
  - — optional or mandatory
  - — how much storage space is saved?
- Data limits, number of:
  - — record or segment types
  - — searchable fields per record
  - — occurrences of a repeating group
- Relationships with non-DBMS files
  - — flat files as input
  - — flat files as output
  - — types of flat files
  - — is database file organization standard and readable by non-DBMS programs?

Database Access

- Sequential
- Random
  - — support for large keys
  - — support for own randomizing routines
  - — single key access
  - — multikey access
- Indexed
- Ability to dynamically select indexed or sequential search based on frequency of data values—is this ability automatically exercised by the DBMS or invoked by the application?
- Database navigation techniques
  - — backward searches
  - — forward searches
  - — direct return to owner or parent
- Binding
  - — at run time
  - — at compile time

Concurrency

- Multiple concurrent queries
- Multiple concurrent updates
- Lockouts
  - — record level
  - — file level
  - — set level
  - — optional or mandatory
- Deadlock prevention

Backup, Recovery and Security

- Modularity (if part of the DBMS is down, which other parts continue to operate?)
- Before-and-after imaging
- Logging
- Consolidated database/data communication journaling
- Forward/backward recovery
- Coordinated transaction/database recovery
- Checkpointing
- Restart
- Audit trail
- Program isolation
- Data encoding/decoding
- Dynamic backout
- Reentrant code

Volume and Performance

- Ability to handle large transaction volumes
- Ability to handle large database volumes
- Efficiency of batch vs. on-line processing
- Efficiency of on-line retrieval vs. on-line updating
- Largest volume installed applications

Change Flexibility

- Levels of data independence
- Ease of change
  - data elements
    - definitional changes
    - new data elements
  - relationships
    - structural changes
    - definition changes

Operational Characteristics

- Central copy vs. copies for each user for on-line processing
- Central copy vs. copies for each user for batch processing
- Dynamic allocation of resources
- Variable page sizes

Data Description Language

- Type
  - keyword
  - positional
  - free format
- Readability
- Ease of learning and use
- Quality reports and ease of production
- Security (authorization)

- Elements of description
  — data type
  — size
  — name
  — alias

Data Manipulation Language

- Interface to:
  — Cobol
  — PL1
  — Fortran
  — BAL
  — other
- Ease of use
- Data independence

Query Language

- Easy to use
- Boolean capabilities
- Flexible syntax
- Ad hoc searching (and relating previously unrelated files)
- Compileable or interpretive

Report Language

- Ease of use
- Command set
- Operating efficiency

Data Dictionary

- Ease of use
- Support of non-DBMS information
- Degree to which it is "active"

Development Tools

- Screen formatter
- Test data generator
- Trace and other testing aids
- Code generator
- Path optimizers
- Data analysis support
- Simulation software
- Modelling software
- Prototyping language

Utilities

- Performance tuning tools
- File conversion

- Load/unload
- Reorganization
- Performance monitoring and statistics
- Data integrity check
- Data linkage patch
- Database restoration

Hardware and Software Requirements

- Memory
- Operating system needed
- Teleprocessing monitor
  - single monitor that must be used
  - choice of monitors
  - message/transaction handler
  - interface with other communication protocols
- Compatibility with other installation software
- Storage device support
- Transportability to other hardware

Cost

- Initial rent or purchase
- License fees
- Maintenance
- Training and installation
- Supporting products
- DBMS components priced separately
- Cost of consulting services

Documentation and Training

- Availability
- Extra cost
- Quality
- Quantity

Vendor Characteristics

- Stability
  - financial
  - personnel
- Customer base
- Availability of supporting products
- Service quality
  - fixes
    - frequency
    - applied by customer or by vendor
    - object code updated via dial up to client's computer
  - version control
  - user group
  - response time

      — hotline
      — local support
      — size of technical support staff
- Amount of support
      — installation done by vendor or customer people?
      — free vs. pay support
- Consulting group available

DISCUSSION QUESTIONS

Who should be on a DBMS acquisition team and why?

Describe the kinds of application requirements that must be taken into account.

Name the two other major needs that must be considered besides application requirements.

Why is a Request for Proposal useful? What does it normally contain?

Identify three factors that may serve to remove a product from consideration right from the start.

What kinds of questions should users of candidate products be asked during customer visits?

Describe the difference between modelling, simulation and benchmarking. What are their drawbacks?

Describe the importance of evaluating backup and recovery features in a DBMS.

4

ORGANIZING
THE DATABASE
ENVIRONMENT

INTRODUCTION

The introduction of database technology must be accompanied by changes in organization structure, changes in the way computer people do their job and, perhaps most importantly, changes in the way people think about systems. Unless these organizational and perceptual changes occur, a company will not gain the advantages DBMS technology offers. Worse, management may find themselves in bigger trouble than if they had not acquired the DBMS in the first place!

This chapter outlines the major differences between non-DBMS and DBMS environments and describes the required new functions.

MAJOR DIFFERENCES BETWEEN TRADITIONAL AND DBMS ENVIRONMENTS

New Functions

The key organizational difference is the presence of one or, optionally, two new functions: Database Administration (DBA) and Data Resources Management (DRM). Together they form the most visible evidence of the "new" organization. DBA and DRM are described later in this chapter.

Almost all companies that use a DBMS need a DBA function. In addition, many companies—particularly larger ones—also have a DRM function. (Incidentally, DRM is sometimes used as an umbrella term to cover all data-related functions, including DBA. In this book, it will be used in a more restrictive way to describe only corporatewide, essentially nontechnical data functions.)

Standards

Standards have always been important to a well-run data processing organization. However, they are even more important in a DBMS environment. The reasons for this are threefold: much more interaction between organizational units is required and this interaction becomes chaotic unless some degree of consistency is enforced; integration between systems is usually increased—making compatibility a very important issue; and more people interact with a wider variety of systems because of the increased ease of access provided by user-friendly software tools.

System Integration

Unless a serious attempt is made to integrate related systems, much of the value of a DBMS will be lost. System integration requires analysts to examine relationships between the applications they are building and other systems—both manual and automated.

This analysis must be directed primarily at identifying common data and ensuring compatibility in data element definitions and relationships. It should also encompass processes. That is, the system under development should be designed to enable movement of data between related systems.

In theory, the job of ensuring system integration rests primarily with DBA and DRM. In practice, it cannot be accomplished without a high degree of effort and cooperation by line data processing people—the folks who are actually developing new applications.

Global View of Data

System designers must learn to think of data in a more comprehensive, companywide fashion. They must stop thinking of data as belonging exclusively to a specific application and become alert to its implications across organizational units and systems. This is primarily the responsibility of DBA or DRM. However, as with system integration, the cooperation of line people is essential.

Organizational Interdependence

A DBMS impacts many worlds: users, application developers, technical support staff, telecommunications analysts, computer operations, and, of course, staff functions such as planning. No other software product has such a pervasive influence.

Traditionally antagonistic groups, such as System Development and Operations, must learn to work more harmoniously in a DBMS environment. On-going cooperation is absolutely vital. In addition, each group must learn to share responsibilities. For example, file (i.e., database) design is no longer the exclusive preserve of systems analysts.

Successful organizational interaction requires management commitment to make it happen (the most important ingredient); standards and procedures that govern interaction; plenty of practice (i.e., on-going interaction—not just in problem situations); and a realization by everyone that systems can no longer be built without extensive cooperation between groups.

Technical Complexity

No matter how easy the software dream merchants claim their products are to use, there is no such thing as a "simple" DBMS. It might be simple by the time a user formulates an on-line request with a friendly, high-level language; but that's just the tip of the iceberg.

A DBMS increases the overall complexity and, therefore, the technical sophistication of a data processing shop. This translates into the need for more training, the need for higher-priced people, and the willingness of people to master the new technology.

Increased Software and Data Maintenance

A DBMS represents an additional layer of software between the operating system and the application program. As with any product that is appended to an already complex battery of components, we pay a price, which includes:

- Increased "tuning"—that is, tinkering with the rules that govern data storage and manipulation in order to increase performance
- Implementation of fixes and enhancements provided by the vendor
- Greater data integrity oriented processing, such as database backup, purges of records that are out-of-date or in error, and the repair of destroyed linkages or other connections between related records
- Execution of data reorganizations, which serve to distribute data more efficiently after a period of vigorous updating

Any complex software component requires maintenance. However, this burden is frequently greater in a DBMS installation.

Increased User Demand

The history of data processing shows that the implementation of new technologies is invariably accompanied by increased demands to provide more and more benefit to the user community. A successful DBMS installation will, therefore, increase rather than decrease the "application backlog." As data becomes available in accessible, useful form, the audience for that data will increase.

DATABASE ADMINISTRATION

The purpose of the DBA function is to provide technical expertise and the planning and coordination needed to support use of DBMS technology. Specific DBA responsibilities are discussed below.

Planning

DBA's planning role is to help acquire a DBMS (if the database administrator was hired prior to the selection process), to suggest the types and magnitude of the hardware and software needed to support the DBMS, and to plan for future expansion and enhancements.

DBA people are the resident database experts. Like their peers in Software Support, Operations, and Systems Development, DBA personnel must participate in hardware, software, and applications planning.

Coordination

DBA monitors and coordinates the data design activities of application development groups. This is done to ensure the consistency of data definitions and usage between applications, to the extent that this is possible.

DBA has two means of controlling data design: personal contact with application developers and the use of a data dictionary.

Despite the current emphasis on data dictionaries, coordination cannot take place without a very significant amount of personal interaction. The data dictionary is an invaluable tool but is not a substitute for the trust and confidence engendered by personal contact.

Personal contact must begin during the feasibility study phase of the development cycle. It is at this early stage that an organization makes tentative decisions concerning the integration of the new system with existing and planned systems. The most effective vehicle for DBA involvement at this stage is to discuss the proposed system with development people and to comment on the preliminary draft of the feasibility study report.

DBA involvement increases as needs analysis and technical design proceed. Needs analysis should take into consideration the data definitions that currently exist in the data dictionary. As data elements are defined by the application development team, DBA must check them against similar elements already in the data dictionary for redundancy. Minor discrepancies in definition, names and usage are resolved whenever possible.

Database design, which takes place after needs definition, is also subject to coordination. DBA must ensure that data relationships for a new system do not contradict the relationships defined for existing systems and for the corporate data model. Discrepancies are not necessarily wrong—they may stem from genuine differences in data usage and terminology; however, they must be investigated and discussed.

Incidentally, the ability of application development personnel to add data elements and records to a data dictionary is limited in many installations. This gives DBA the "middleman" control needed to monitor the data definition process.

Training

The process of learning how to develop systems under a DBMS is, unfortunately, not fully accomplished by taking a vendor-sponsored one-week course. Training must be ongoing and must be installation specific—that is, the limitations and standards applicable to a given installation must be taught in addition to product oriented characteristics. An important DBA responsibility is to ensure that such training takes place.

Standards

DBA is the logical source of database standards. These include:

- Naming conventions for data elements and records
- Usage (and prohibition) of various DBMS features
- Programming conventions for database retrieval
- Backup and recovery requirements
- Logging and journaling requirements
- A methodology for performing database design
- Relationships and responsibilities between DBA and other organizational units

The primary impetus for developing DBMS-related standards should come from the DBA. However, as is the case with all other data processing standards, the people who will actually have to comply with the standards should also be involved.

A suggested approach is for DBA to work in a committee-like setting with key data processing people (and, possibly, users) to define major standards in outline form. DBA should then write the standards, elicit comments, make appropriate modifications, and put the standards into use. It is a serious mistake to develop standards without consultation or, on the other hand, to expect perfect agreement from all parties (an impossibility). Naming conventions and other less technical standards can be developed by DRM, if this function exists.

Database Design Consultation

Although the primary responsibility for database design belongs with the application development team, a significant amount of assistance from DBA may be needed. Application development people will not necessarily know how to design databases—especially in a new DBMS environment. In some installations, database design is done entirely by DBA. Although this is tolerable in the short term if DBA is the only source of expertise, it is detrimental in the long run.

The nature of DBMS technology is too pervasive and important to be left entirely in the hands of a staff group. To do so makes for dangerous dependency on a small number of people, removes design activities from the crucible of close user contact, and results in morale problems for development people who feel left out of an exciting technology.

Physical Design and Tuning

Since physical design is concerned with "internals," or how the database actually manipulates data, it is the responsibility of DBA. Physical design consists of translating the logical relationships defined by the applications development team into a viable database that will perform adequately.

Database tuning is an iterative process that is part of physical design. It consists of experimentation with various storage and access alternatives for the selected logical design. It also involves potential redesign of some logical relationships that cannot be successfully implemented.

Database Security, Backup and Recovery

The techniques available in a DBMS for preventing unauthorized database access, and for ensuring recoverability in case of hardware or software malfunction, are best known to DBA. Implementation of appropriate procedures can be a subtle, complex task often made unnecessarily difficult by poor vendor documentation.

System development people are expected to determine the need for application-specific data and the costs of recreating it. However, only a knowledgeable database technician can assess the desirability of various backup and recovery alternatives in terms of performance degradation, increased system complexity, increased disk storage requirements and other trade-offs.

Backup and recovery procedures for databases used extensively across different applications may fall through the cracks if left up to analysts who are responsible for only parts of the data. This is another good reason why DBA should be a key participant.

DBMS and Database Maintenance

DBA's maintenance role is twofold: to apply fixes and enhancements to DBMS software; and to perform "generic," or nonapplication-specific, maintenance on the application data itself. The former is needed in order to keep the DBMS up to date. The latter is needed in order to maintain data integrity, enable adequate system performance, and keep computing resource usage to a reasonable level.

The most common database maintenance activities are:

- Unloading and reloading data when definitional changes require physical rearrangements
- Reorganizing data when the volume of additions and changes impacts performance
- Purging data when "deleted" (i.e., unavailable but physically present) records are taking up a significant amount of disk space and impacting performance

■ Operating "patch" programs to identify and fix damaged indexes or linkages between related records.

ORGANIZATIONAL PLACEMENT OF DBA

The position of DBA in the organization depends on the degree to which that function is strictly technical, the extent to which it is sensitive to the needs of applications development, and the degree to which it is intended to be a precursor to DRM. Figures 4.1 to 4.3 illustrate three popular organizational alternatives.

Alternative 1 places DBA under the Systems and Programming group. This usually provides the best support for applications development but may result in too much concentration on the needs of the moment. Programming groups are always concerned with implementing a specific application and are reluctant to make the time-consuming effort needed to integrate their data with other systems or with the corporate plan.

In Alternative 2, DBA is part of the technical support function. This highlights the importance of DBA's technical role but removes it from any stewardship of corporate data. It also lessens the sensitivity of DBA to the needs of the Systems Development organization.

In Alternative 3, DBA is placed on the same level as the other functions that report to the Director of Management Information Systems (MIS). This provides DBA with power and visibility and is a good interim step towards the establishment of a DRM function. Unfortunately, it may also result in decreased emphasis on important technical functions. DBA may end up achieving a corporate viewpoint at the expense of being useful to the troops in the field.

The best alternative depends on the specific situation. Two factors should play a major role: the kinds of problems an organization is experiencing in its efforts to imple-

Figure 4.1 Organizational Placement of the DBA Function
Alternative 1: Reporting to Application Systems Development

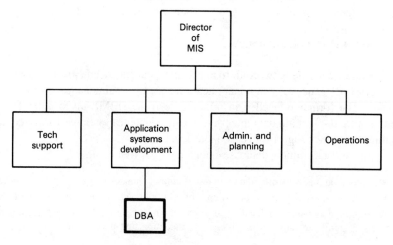

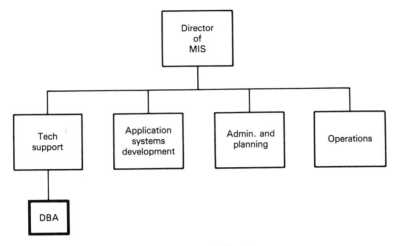

Figure 4.2 Organizational Placement of the DBA Function
Alternative 2: Reporting to Technical (Software) Support

ment database systems, and the level of experience an organization has achieved in database technology.

Alternative 1 is most suitable for companies that are in the process of developing their first database systems. Since few or no DBMS skills exist in the applications area, extensive support must be provided by DBA. This is best done by integrating the DBA function into the development team.

In general, however, this alternative is a temporary expedient. It should be continued only as long as inexperience or lack of cooperation between Development and Technical Support hampers the successful use of DBMS technology.

Alternative 2 is appropriate when the software environment is highly complex and extensive tuning of databases must be done. Placement under the software manager tends to encourage technical skills and facilitate cooperation with other technical groups

Figure 4.3 Organizational Placement of the DBA Function
Alternative 3: Reporting to the Director of MIS

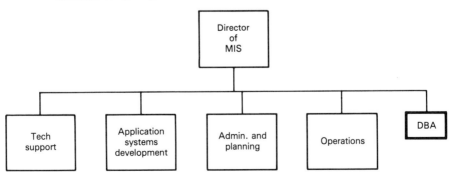

(telecommunications, systems programming, etc.). This alternative is particularly suitable for an organization that has already implemented several database applications.

Alternative 3 is appropriate for a more mature organization. After a number of database applications have been successfully implemented, an organization is faced with the problem of controlling future development to ensure a reasonable degree of data integration.

Therefore, the DBA may need to be removed from the pressure exerted by Development and Technical Support to satisfy immediate requirements quickly without regard to longer-term needs. The possibility of achieving this goal is greater if DBA reports directly to the Director of MIS. In addition, this is a natural lead-in for the later creation of a DRM function, which should never report below the MIS Director level (see next section).

DATA RESOURCE MANAGEMENT (DRM)

The job of the 1970's-style "database administrator" (from which the more widely used "database administration" acronym was derived) has been sliced in half. This function is now exclusively technical; the companywide responsibilities have been assumed by DRM.

DRM has also been given additional responsibilities—partly as a result of better data dictionaries, which have made the maintenance of corporate data easier; and partly through increased emphasis on data as a corporate resource. The specific roles of DRM in most organizations are described below.

Corporate Data Modelling

This type of modelling is an attempt to describe the data relationships that constitute the heart of a company's business. Corporate data modelling usually results in an Entity-Relationship diagram or other pictorial representation of data. However, a "real" database—that is, one that contains live data—is not built. Rather, the conceptual model is used to gain a better understanding of how the company works, to point the way for future "subject" (i.e., application) databases, and to provide a context for planning future systems.

In addition, a corporate data model should be developed if "enterprise modelling" is done. (Enterprise modelling is the development of a flowchart or other representation of major company processes and data flows.)

The steps of corporate data model development are as follows.

- Identify major corporate functions. What is the major business or businesses of the corporation and what functions must be performed in order to operate successfully?
- Define the types of information needed by each function. What does each function need to know in order to do its work?

- Identify the relationships between major data categories. What is the interaction between data?
- Document the above visually and with supporting narrative. An Entity-Relationship diagram may be used (see the chapter on database development).

The level of detail a data model should follow is open to question. All known data that is, or should be, used to run the business can be defined. Or, a less detailed approach that identifies only entities (e.g., customer, customer order) and important categories of information (e.g., customer order history, customer address information) may be used.

More detail is costly in terms of DRM time, may bury critical information in a mass of detail, and may duplicate work that has already been done (or will need to be done) to develop databases for specific applications.

On the other hand, insufficient detail can make data modelling a trivial exercise. A good rule of thumb is to limit development of the corporate data model to less than three person-months of effort.

Development and Maintenance of the Corporate Data Glossary

This is perhaps the most difficult but most useful function of DRM. Most organizations experience communication difficulties because some products, processes or entities are called by different names, even though they are the same (synonyms); are called by the same name, even though they are different (homonyms); or are defined differently across departments within the company. Imagine the life-threatening chaos in a hospital operating room if two or more surgical instruments were called by the same name while others each had three or four names!

A less dramatic example is the definition of a bank "customer." Is the Pontiac Division or General Motors the customer? If I am a loan officer on the Pontiac account, Pontiac is the customer; if I am on the credit review committee, General Motors is the customer because Pontiac's line of credit is guaranteed by the General Motors corporation. In personal banking, am I a customer if I have a bank credit card? An outstanding loan? A checking account with $3.47?

Terminology problems such as these are not merely semantic curiosities. They may cause endless delays and disagreements in the development of application systems and may result in distorted or misleading information.

Some definitional problems can never be resolved to everyone's satisfaction because of legitimate differences in usage from department to department. These differences may be perfectly natural and may be necessary to promote understanding. However, many definitional problems exist simply because terms were invented by different people at different times with no attempt at standardization. This is where DRM comes in.

Usages across the organization should be researched and standardized where possible. DRM definitions can then be used when application systems are developed. (Incidentally, all important terms that are in general use should be documented, even if they are not part of a computer system.)

The key ingredients of a useful glossary entry are:

- Business name of the term
- A short data processing name that follows standard naming conventions, if this term represents a data element already used by a computer system
- A clear, concise business definition
- Synonyms or "AKAs" (also known as)—that is, other names by which this term is known
- Ownership of the term (the functional area of the company that is primarily responsible for the term's definition)

The data glossary does not contain the detailed data element definitions needed to develop computer systems. Rather, it provides the foundation for such definitions.

Participation in Corporate MIS Planning

DRM enjoys a unique corporate perspective of data needed to run the business. Therefore, DRM representatives can be (but are not always) important participants in formulating long-range EDP plans. The bird's-eye view provided by DRM is needed when establishing systems development priorities.

Data definitions prepared during development projects should be monitored for general conformance to the long-range plan. Naturally, some projects won't conform—the plan is, after all, a road map and not necessarily the actual route. However, the destination should be the same. If it isn't, either the plan or the development project should change.

Security and disaster recovery planning is another area of DRM interest. Issues such as protection against unauthorized access to confidential data, the off-site storage of critical files, and protection against data theft should be covered from corporate as well as application-specific perspectives.

Although DBA and others may be responsible for the technical implementation of disaster recovery procedures, DRM should be at the forefront of planning for them.

Participation in System Development Activities

To be effective, DRM must be a positive presence in system development projects. One critical task is to help analysts identify application data that has already been defined in other systems or in the corporate data model. The glossary that contains data definitions is used for this purpose.

Participation in Standards Development

The following standards have a direct bearing on the DRM function:

- Data naming conventions
- Glossary access and usage
- Data Dictionary access and usage (DRM is a major Dictionary user)

DRM must, therefore, participate in the development of standards for these areas.

Development of Improved Access to Corporate Data

Each department or group in the organization has its own notions of user-friendly access to data. This invariably leads to the acquisition of incompatible query languages, report generators and other software tools. It is not at all unusual to find "one of each," even in relatively small installations.

More importantly, parochial viewpoints lead to redundant storage of data, fragmentation, and denial of data to "foreign" systems—precisely the situation we are trying to correct with a DBMS.

Since DRM has a corporate perspective, it is logical for DRM representatives to research and recommend tools that will provide maximum corporate benefits.

ORGANIZATIONAL PLACEMENT OF DRM

The position of DRM in the organization depends on the degree to which management considers DRM to be a "corporate" versus "data processing" function. To put it more candidly, it depends on the degree to which DRM is taken seriously. Figures 4.4 and 4.5 illustrate alternate organization structures that accommodate the DRM function.

In Alternative 1, DRM is part of the data processing organization. The head of DRM reports to the Director of MIS and, in theory at least, is on an equal footing with Operations, Systems Development, Technical Support, and Planning.

In reality, DRM is essentially a staff function whose clout depends entirely on the support of the MIS Director. Unlike Development or Operations, DRM does not have a large staff and does not perform an immediately critical function. If DRM reports to the Director of MIS, a "Data Administration" function can be established that includes both DRM and DBA.

The advantage of reporting to the MIS Director is the close link that is maintained between data processing and DRM. This helps keep DRM securely anchored to

Figure 4.4 Organizational Placement of the DRM Function
Alternative 1: Reporting to the Director of MIS

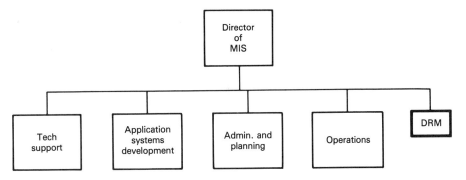

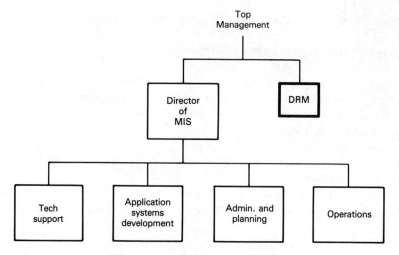

Figure 4.5 Organizational Placement of the DRM Function
Alternative 2: Same Level as Director of MIS

reality. The disadvantage is that DRM can become too parochial. Data processing systems, files and databases constitute only part of the information used in running a company.

In alternative 2, DRM is on the same level as the Director of MIS. Although the position is now enhanced, it still occupies a staff function with little influence in the company. The advantages and disadvantages of Alternative 2 are the opposites of Alternative 1: DRM is potentially more effective from a corporate perspective but runs the danger of getting out of touch with data processing.

In organizations that have a DRM function, the role of DBA is almost entirely technical. DBA is responsible for supporting logical design of application databases and taking the leading role in physical design.

If there is no DRM, DBA takes on more wide-reaching functions. In addition to a technical role, it attempts to integrate database design efforts in various application areas and may attempt to perform corporate data modelling.

Organizations that are seriously committed to the concept of ''data as a corporate resource'' will contain both DBA and DRM functions. Their respective roles will roughly follow the guidelines established earlier in the chapter.

COMMENTS ON THE ROLE OF DBA AND DRM

In the early days of DBMS—roughly 1970 to 1975—many gurus were advocating the establishment of corporate databases that would integrate all the data needed by an organization to run its business. Presiding over this was a Database Administrator, or ''information czar,'' who was to be both a technical wizard and a corporate generalist with an intimate knowledge of the business.

This approach failed for three reasons: the notion of a corporate database was faulty, the combination of skills needed by a Database Administrator was almost impossible to find, and the power of DBA which is, after all, a staff function, was never commensurate with expectations.

The corporate database concept proved faulty because it was frequently interpreted in a very literal sense—that is, people expected a single database that could actually be used by many applications in a production environment. This didn't work. A corporate database cannot possibly include all needed data because all needed data can never be known. Even if this were possible, such a database would not be capable of adequate performance given the state of current technology. By definition, a corporate database is all things to all people—a concept totally incompatible with the real world.

The concept of an all-powerful Database Administrator failed because of the impossible combination of skills postulated for one person. The ability to deal on a corporate level and possession of in-depth business knowledge is rarely compatible with the bits-and-bytes orientation needed to be a successful database technician.

Even when these skills were split between two or more people, a neither-fish-nor-fowl situation developed. The corporate data stewardship role was too far removed from the highly technical DBMS software role, resulting in two temperamentally different functions coexisting uneasily beneath the same roof.

The power of the Database Administrator to accomplish great things was undercut because of a remoteness from line functions. It became clear that a project team representing a specific, immediate need (e.g., implementation of an inventory system) would invariably wield more influence than the DBA.

Applications people had an understandable reluctance to let staff people (read DBA) slow down development or compromise user needs. Being good corporate citizens was not their top priority.

The result of all this was a retrenchment of the Database Administrator's role. This individual's data stewardship functions were deemphasized in favor of a strictly technical orientation. In some cases, the DBA's people were even assigned to work on application development teams in order to ensure maximum cooperation. What began as a stellar new corporate function turned into a group of software jocks that helped design and tune databases.

At about the time that the ''old'' DBA function was dying, a new concept was born. The *Harvard Business Review* and other influential journals began touting data resource management. This was an expansion of the original corporate role of DBA and was based on the theory that information is a valuable corporate resource and should be treated as such. The technical aspects of DBMS were downplayed in favor of the new DRM function: the stewardship of corporate data.

The notion of data as a corporate asset is laudable but only partially correct. Data is not useful unless

- It is accurate.
- It is comprehensive.
- It is meaningful.

- It is timely.
- It is easy to get.
- It is not prohibitively expensive.
- People actually use it once they get it.

These are all "Big Ifs." Data per se is without value. It is an asset only to the extent that the corporate culture encourages its use, the corporate infrastructure makes accurate and timely collection possible, and effective delivery mechanisms exist. Unless these factors are present, data resource management becomes nothing more than a marginally useful exercise in producing attractive charts for Board presentations.

Figure 4.6 Comparison of DBA and DRM Functions

FUNCTION	DATA RESPONSIBILITY	DRM RESPONSIBILITY
Planning	DBMS acquisition, enhancements and maintenance Hardware/software upgrades and changes needed to support DBMS	Data dictionary acquisition Corporate data modeling
Coordination	Use of data between applications Consistency of data definitions between applications	Compatibility of application databases with corporate data model
Application Development and Data Design	Technical consulting for databases design Database tuning Database-oriented backup Utility software for database reorganization and other maintenance	Applications compatibility with corporate EDP plan Corporate perspective on data and applications Improved corporate access to data Corporatewide consistency of data definitions and usage Corporate data security
Standards	Technical conventions	Corporate glossary and data dictionary
Training	Technical	Use of data

To be really effective, DRM must pay a great deal of attention to organizational and delivery factors. The problem is not recognition of data as a corporate resource; it is the collection, delivery, interpretation, and use of data.

The solution is not to spend a lot of time and money preparing corporate data models but, rather, to focus on technical and organizational roadblocks. All too often a preoccupation with the former leads to neglect of the latter. Although some form of high-level data analysis is necessary, it should not be the most important part of DRM's job.

DRM should participate in the activities described in this chapter. However, its role in the corporation should not be exaggerated. The following problems must be recognized:

- DRM lacks real power. Its influence is by persuasion, not by fiat.
- A conflict between corporate and application-specific data definitions is inevitable. The needs of specific applications usually win out because of their immediacy. For example, the development of application systems cannot wait for the consensus needed to agree on common data definitions.
- DRM lacks application familiarity. DRM people are, therefore, at a disadvantage in pushing corporate interests when confronted by the specific knowledge of a development team.

A comparison of proposed DBA and DRM responsibilities is illustrated in Figure 4.6.

This chapter marks the end of the "nontechnical" part of this book. We will now examine the properties of the three most popular data models—hierarchical, network and relational—in order to gain an understanding of how DBMS software actually works. These chapters will be followed by a detailed methodology for developing databases.

DISCUSSION QUESTIONS

Name and describe three major differences between a traditional, or flat file, environment and a DBMS environment.

Who is responsible for the technical aspects of DBMS maintenance—the DBA or the DRM? Explain.

Explain the advantages and disadvantages of having the DBA report to Applications Development, Technical Support or directly to the MIS Director.

What is corporate data modelling and what role should it play in a DBMS environment?

What is a corporate database? Is it a practical alternative to "subject" databases?

Describe and critique the "data as a corporate asset" philosophy.

5

THE HIERARCHICAL MODEL

INTRODUCTION TO DATA MODELS

The evolution of commercial DBMS products has been influenced by some theoretical notions of how data should be organized and viewed. Although the features, advantages and disadvantages of these ''data models'' are sometimes the subject of acrimonious debate, none of the popular systems available today are pure examples.

Therefore, heated advocacy of one model or another should be relegated to coffee-break time. The concern of the selection team is to provide the product that best meets the needs of the organization. Attention to labels simply clouds more important issues.

Having struck that cautionary note, knowledge of the three major models—hierarchical, network and relational—is an important educational exercise. It gives database designers much-needed familiarity with data structures. The specific products that are discussed in this and the next two chapters provide examples of how these models are reflected in real-life systems.

The major differences between models revolve around how data relationships are represented; what a programmer, analyst or end-user must know in order to access data; the degree to which dynamic vs. predefined data relationships are needed; how data is stored and retrieved; and the data controls that are available to the user.

Each of these differences is summarized below.

Data Representation

The way we think about data and the way we graphically express our ideas will vary depending on the DBMS model that is ultimately selected. Hierarchical models discussed in this chapter represent data arrangements using the tree structure. Networks use the plex structure, which is a variant of the tree. Relational models do not use any structural representations. Instead, they rely on two-dimensional tables.

Structural Knowledge That Is Needed

The knowledge that a programmer needs to write programs also varies from model to model. More information on how the database is structured is needed by programmers working with hierarchical and network databases than with relational models. This is because relational databases don't have a structure as such. Navigation is done internally through use of indexes and various search techniques rather than through physical linkages.

Dynamic vs. Predefined Relationships

Establishment of dynamic vs. predefined routes to data also differs from model to model. Although some leeway exists, hierarchical and network databases tend to be limited in providing different ways of accessing data "at run time" (versus at the time the system is initially defined).

However, relational DBMS's also have limitations in this regard. Although practically any piece of information should be accessible in conjunction with any other piece of information, this capability is costly and exists only if the database is skillfully designed. At this time, no "pure" relational model has been successfully implemented—and it may never be.

Physical Storage and Retrieval

The physical makeup of data will vary depending on the model. In theory, this should not happen: logical representation is not supposed to imply any particular physical arrangement. In practice, the way we wish logically to structure data has some influence on its physical implementation.

Hierarchical and network databases make extensive use of pointers embedded in each record, enabling us to find related records. Relational databases use flat files in conjunction with indexes, which lead us to records containing desired values. Hierarchical and network databases also make use of indexes. Most DBMS products, regardless of which model they follow, also place frequently used records in physical proximity to enhance performance.

Data Controls

Hierarchical and network models generally provide a greater degree of automatic control over the integrity of data than do relational models. They also tend to provide more comprehensive backup and recovery facilities.

Nonrelational DBMSs were developed before relational systems and had to carry the brunt of massive batch processing applications, which require extensive controls. Most relational products, on the other hand, were designed primarily to support interactive, ad hoc, management information systems—not transaction processing. Therefore, controls have not been emphasized.

A General Comment on Data Models

The sequence in which the three data models are presented—hierarchical, network and relational—is not an indication of their importance (indeed, the relational model currently enjoys the greatest attention and the hierarchical model, though widely used, is no longer considered a "modern" product). The sequence of presentation provides a convenient learning progression that leads from a fairly simple* but restrictive structure (hierarchical), to a more flexible structure (network), to a "nonstructure" (relational).

In keeping with the pragmatic tenor of this book, I have described actual implementations of each data model, thus illustrating how hierarchical, network and relational concepts work in real life. The examples I have chosen are IBM's IMS (Information Management System), Cullinet's IDMS (Integrated Data Management System),** and IBM's DB2 (Database 2).

Of necessity, the description of each of these products is not comprehensive and contains generalizations that experts may argue with. The reader is therefore urged to consult appropriate vendor manuals and specialized books if a thorough understanding is desired.

Although I discuss three models, many commercial database products are a hodgepodge of concepts and cannot easily be pigeonholed. There are, in a sense, as many "models" as there are DBMS products.

It is sometimes impossible accurately to define terms across products or across theoretical models. For example, the term "record" is used by most people (including the author) in a generic sense. It is also used in a very specific sense to describe one thing in IMS and something quite different in IDMS.

I have, therefore, defined and redefined many of the same terms (record, pointer, index, etc.) for each model. This has resulted in some redundancy in the interests of covering definitional differences and providing a complete package of terms for each model.

---

*However, the implementation of the hierarchical model—at least in the case of IBM's IMS—is anything but simple.

**Since Release 10, the latest version of IDMS, the product has been renamed IDMS/R, the "R" standing for "Relational." This is an attempt by Cullinet to reflect the addition of some relational capabilities in Release 10. I will, however, continue to refer in this book to Cullinet's product by the old name IDMS, which is still what it is commonly called.

HIERARCHICAL	NETWORK	RELATIONAL
Field	Field or data item	Attribute (or column)
Segment	Record type (or record)	Row (or tupple)
Logical record	N/A	N/A
Physical record	N/A	N/A
Parent/child	Owner/member	N/A
Key	Key	Primary key
N/A	Set	N/A
Pointer	Pointer	N/A
Index	Index	Index
File	File	Table (or file)

Figure 5.1 Terms Equivalency Table

Figure 5.1 is a terms equivalency chart to help lead you through the sometimes confusing thicket of product-specific terminology.

Finally, it is almost impossible to make ironclad generalizations about the advantages and disadvantages of each model because so much depends on the specific implementation—and we have only covered three products. The reader should keep this in mind when making the DBMS selection.

The normalization chapter describes a method of data decomposition that is sometimes (incorrectly) ascribed exclusively to relational models. It is not presented here as a complete database design methodology but, rather, as an aid to understanding data. The Entity-Relationship Approach described in the Database Development chapter, on the other hand, has been expanded into a comprehensive development methodology. That approach was created for network databases but, like normalization, is also suitable for use with other models.

INTRODUCTION TO HIERARCHICAL DATABASES

The first widely used commercial DBMS, IBM's Information Management System (IMS), was based on the hierarchical data model. Or, perhaps more accurately, the model and IMS grew up together in a symbiotic relationship, one explaining the other.

Although the limitations of this structure seem in hindsight to have made it a peculiar basis for a major new product, the primitive computer technology of the 1960's precluded greater sophistication. After all, when IMS was first introduced in 1968, even very large commercial computers could not rival the speed and memory capacity of today's top-of-the-line personal computers.

Early versions of IMS were crude by today's standards. However, the product has changed substantially over the years and now includes many state-of-the-art features. IMS is a powerful, popular, extremely complex DBMS that is still going strong. It is a mistake to dismiss it out-of-hand—as some academics do—because it was based on a simplistic concept of data: the tree structure described below.

THE TREE STRUCTURE

People intuitively understand hierarchies because hierarchies represents superior/ subordinate relationships between people and between things. Our everyday experience with school, work, the military and sometimes even the church corroborates the pervasive nature of hierarchies.

A hierarchy is represented in its theoretical form by a construct that looks like a tree uprooted by a hurricane and deposited upside down. Examine Figure 5.2. Each small numbered circle represents a *node*. The topmost node is called the *root* and the nodes on the bottom are called *leaves*. This is where the tree analogy ends and the family analogy begins.

Each set of nodes connected by a line represents a parent/child relationship. Node 1 is a *parent*. Nodes 2, 3 and 4 are its *children* and are, in turn, parents to other children. Note that in a hierarchy each child has only one parent (computer people are not very good at thinking up accurate metaphors).

Each "generation" of children is referred to as one *level* of the hierarchy. Our example consists of four levels. Level one is the root; level two consists of nodes 2, 3 and 4; level three consists of nodes 5–11; and level four consists of node 12.

Now look at Figure 5.3. A *family* consists of all the children of one parent. Its size is called a *dimension*. Thus, nodes 5–8 are a *family of dimension 4*. The number of children of a single parent is called a *degree*. Node 4 is thus a *node of degree 2*. A *count* refers to the total number of nodes in a level. level three has a count of 7.

The dotted lines surrounding nodes 1, 3 and 9, nodes 4 and 10, and nodes 1 and 2, are examples of *paths*. The first path is *maximal* because it starts at the root and follows one branch of the tree all the way down to a leaf. The other paths, of *length 2*, do not go

Figure 5.2 A Tree Structure: Root, Leaves, Parents, Children and Levels

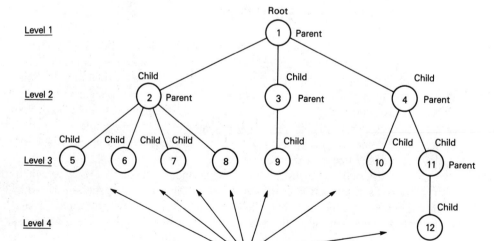

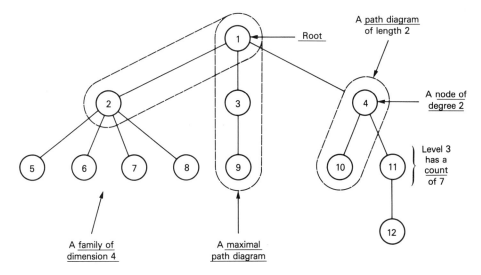

Figure 5.3 A Tree Structure: Families, Dimensions, Degrees, Counts, and Paths

all the way down. Paths are an important concept in the design of hierarchical and network databases because they can provide an indication of how records are accessed.

Here, then, are the salient features of tree structures:

- A tree structure contains a hierarchy of nodes.
- The top of the structure contains one and only one node, the root.
- Each node except the root must be connected to one and only one higher-level node.
- Each parent may have one or more children.

Some relationships can be represented very nicely by a tree structure, and some cannot.

In a Customer Order database the relationship between a Customer record and an Order record is hierarchical. A customer may have many Orders at any given time but a specific Order can only be for one Customer. This is known as a *one-to-many* relationship and is illustrated in Figure 5.4. Customer is the parent and Order is the child.

But in the case of an Order and a Part, the hierarchical relationship breaks down. Figure 5.5 illustrates a *many-to-many* relationship. An Order can consist of many Parts, but, at the same time, a specific Part can appear on many different Orders. This situation defies a conventional parent/child representation in a tree structure because it violates the hierarchical principle that a child can have one and only one parent.

We can get around this limitation by decomposing a many-to-many relationship into several one-to-many relationships. In our Order/Part example, we create two relationships: a one-to-many relationship between Order and Part, and another one-to-many relationship between Part and Order. Figure 5.6 illustrates this translation. The resulting structures meet our criteria for a tree.

However, we pay a price in data redundancy. As Figure 5.5 shows, instead of having one and only one record for a ⅛″ NUT, a 1″ BOLT, a NO 15 SCREW, and a

A customer may have multiple orders but an order can apply to only one customer.

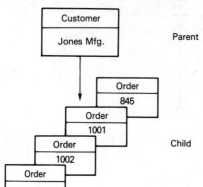

Figure 5.4   A One-to-Many Relationship

SMALL CLIP, as well as one record for each Order, specific Part and Order records must be repeated each time they appear in combination. Even in our small example, the NO 15 SCREW appears twice, the SMALL CLIP appears three times, etc. We can reduce some of this redundancy by simply keeping only one part of the relationship: Order and Part, as in the top of Figure 5.5, or Part and Order, as in the bottom of Figure 5.5. This would mean that only Parts, in the former case, or only Orders, in the latter case, would need to be repeated.

Unfortunately, representing only one half of the relationship may hinder our ability to find quickly all the Orders for a given Part, in the first case, or all the Parts for a given Order in the second case. The physical structure that is likely to result from this logical structure is not amenable to finding quickly the information we need.*

We can, of course, maintain *both* relationships illustrated in Figure 5.5 and give ourselves the benefit of being able to access data either through the Order/Part relationship or through the Part/Order relationship. However, this doubles the size of an already redundant structure.

There is a reasonable solution to this problem but it lies in the workings of the DBMS software itself and not in the character of the tree structure. We shall see how IMS accommodates many-to-many relationships in the next section.

IMS CONCEPTS

This is a brief summary of how IMS arranges and manipulates data. A good way to understand the basic concepts is to learn IMS terms, the most important of which are described below and illustrated in Figures 5.7–5.10. A Customer Order database is used as an example.

---

*As indicated in earlier chapters, even though a logical structure should not influence the way data will be physically arranged, in practice the two are related.

A customer can order many different parts with one order;
a part can appear on many invoices.

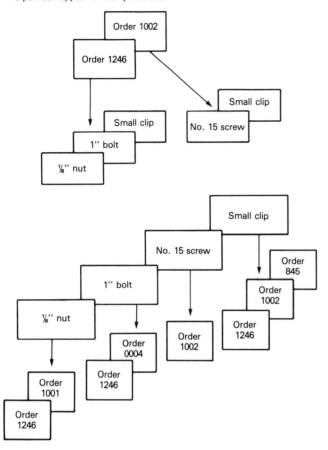

Figure 5.5 A Many-to-Many Relationship

- A *field* is the smallest unit of data recognized by IMS. Per Figure 5.7, examples of fields are Customer Name, Invoice Number, and Part Number.
- A *segment* is a data aggregate containing one or more fields. A segment is analogous to a record in a flat file and is the basic unit of data accessed and manipulated by IMS. Examples of *segment types* are Customer, Address, Salesperson, Order, and Part.
- A *root segment* is at the top of the hierarchy. In Figure 5.7 this is the Customer.
- A *dependent segment* relies on a higher-level segment for its full meaning or identification. For example, the Address segment in Figure 5.7 is meaningless if taken by itself—anyone can live at, say, 425 Main Street. It is only when we know that the segment to which it is attached is the Jones Manufacturing Company that the address becomes useful.
- Order and Part have their own identifiers, and are thus *independent segments*. They are related to, but not dependent on, higher-level segments for their identity.

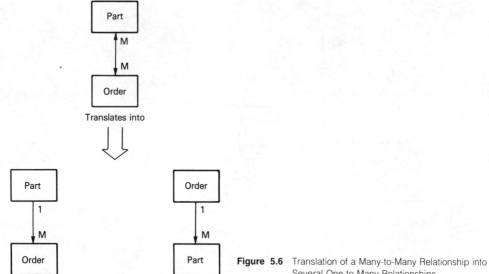

Figure 5.6 Translation of a Many-to-Many Relationship into Several One-to-Many Relationships

- *Parent* and *child* segments have a superior/subordinate relationship to each other. The Customer segment is the parent of Address, Salesperson and Order, and they, in turn, are the children of Customer. The Order segment is the parent of Part, as well as the child of Customer.

- *Twin segments* are occurrences of one segment type. In Figure 5.8 Parts 950, 122 and 1300 attached to Order 1246 are twin segments, as are Parts 1240 and 1300 attached to Order 1002. Orders 1246 and 1002 are also twins because they are attached to the Jones Mfg. Co. customer segment.

- A *logical record* is a set of hierarchically related segments passed to the application program. This is what the programmer or end-user actually sees. A logical record may be

Figure 5.7 An Illustration of IMS Terminology

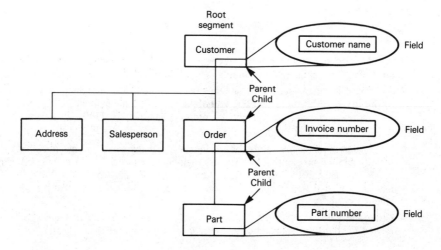

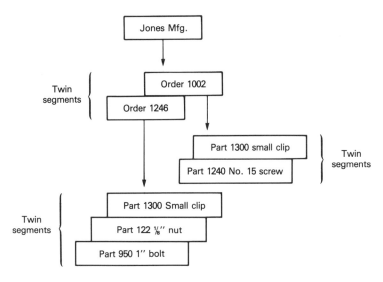

Figure 5.8 An Example of Multiple Occurrences

comprised of segments from one or more physical records. The logical record for Jones Manufacturing Company, illustrated in Figure 5.9, was derived by traversing the data structure in Figure 5.8 from top to bottom, left to right, pulling in each segment along the way. This is an *instance* of the Jones Manufacturing Company record.

■ A *physical record* is a group of hierarchically related segments stored as one consecutive record on the database. A physical record may or may not correspond to a logical record.

■ A *logical database* is the way the database appears to an application programmer or end-user. The purpose of the logical database concept is to allow the user to see data in a functionally useful manner without being limited by its physical structure. Figure 5.10 is an example of a logical database.

■ A *physical database* is the arrangement of the logical database on a storage device.

The alert reader will notice a problem with the database in Figure 5.8: we haven't solved the redundancy associated with representing many-to-many relationships in a tree struc-

Jones Mfg.
Order #1246
Part 950 1″ bolt
Part 122 ⅛′ nut
Part 1300 Small clip
Order #1002
Part 1240 No. 15 screw
Part 1300 Small clip

Figure 5.9 A Logical Record

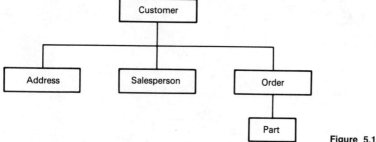

Figure 5.10 A Logical Database

ture. We are simply repeating the Part segment each time a specific part is ordered (e.g., the Small Clip for Orders 1246 and 1002.)

The solution lies in the interrelationship of physical databases, illustrated in Figure 5.11. Since the software does not restrict access to multiple trees, the "real" Part segment can be placed in a second tree structure. The creation of a second tree is reasonable because we will probably wish to store more information about parts than is needed strictly to satisfy customer order information requirements. Some of this additional data may include Part Description, the Warehouse the part is stored in, and the Parts Supplier, as shown on the right-hand side of Figure 5.11.

The Part segment in our Customer Order tree will then become a *pointer segment*

Figure 5.11 Relationships between Two Physical Databases

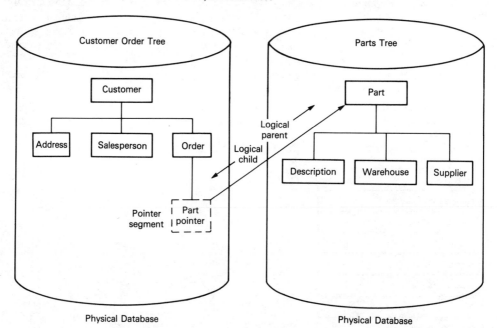

that contains little more than the address of the part we are looking for. The address will bring us into the Parts tree where the "real" Parts segment is stored. This approach is less redundant and more flexible than maintaining two sets of records, as in Figure 5.5.

The Part segment in the Customer Order tree is the *logical child* of the Part segment in the Parts tree and the *physical child* of the Order segment. Conversely, the Part segment in the Parts tree is the *logical parent* of the Part Pointer segment. Figure 5.12 illustrates these relationships in greater detail.

The need to interrelate tree structures is quite common. We could include a pointer to the Personnel database for information about the salesperson, a pointer from the Parts database to a Purchasing and/or Manufacturing database to facilitate requirements generation, a pointer to an Accounts Receivable database to track customer payments, and so on. In fact, performance considerations are more likely than business needs to limit the use of these pointer segments.

It is interesting to note that in most many-to-many relationships important information exists in common between two or more related segments. This information is often unique to the specific records and is called *intersection data*. It is stored in the pointer segment along with the address of the physical parent. Figure 5.13 illustrates three examples of intersection data.

In a school database, an instructor teaches several courses and a course may have several instructors. The intersection data includes the time and place of the course section that the instructor is teaching.

In a Personnel database, an employee may have many skills and a skill may be possessed by many employees. The intersection data may be the date a person became officially qualified in a specific skill.

In our Customer Order example, the intersection data is the Quantity of a specific part that was ordered, the quantity that was shipped and the dollar amount the customer owes. The Part Pointer segment in the left-hand database in Figures 5.11 and 5.12 can thus become a Quantity segment and can carry quantity and dollar data for a specific Order/Part combination.

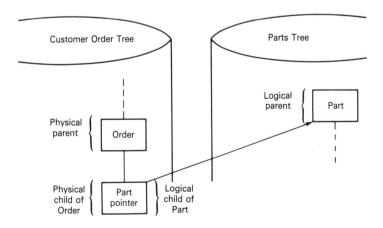

Figure 5.12 Physical/Logical Relationships between Two Trees

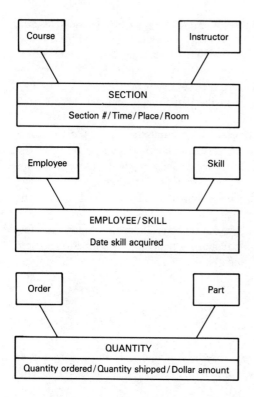

Figure 5.13 Examples of Intersection Data

PHYSICAL CONSIDERATIONS

Most of our discussion has centered around the "logical" aspects of the hierarchical data model. This is what the programmer and systems analyst are most concerned with. However, physical considerations cannot be ignored.

Here are the major physical features of IMS.

Pointers

In addition to carrying application data (Customer Name, Customer Number, etc.) each record or segment in a hierarchical database may contain one or more *pointers*. A pointer is a field containing the address of the next logically related record.

A *child* pointer resides in the parent segment and contains the address of the first occurrence of the child segment. A special type of child pointer can also be used to point to the last occurrence. A *twin* pointer points to the next occurrence of the same segment type. *Forward* and *backward* pointers can be used to provide reverse addressing.

A variety of pointers is illustrated for a specific instance of the Customer/Order/Part hierarchy in Figure 5.14.

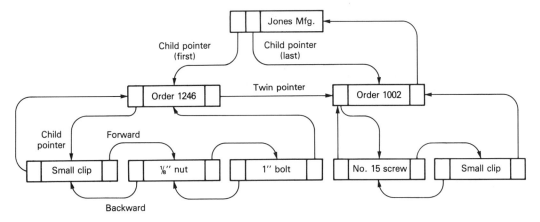

Figure 5.14 Examples of Pointers

Storage Space

Space on a mass storage device must be allocated before a database can be built. Although this is usually the job of database technicians, the information on which allocation decisions should be made is provided by application designers. Two considerations of particular interest are *free space* and *overflow*.

Free space consists of small pieces of disk storage reserved for expansion and scattered throughout the main storage areas allocated to the database. If application designers believe that the business will expand, they must attempt to predict how that growth will affect the database. Will the number of customers increase? The number of orders per customer? The number of parts per order? Or a combination of all of the above?

If orders increase by 20 percent, and if the current number of orders per customer is four or five, it may be advisable to leave unused space to fit one or two additional occurrences of Order for each customer.

Overflow is a contiguous chunk of disk storage that is used when the number of occurrences for a given segment exceeds the space we have allocated to it. Overflow areas are allocated outside main storage for a data structure. Since the search for records that have been pushed into overflow may be slower than the use of free space, careful analysis should be done to accommodate new segments without resorting to overflow areas.

Figure 5.15 illustrates free space and overflow concepts for the Order and Part segments of our Customer Order database. If we have allocated enough room for three occurrences of the Part segment, the fourth occurrence (e.g., Small Clip) will be placed into the overflow area.

Secondary Indexing

This is a technique used to keep track of the location of segments that contain nonkey fields with specific values. We may, for example, wish to retrieve orders by Order Date as

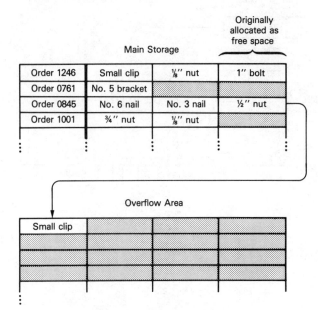

Figure 5.15 Free Space and Overflow

well as Invoice Number. Use of a secondary index based on Order Date (see Figure 5.16) eliminates the need to examine each Order segment sequentially.

File Organization

We are given a choice of file access techniques for physically implementing all or parts of our tree structure. The two generic techniques for accomplishing this are *sequential* and *direct*.

The sequential method is the oldest technique for storing and accessing records. In a database context, this means the adjacent storage of all the segments that comprise a logical record. Figure 5.17 illustrates this concept.

An index may be used to bring us to the root segment occurrence of each physical record. In that way the entire file need not be read to find the group of segments that comprise the record of interest.

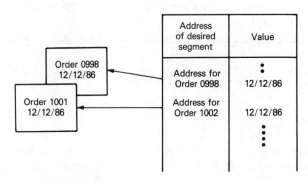

Figure 5.16 Secondary Index on Order Date

	First Record								Second Record		etc...
Jones Mfg.	Order 1246	Part 1300	Part 122	Part 950	Order 1002	Part 1300	Part 1240	ABC, Inc.	Order 0761	Part 715	etc.

Figure 5.17 Physical Records

The direct method uses a mathematical formula called a *hashing algorithm* to convert a symbolic key, such as Customer Number, into a specific physical storage location. This results in a scattering of data across the entire storage area allocated to the tree structure. Dependent segments may or may not be in physical proximity depending on the use of twin pointers.

IBM's access methods are illustrated in simplified form in Figures 5.18–5.20. They are:

- *HSAM*, which stands for Hierarchic Sequential Access Method. This is a database access method in name only. It is simply the ancient sequential access technique used since the early days of computers.
- *HISAM*, which is the Hierarchic Indexed Sequential Access Method. This is indexed access to a root segment followed by sequential access to dependent segment occurrences.
- *HDAM*, which is the Hierarchic Direct Access Method. This is random (hashed) access by key to a root segment followed by either sequential or pointer-based access to dependent segments.

Figure 5.18 IMS Sequential Access Methods—HSAM and HISAM

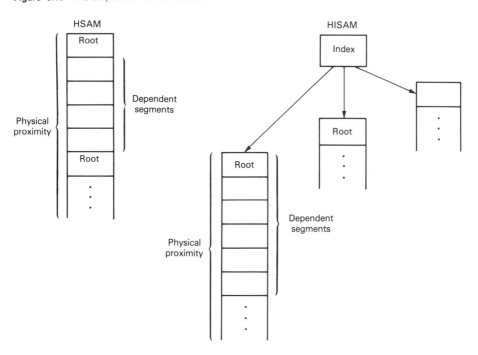

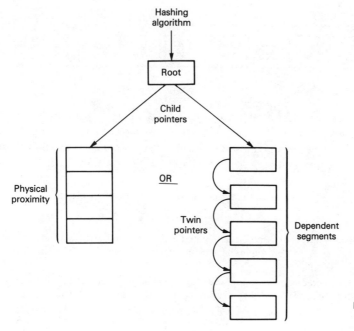

Figure 5.19 IMS Direct Access Methods—HDAM

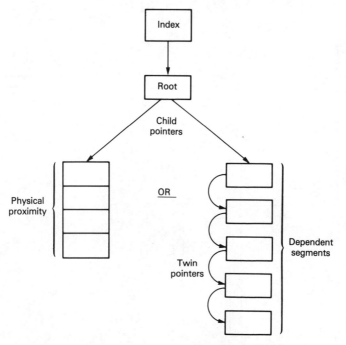

Figure 5.20 IMS Direct Access Methods—HIDAM

- *HIDAM*, which stands for Hierarchic Indexed Direct Access Method. This is indexed access to the root segment followed by either sequential or pointer-based access to dependent segments.

The choice of physical file organization techniques depends on many complex factors. These include the frequency of access to various segments, the size and number of segment types, the volatility of the database, and so on.

ADVANTAGES AND DISADVANTAGES

Here are some comments about hierarchical databases in general and IMS databases in particular. A product such as IMS is appropriate under the following circumstances:

- Most relationships are one-to-many. Although many-to-many relationships are accommodated in some hierarchical systems, the natural structure for these relationships is a network.
- Most data manipulation is routine and predefined. Extensive ad hoc queries are handled better in relational models.
- Performance is important. Hierarchical (and network) databases often outperform today's relational databases when large amounts of data are processed in a predictable fashion.
- The installation is large enough to absorb the start-up and training costs of an extremely complex product. IMS may, in fact, have the dubious distinction of being the most complex, option-packed DBMS on the market. Its age has resulted in an accretion of rules, features and limitations that are not always clear or logically consistent.
- The database design is fairly static. It is no small matter to make significant structural changes to an IMS database.

DISCUSSION QUESTIONS

What relevance does a discussion of models have in learning about databases? Can it be counterproductive? Explain.

Name the chief characteristics that can differ between models.

Name three important characteristics of tree structures.

What type of relationships cannot be described using a "pure" hierarchical model? How do real-life hierarchical DBMS packages get around this?

What is a segment? A root segment? A dependent segment?

What is a record in IMS? Give an example.

What is the purpose of free space? Overflow?

What is the difference between a child pointer and a twin pointer?

Name and describe, in general terms, the four main access methods used by IMS.

6

THE NETWORK
MODEL

INTRODUCTION

In 1971, the Conference on Data Systems Languages (CODASYL), representing various computer manufacturers and large users, established a set of industrywide DBMS standards. These standards defined database terms and described the concepts vendors should use in developing their products.

CODASYL recommended a network architecture that was followed by some vendors but ignored by others. The most popular network DBMS products to emerge were Cullinet's Integrated Database Management System (IDMS), and Cincom Systems' TO-TAL.

A network DBMS has many features in common with its hierarchical counterpart. Both make use of pointers embedded in database records to find related records. Both require that programmers know the database structure in order to use the product. And both rely heavily on predefined rather than dynamically selected access paths.

However, there are important conceptual as well as terminological differences that will become clear as we examine the network model. Because network-based products usually follow at least some CODASYL standards, we will use CODASYL terminology whenever possible. As in the section on hierarchical models, we will examine network theory and follow that with a discussion of how a CODASYL product actually works.

THE PLEX STRUCTURE

A *plex* or *network* structure—the terms are used interchangeably—is one in which any node can be linked with any other node. It is less restrictive than a tree structure because there are no hierarchical implications and because many-to-many, as well as one-to-many, relationships are allowed. Unlike a tree, which points downward from the root, the nodes multiplying like so many amoebas, a network shows nodes that can be interrelated in any fashion—up, down, sideways.

Figure 6.1 illustrates how plex structures differ from trees. Trees conform to an orderly hierarchy. Networks, on the other hand, can sustain any conceivable connections between nodes.

Note the duplication that occurs when we attempt to use a tree structure in situations where a network is more suitable. In the first example of Figure 6.1, Node 4, which happens to have two parents, must appear twice in the tree. Node 6 also appears twice. The second tree is even more redundant: what was accomplished in seven nodes in a plex structure requires eleven nodes in a tree.

A network can be *simple* or *complex*. A simple plex structure is one that contains

Figure 6.1 Comparison of Plex and Tree Structures

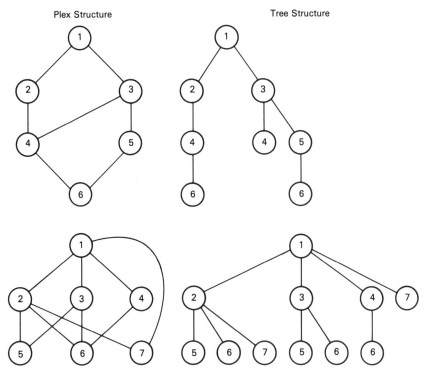

only one-to-one or one-to-many relationships. Figure 6.2 illustrates such a network, the "1" and "M" on each line indicating the association.

A complex network, illustrated in Figure 6.3, accommodates many-to-many as well as one-to-many relationships. Most implementations of the network model support the simple but not the complex structure. But, in most cases, this is not a serious drawback.

If we think carefully about Figure 6.3, we will notice that certain needed data cannot be placed into the entities illustrated on the diagram: where can we express the quantity of a specific part on a specific order? Where can we record the amount of a given part stored in a warehouse? Where do we go to find out what a specific supplier is charging us for a specific part?

This is called *junction* or *intersection* data. It exists uniquely within the confluence of two or more records connected by a many-to-many relationship.

The quantity of each Part that was ordered by a customer, the quantity that was actually shipped and the dollar amount this represents is an example of intersection data. This information is stored in the newly created Quantity record, which sits between the Order and the Part records in Figure 6.4. The Part/Warehouse and Part/Supplier relationships also result in the creation of junction records:

- The amount of each part supplied by a vendor (Part Supplied).
- The on-hand quantity of a specific part in a specific warehouse (Stock Status).
- The bids that were made by suppliers to sell us parts (Quotation).

Notice that the creation of these new record types has resulted in the transformation of each many-to-many relationship into several one-to-many relationships. As we shall see in Chapter 10, The Steps of Database Development, the resolution of many-to-many relationship into one-to-many relationships is an important part of the design process.

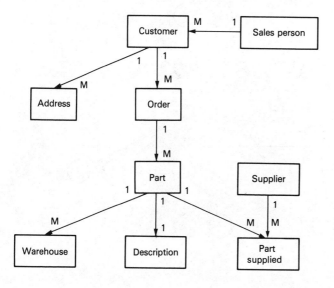

Figure 6.2 A Simple Network Structure

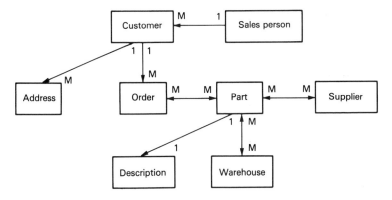

Figure 6.3 A Complex Network Structure

So far, we have illustrated relationships only between different record types: Customer and Order, Order and Quantity, Part and Stock Status, etc. But what if we wish to express a relationship between occurrences of a single record type?

In our Customer Order database, some salespeople, because of their experience and skills, are given management as well as sales responsibilities. There is no difference between information that must be kept about ordinary salespeople and salespeople with management responsibilities—let us call them ''sales managers.'' As a result, the creation of separate ''salesperson'' and ''sales manager'' record types is logically, if not physi-

Figure 6.4 A Network Structure with Intersection Data

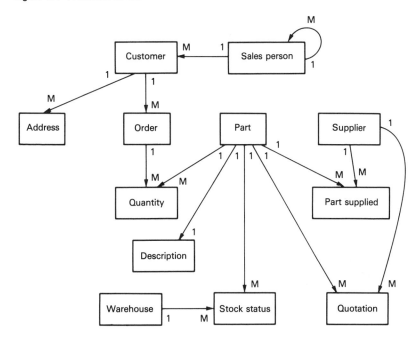

cally, redundant. We can avoid this situation simply by defining a Sales Manager/ Salesperson relationship between occurrences of the same record type. This is called an *iterative relationship* or *loop* and is illustrated in Figure 6.5.

Our specific example is a one-to-many loop. It is one-to-many because a salesperson designated as a sales manager can have many salespeople reporting to him or her, but each salesperson can have only one manager.

A fancier loop is illustrated in the middle of Figure 6.5. In this case, salespeople and sales managers are interchangeable, depending on customer accounts. For example, Jones manages Smith for one group of customers and Smith manages Jones for another group. Furthermore, Jones can have Smith as a manager on one account and Thomas as a manager on another. Both salespeople and sales managers can relate to each other in a many-to-many fashion. This is called a many-to-many loop and, like other many-to-many relationships, requires resolution into a one-to-many form through the creation of an additional record type. This is illustrated at the bottom of Figure 6.5.

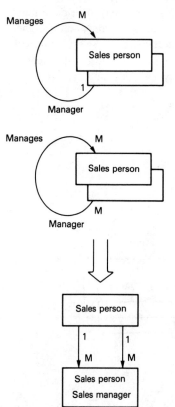

Figure 6.5 An Iterative Relationship

CODASYL CONCEPTS

So far, we have discussed the inherent characteristics of plex structures with little regard to specific CODASYL standards or products. This section continues to describe network principles but we shall now include terminology and concepts used by CODASYL-based DBMS products—specifically, Cullinet's Integrated Database Management System (IDMS). This is perhaps the most popular network DBMS.

A *set* is a two-level tree consisting of one (and only one) *owner* record type and one or more *member* record types. The top of Figure 6.6 illustrates a set relationship and the bottom illustrates an *instance* of a set, consisting of one *occurrence* of the owner record and all the occurrences of the member. Incidentally, the CODASYL meaning of the word "set" should not be confused with its usage in mathematical set theory.

A *record* in CODASYL parlance is roughly analogous to a segment in IMS and a table in a relational database (see the next chapter). As you have probably deduced from the previous section, the term *record type* refers to a category of records such as Customer. The term "record" can have either a generic (e.g., Customer) or specific (e.g., Jones Mfg.) meaning, depending on context.

There can be as many sets as there are relationships between individual records. For example, the database illustrated in Figure 6.4 can be defined to contain thirteen sets:

- Salesperson/Sales Manager (the Salesperson loop)
- Salesperson/Customer
- Customer/Address

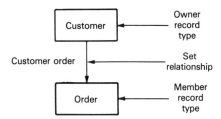

An Instance of the Customer / Order Set

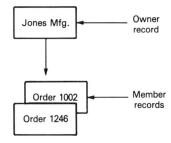

Figure 6.6 A CODASYL Set

- Customer/Order
- Order/Quantity
- Part/Quantity
- Part/Description
- Part/Stock Status
- Warehouse/Stock Status
- Part/Quotation
- Part/Part Supplied
- Supplier/Part Supplied
- Supplier/Quotation

If appropriate, we could define fewer sets with more members in each set. Figure 6.7 illustrates part of Figure 6.4 using the following new set definitions:

- Part/Quantity/Stock Status/Quotation/Part Supplied
- Supplier/Part Supplied/Quotation
- Warehouse/Stock Status

We can also define two different sets using the same record types. For example, suppose we wish to access active orders most of the time, but are also interested in a customer's buying history. We can define the Customer and Order records as belonging to both a Past Orders set and an Outstanding Orders set as illustrated in Figure 6.8. We can now access Outstanding Orders using one set and Past Orders using the other.

A *singular set* can also be defined. This is a set containing only one record type with the owner defined simply as ''system.'' This permits the record to be treated independently of its other relationships. For example, if the Order record contains a unique

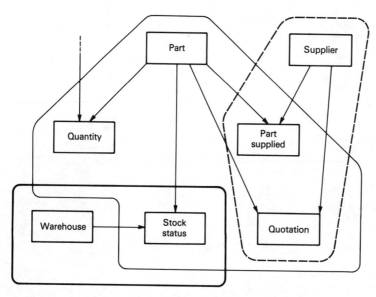

Figure 6.7 Example of Sets

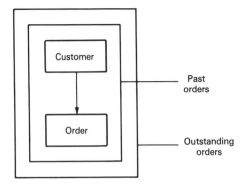

Figure 6.8 Two Sets Covering the Same Record Types

key, it can be defined as a singular set and, therefore, accessed without the need to first get the Customer record to which it is attached. Figure 6.9 illustrates a singular set.

Specific occurrences of a record type can participate in a set in a variety of ways. These are called set membership types and can be *mandatory* or *optional*. Mandatory membership means that, once added to a set, a record occurrence cannot be deleted—only modified. This helps ensure that a Customer record, for example, is not deleted, leaving Order records without an owner. Optional membership allows a record to be removed from the set or deleted from the database.

Membership can also be *automatic* or *manual*. Automatic membership permits the DBMS software to establish the linkages necessary to make a new record occurrence part of a set. Manual membership means that these linkages must be established—or selectively ignored—by the application program.

The Mandatory/Automatic choice provides the greatest margin of safety for most applications. In fact, the specification of membership is an important consideration in *referential integrity*. This is the notion that in most relationships there is an implied hierarchy between records in a set—that is, they "go together" in a specific direction. Thus, orders should not exist without customers, a stock item always belongs to a warehouse, etc.

Referential integrity is one of the strong suits of structurally oriented (e.g., hierarchical and network) database models.

Set selection is the means specified to retrieve an occurrence of an owner record and/or the members attached to it. Keys and sequential searches are the most commonly used techniques.

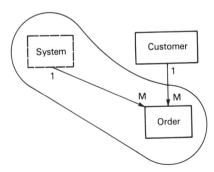

Figure 6.9 A Singular Set

The key method, sometimes called CALC for the statement used to define it in the CODASYL Data Definition Language, requires a unique key for the record. A hashing algorithm converts the key to the physical location in the database area where the record will be stored.

VIA sets are used to find member records after the owner has been reached through the use of a key. VIA indicates to the DBMS software that each occurrence of the member is to be stored on or near the physical page in which the owner is stored.

Figure 6.10 illustrates set selection techniques. Suppose we wish to determine how many Small Clips (part 1300) are available in Warehouse 12. First, we find the desired Part record directly through the use of a hashing algorithm. Then we read all the Stock Status records attached to it until we reach the one for Warehouse 12. This is the record we are looking for. Note the approximation of the physical layout at the bottom of Figure 6.10. (Incidentally, the software can automatically reject the addition of a Part record with an already existing Part Number. The rejection of duplicate records can be specified by the designer for any CALC record.)

The order in which new record occurrences in a database are available for retrieval can also be specified in CODASYL models. This is illustrated in Figures 6.11 to 6.13.

Figure 6.10 Use of CALC and VIA

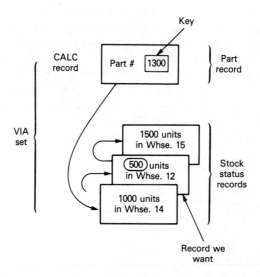

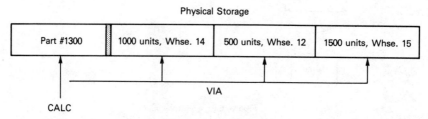

ORDER IS FIRST

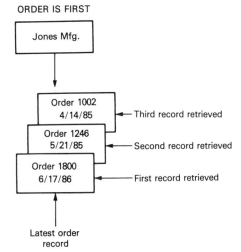

Figure 6.11 Order Is First

We can specify ORDER IS FIRST for new occurrences of the Order record. This ensures that the latest Order for a customer will be retrieved first—a sequence that may be convenient for customer inquiry and billing purposes. We could also specify ORDER IS LAST. This may be a convenient sequence for accessing new Quantity records, since we may wish to access them in the sequence in which line items appear on the invoice form.

ORDER IS SORTED rearranges the retrieval sequence each time a new record is added. This can be a very slow process but may be useful when we wish our records always to appear in a certain order. We may, for example, wish to use sorted order when listing Suppliers. That way they will appear on all of our purchase reports in identifier sequence.

ORDER IS LAST

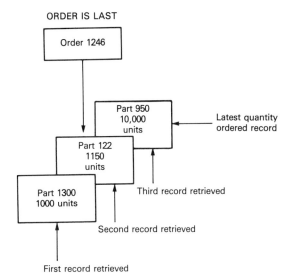

Figure 6.12 Order Is Last

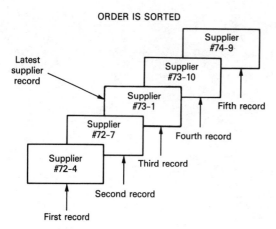

ORDER IS SORTED

Figure 6.13   Order Is Sorted

It should be noted that the sequence of records specified in the ORDER clause is a *logical* sequence. It determines the order in which records will be presented to the application program or end-user. Although pointers are affected, ORDER does not necessarily correspond to the *physical* placement of records.

PHYSICAL CONSIDERATIONS

Although the logical and physical aspects of database design are theoretically independent, almost all design decisions have physical implications. In the case of a network database, "logical" decisions such as the use of keys, the sequence in which records are to be retrieved, and the way records are related to one another by sets, necessarily limits our choice of physical arrangements. The most important of these arrangements concerns *areas*, *physical contiguity* and *pointers*.

Areas

An area is that portion of mass storage reserved for the physical storage of specified record types. We may subdivide our database into several areas in order to achieve greater storage efficiency, access speed and processing convenience.

Here are two examples of the potential benefits the kind of area arrangement illustrated in Figure 6.14 can achieve:

- A small portion of mass storage can be densely packed with one type of record to enhance processing speed. For example, we can assign an area to carry Customer and Address records exclusively. This ensures very fast access to customer address information.
- Since many security and integrity controls cover an area rather than the entire database, we can perform certain functions on two related records in different areas at the same time. Although care must be exercised, this independent processing capability can be a useful feature.

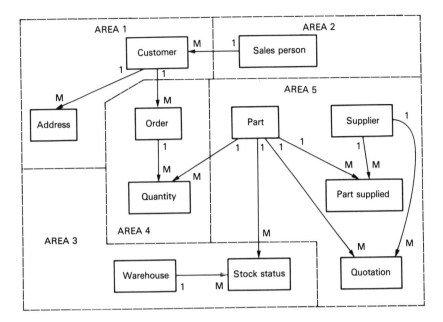

Figure 6.14 Areas

Physical Contiguity

Physical contiguity (or proximity, as it is sometimes called) refers to the placement of member records next to their owner. This technique can greatly reduce the time it takes to find member records.

Figure 6.15 illustrates the placement of Quantity records next to Order records. Since a large chunk of mass storage can be accessed by the computer with one command, once we have found the right owner record we will probably also pick up all the member occurrences associated with it. Without such contiguous placement, each member may require a separate read operation, a time-consuming mechanical task.

The specification of *free space* and *overflow*, illustrated in the lower portion of 6.15, allows room for future expansion. However, excessive use of overflow and/or the underutilization of free space can negate the advantages of physical contiguity.

Furthermore, physical contiguity is part-and-parcel of the VIA record definition. This means that once we have decided to use physical contiguity we cannot, in most database products, access member occurrences without first finding the appropriate owner record—a potential disadvantage. These and other issues are something the database analyst must consider when designing the database.

Pointers

A pointer is a field in a database record that contains the address of a related record. Pointers allow us to navigate a set of records without the need for physical contiguity. Figure 6.16 illustrates each major type of pointer generally available in network

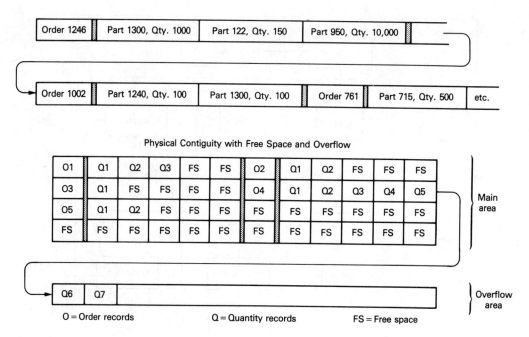

Figure 6.15 Physical Contiguity

databases. A *next*, or *forward*, pointer contains the address of the first occurrence of the member record. A *prior*, or *backward*, pointer can be defined to point to the last occurrence. An *owner* pointer contains the address of the owner record. It enables us quickly to return to the owner once we have found the member record we are looking for.

Unless a record type is at the bottom of our network, it will contain at least two pointers: one pointing to the first occurrence of the member record type; and the other pointing to the next occurrence of the same record type. The latter is called a twin pointer and is illustrated in figure 6.17. Incidentally, the forward twin pointer in the last occurrence of a record always points back to the owner, as does the backward pointer in the first occurrence.

Figure 6.17 illustrates all these pointers in the context of our Customer Order database:

- Next and prior pointers in the customer record enable us to see the newest and the oldest outstanding Orders for Jones Manufacturing Company without the need to see any intervening records.
- Backward (prior) and forward (next) twin pointers permit us to read Quantity records in either direction. This backward and forward scanning may help order entry clerks when correcting errors.
- Owner pointers enable us to go directly back to Jones Manufacturing after we have read the Order record of our choice. Without this facility we would have to read all the remaining Order records before returning to the owner.

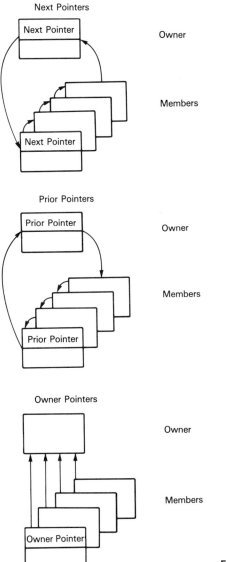

Next Pointers

Next Pointer

Owner

Members

Next Pointer

Prior Pointers

Prior Pointer

Owner

Members

Prior Pointer

Owner Pointers

Owner

Members

Owner Pointer

Figure 6.16 Pointers

The selection of pointers depends largely on the number of member record occurrences we expect for a given owner record type, the way the set will be processed, and the amount of space we can afford (each pointer requires about six bytes per record).

A long string of member occurrences and the need for very fast inquiry response time may necessitate extensive pointer arrangements. But this must be balanced off

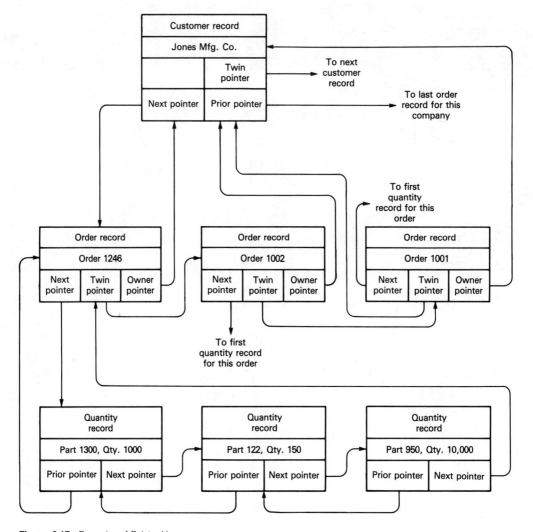

Figure 6.17 Examples of Pointer Usage

against the extra time needed to maintain pointers when updating the database and the extra space pointers require.

The alert reader may have noticed that Figures 6.15 and 6.17 actually reflect alternate ways of storing an Order/Quantity set. Whereas access to data in Figure 6.15 relies on the physical proximity of members to their owner, Figure 6.17 uses pointers.

This brings up an interesting dilemma. The Quantity record actually has two owners, Part and Order (see Figure 6.4). These relationships are, of necessity, defined in two different sets since a set can have only one owner record.

We cannot have physical contiguity between the Part/Quantity set *and* between

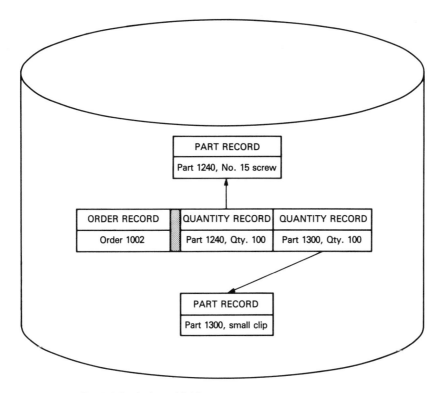

Figure 6.18 Physical Contiguity and Pointers

Figure 6.19 A Ring Structure with Two Record Types

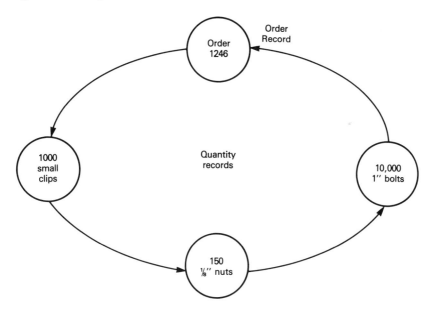

the Order/Quantity set. A Quantity record cannot be adjacent to both an Order and a Part record—that is physically impossible! Therefore, a choice must be made. For the Order/Quantity set we may wish to use physical contiguity because Quantity is almost always updated and accessed along with Order. In fact, the Quantity record is meaningless outside the context of a specific order. The less frequently used Part/Quantity set, on the other hand, may be connected through the use of pointers, leaving physical proximity to the other set. Figure 6.18 is a simplified illustration of this new arrangement.

Figure 6.20   A Ring Structure with Three Record Types

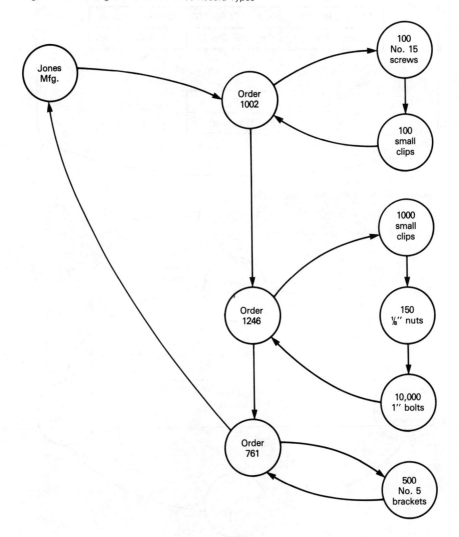

The use of pointers leads to the creation of *rings* or *chains*. Figure 6.19 illustrates a simple ring structure between the Order and Quantity records. Figure 6.20 is a more complex example that includes three different record types. Here is a guide to interpreting Figure 6.20:

- All Orders are for Jones Manufacturing Company.
- Order 1002 consists of Number 15 Screws and Small Clips, both of which were ordered in quantities of 100.
- Order 1246 consists of Small Clips, ⅛" Nuts and 1" Bolts, which were ordered in quantities of 1,000, 150, and 10,000 respectively.
- Order 761 consists only of Number 5 Brackets. Five hundred units were ordered.

The significance of chains is that, if they are excessively long, we face two problems:

- It can be a lengthy process to traverse the ring in search of a specific record (each access may require a separate read operation).
- A computer malfunction may result in the destruction of pointers. The entire chain beyond the damaged record may thus become inaccessible and painstaking reconstruction may be needed.

A potential alternative to chaining is the use of indexes between an instance of the owner record and its member occurrences. This intermediary may enable quicker access to desired members than traversing the chain. Thus, instead of having to read twenty large records in order to get to the twenty-first one, we may be able to read one physical index record which points us to the desired member. As with other features, indexes are not necessarily supported in all network products.

ADVANTAGES AND DISADVANTAGES

A network model may be a good choice when there are a significant number of many-to-many relationships, where access from different points in the structure is desirable, and where performance is an important consideration. Like the hierarchical model, most access paths are predefined at the time data is loaded.

In general, IDMS and other CODASYL products share many of the same virtues and vices as hierarchical systems:

- They are complex.
- They have many tuning and physical storage options.
- They have strong backup, recovery and integrity features.
- They are ill-suited for extensive ad-hoc data access.
- Database redesign and restructuring can be difficult and disruptive.

DISCUSSION QUESTIONS

What is the major conceptual difference between a hierarchical and network model?

What is intersection data? Give an example.

How does a loop or iterative relationship differ from other kinds of relationships between records?

What does a set consist of?

What is referential integrity and how is it related to the automatic/optional membership option?

What is the difference between CALC and VIA sets?

What is meant by a ring or chain in network terminology?

7

THE RELATIONAL
MODEL

INTRODUCTION

Relational database technology is one of the hottest subjects in data processing. Its proponents claim that it is the wave of the future and that all other models are out of date. Much development work in the DBMS world today is, in fact, directed toward developing and improving relational products. New companies are springing up and established vendors such as IBM and Cullinet are busy providing their older products with "relational-like" capabilities.

That's the good news. The bad news is that some products marketed as "relational" are extremely limited. They lack performance for even modest amounts of data, cannot support multiple users, fail to provide adequate backup and recovery facilities, and cannot be used with standard programming languages.

Examples of good mainframe relational technology are IBM's DB2, Oracle Corporation's Oracle, Applied Data Research's DATACOM, and Information Builder's FO-CUS. This is certainly not a complete list and none of these packages would meet a purist's definition of a "true" relational system. However, they are among the best we have today.

It is interesting to note that virtually all DBMS products for personal computers are based on the relational model. This is because it is conceptually the easiest to master, is the most flexible and provides the inexperienced user with workable applications in the shortest amount of time. The problems currently associated with relational systems—performance, data integrity, etc.—are not particularly relevant to the low-volume, single-user environment of the typical PC.

123

TABLES AND TUPLES

A relational database consists of one or more two-dimensional flat files called *tables* or *relations*. I prefer the former term for its simplicity and will use it whenever possible.

Each table contains *rows* and *columns* roughly analogous to records and data elements in a nonrelational setting. Figure 7.1 illustrates the Order Table of a Customer Order database. Figure 7.2 illustrates relational terminology. Incidentally, Figure 7.1, and all subsequent figures, show data in an abbreviated, easy-to-read form—not necessarily the way it is actually stored in the computer.

Each row in a table is called a *tuple*, which is an obscure suffix meaning "a group of." An *n-tuple* is its generalized form and indicates the number of columns it contains. Our sample table contains six columns and is, therefore, a 6-tuple relation. Another way of expressing this is to say that it is of *degree 6*.

A tuple is an ordered set of values analogous to an entity. It contains all or part of the information we are storing about a person, place or thing of interest to our application. We will use the terms tuple and row interchangeably.

Columns are called columns. (Perhaps through an oversight, the fathers of relational theory failed to provide us with a more esoteric term.) Each column represents the values for a specific *attribute* (Invoice Number, Order Date, etc.).

A *domain* is the set of all possible values for an attribute. The domain of Customer Number is 0001 to 9999. The domain of Order Terms is CASH, NET 30, NET 60, NET 90 and PREPAID. Note that all domains are application-specific. They do not necessarily represent any inherent qualities of the attribute.

For example, if we wished to begin our Customer Numbers at 1000, the domain of Customer Number would be 1000 to 9999. There is no reason that we must fill in every number. Domains change as business conditions change. The Order Terms domain may be expanded to include NET 180, NET 15, etc., as we gain a larger clientele. Furthermore, some domains such as dates, amounts and identifiers, may be applicable to more than one attribute.

A *cell* represents the data that lies at the intersection of a column and a row. It contains only one value.

A Customer Order Table

Invoice number	Order date	Customer number	Sales person	Terms	Total amount
1246	04-14-85	0127	122	C	23,125.00
0761	06-17-85	0254	003	N30	1,200.00
1002	05-21-85	0127	122	C	95.00
0845	01-13-86	0307	400	N30	12,640.00
0998	12-12-86	5652	400	C	50.00
1001	12-12-86	0914	921	C	2,850.00
0004	03-01-86	5652	003	N60	1,070.00

Figure 7.1   A Customer Order Table

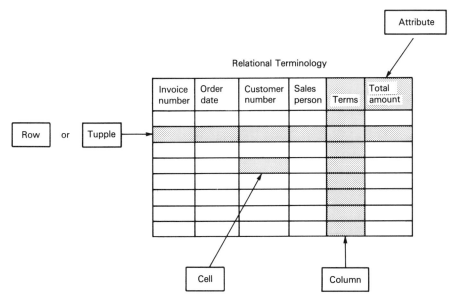

Figure 7.2 Relational Terminology

Cardinality is the number of rows in a given table at a specific point in time. This is equivalent to the number of records in a file. The cardinality of the table in Figure 7.1 is 7. Cardinality is extremely important because it provides us with information on which many important design decisions will hinge. A database consisting of 5,000 Orders with an annual growth rate of 20 percent may need to be designed differently from a database with 1,000,000 orders and the same growth rate.

The *relational universe* consists of all *possible* combinations of attribute values, potential as well as actual. If we were to simplify our example to include only Invoice Number and Order Terms, our relational universe would consist of about 40,000 tuples (9,999 possible order numbers for each of four possible Order Terms). Determining the scope of the relational universe may sometimes provide us with a useful context within which to work. Cardinality, however, is much more important.

Here are the rules a table must satisfy:

- Each column represents one attribute.
- The sequence of attributes throughout the table must be identical. For example, Invoice Number cannot appear as the first attribute in the first row and as the third attribute in the 49th row.
- Every row must be unique. That is, two rows from the same table must differ in at least one cell value.
- All rows must be complete. Thus, six values must be present in each row for a relation of degree 6. Each value must be part of the domain for that attribute.
- Repeating groups are not allowed. That is, only one value is permitted for any cell. For example, if two different dates are needed, two attributes must be defined.

■ The sequence of rows cannot be important to the application. For example, we cannot define and rely on a totals row that always follows detailed transaction rows to give us total amount information.

Keys

A *key* is an attribute or collection of attributes that always makes each tuple within a specific table unique. A key is sometimes called a *primary key* to distinguish it from a *foreign key*, which is a primary key with dual citizenship. That is, it functions as a primary key in one table but also appears in other tables where it is not a primary key. In Figure 7.3, Customer Number is a primary key in the Customer Table and a foreign key in the Order table. The Salesperson identifier is also both a primary and a foreign key.

Foreign keys are important because they establish desired relationships between records, enabling us to pull together data from more than one table. Foreign keys serve the same function in a relational database that pointers serve in nonrelational models.

A key consisting of multiple attributes is called a *composite*, *concatenated* or *compound* key. Invoice Number and Part Number comprise such a key in the Quantity table shown in Figure 7.4. A single attribute key is sometimes called a *simple key* in order to distinguish it from a composite key.

Figure 7.3 Primary and Foreign Keys

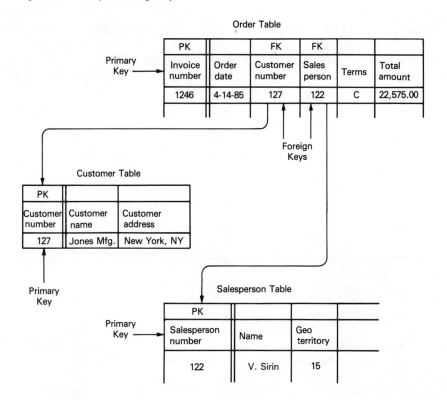

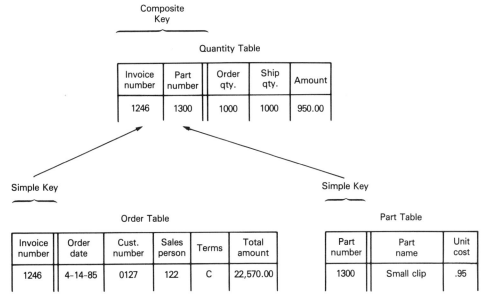

Figure 7.4 Keys

RELATIONAL OPERATORS

If we want to examine data in a relational database, we use variants of three generic operations: *Selection*, *Projection* and *Join*. Unlike Hierarchical or Network models, which require the programmer to navigate the database, extracting information from a relational database is conceptually straightforward. Every relational system has some form of the selection, projection and join operators illustrated in Figure 7.5.

Selection

Selection provides a "horizontal" slice of data. That is, a select operation is used when we wish to extract a row containing an attribute or attributes with specific values. Figure 7.6 shows how a select operation presents all the Order information for Customer 127.

More complex "and/or" logic based on values in several fields is illustrated in Figure 7.7. We can, for example, examine all the cash sales for a specific year by requesting TERMS = C AND ORDER DATE YEAR = 85, or whatever syntactical variant is appropriate for the Data Management Language used by our DBMS.

Projection

Projection provides a "vertical" slice of data. It enables a user to examine specific columns from a table with redundant rows removed. In Figure 7.8 the projection of Customer Number and Salesperson—the only attributes we are interested in viewing—would yield

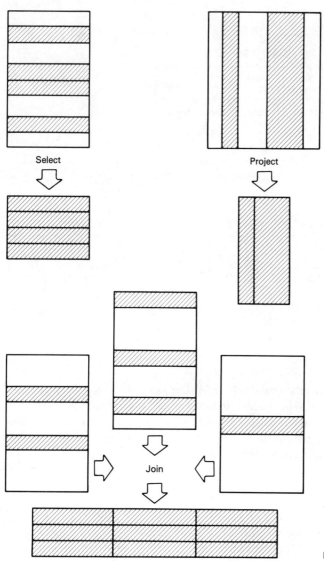

Select

Project

Join

Figure 7.5 Relational Operators

two columns of information containing data from six rows. Notice that the 0127/122 Customer Number/Salesperson combination, which appears twice in the table, appears only once in its projected form (the redundancy is removed).

A projection operates on only one table at a time.

Join

So far we have discussed only operators that work on one table at a time. A join combines data from two or more tables. We use a join if we wish to examine customer and order information for each customer. A join pulls together rows from both tables whenever a

Order Table

Invoice number	Order date	Customer number	Sales person	Terms	Total amount
1246	04-14-85	0127	122	C	22,575.00
0761	06-17-85	0254	003	N30	1,200.00
1002	05-21-85	0127	122	C	95.00
0845	01-13-86	0307	400	N30	12,640.00
0998	12-12-86	5652	400	C	50.00
1001	12-12-86	0914	921	C	2,850.00
0004	03-01-86	5652	003	N60	1,070.00

Select Orders for Customer 127

Invoice number	Order date	Customer number	Sales person	Terms	Total amount
1246	4-14-85	127	122	C	22,575.00
1002	5-21-85	127	122	C	95.00

Figure 7.6 A Simple Select Operation

Customer Number match is found. Figure 7.9 shows how this information would be presented.

In a more complex case, we could list information only about customers who did business with us in 1986. Our program could then calculate each Customer's total dollar

Order Table

Invoice number	Order date	Customer number	Sales person	Terms	Total amount
1246	04-14-85	0127	122	C	22,575.00
0761	06-17-85	0254	003	N30	1,200.00
1002	05-21-85	0127	122	C	95.00
0845	01-13-86	0307	400	N30	12,640.00
0998	12-12-86	5652	400	C	50.00
1001	12-12-86	0914	921	C	2,850.00
0004	03-01-86	5652	003	N60	1,070.00

Select Cash Sales for 1985 (i.e., Terms = C)

Invoice number	Order date	Customer number	Sales person	Terms	Total amount
1246	4-14-85	0127	122	C	22,575.00
1002	5-21-85	0127	122	C	95.00
0998	12-12-85	5652	400	C	50.00

Figure 7.7 A Complex Select Operation

Order Table

Invoice number	Order date	Customer number	Sales person	Terms	Total amount
1246	04-14-85	0127	122	C	22,575.00
0761	06-17-85	0254	003	N30	1,200.00
1002	05-21-85	0127	122	C	95.00
0845	01-13-86	0307	400	N30	12,640.00
0998	12-12-86	5652	400	C	50.00
1001	12-12-86	0914	921	C	2,850.00
0004	03-01-86	5652	003	N60	1,070.00

Project Unique Customer
Number/Salesperson Occurrences

Customer number	Sales person
0127	122
0254	003
0307	400
5652	400
0914	921
5652	003

Figure 7.8 A Projection

Figure 7.9 A Join Operation—All Customers and Orders

Order Table

Invoice number	Order date	Customer number	Sales person	Terms	Total amount
1246	04-14-85	0127	122	C	22,575.00
0761	06-17-85	0254	003	N30	1,200.00
1002	05-21-85	0127	122	C	95.00
0845	01-13-86	0307	400	N30	12,640.00
0998	12-12-86	5652	400	C	50.00
1001	12-12-86	0914	921	C	2,850.00
0004	03-01-86	5652	003	N60	1,070.00

Customer Table

Cust. number	Customer name	Customer address
0127	Jones Mfg.	New York, NY
0254	ABC, Inc.	Concord, NH
0307	Nilges Systems	Seattle, WA
5652	Air-Temp	Chicago, IL
0914	Pollack Corp.	Peoria, IL

Customer and Order Information for All Customers

Invoice number	Order date	Cust. number	Sales person	Terms	Total amount	Customer name	Customer address
1246	04-14-85	0127	122	C	22,575.00	Jones Mfg.	New York, NY
1002	05-21-85	0127	122	C	95.00	Jones Mfg.	New York, NY
0761	06-17-85	0254	003	N30	1,200.00	ABC, Inc.	Concord, NH
0845	01-13-86	0307	400	N30	12,640.00	Nilges Systems	Seattle, WA
0998	12-12-86	5652	400	C	50.00	Air-Temp	Chicago, IL
0004	03-01-86	5652	003	N60	1,070.00	Air-Temp	Chicago, IL
1001	12-12-86	0914	921	C	2,850.00	Pollack Corp.	Peoria, IL

volume for that year. Figure 7.10 illustrates how this data would be presented. Notice that we have omitted Salesperson and Terms information because it is not relevant to our report.

PHYSICAL COMPONENTS: DB2

As with hierarchical and network databases, the actual form a relational DBMS takes in practice depends on the specific product. We will use IBM's family of relational products—specifically, DB2 (Data Base 2)—as an example. Whenever possible, terms of a more universal nature will be substituted for product-specific terminology.

As with the earlier descriptions of IBM's IMS, I have taken some liberties for purposes of clarity. The following description is not, therefore, intended as a rigorous treatment of the subject.

IBM's DB2, as well as most other relational DBMS's, consists of *tables*, *indexes* and a *catalog*. Each table is a flat file whose records represent rows in the table. The logical representation of the table will be referred to as the *base table* and its physical representation will be called the *stored table*. Perhaps more descriptive terms would be *logical table* and *physical table*.

Figure 7.10   A Join Operation—1986 Orders Only

Order Table

Invoice number	Order date	Cust. number	Sales person	Terms	Total amount
1246	04-14-85	0127	122	C	22,575.00
0761	06-17-85	0254	003	N30	1,200.00
1002	05-21-85	0127	122	C	95.00
0845	01-13-86	0307	400	N30	12,640.00
0998	12-12-86	5652	400	C	50.00
1001	12-12-86	0914	921	C	2,850.00
0004	03-01-86	5652	003	N60	1,070.00

Customer Table

Cust. number	Customer name	Customer address
0127	Jones Mfg.	New York, NY
0254	ABC, Inc.	Concord, NH
0307	Nilges Systems	Seattle, Wa
5652	Air-Temp	Chicago, IL
0914	Pollack Corp.	Peoria, IL

Customer and Order Information for 1986 Orders

Invoice number	Order date	Cust. number	Total amount	Customer name	Customer address
0845	01-13-86	0307	12,640.00	Nilges Systems	Seattle, WA
0998	12-12-86	5652	50.00	Air-Temp	Chicago, IL
1001	12-12-86	0914	2,850.00	Pollack Corp.	Peoria, IL
0004	03-01-86	5652	1,070.00	Air-Temp	Chicago, IL

In DB2, stored tables and indexes are physically located in areas called *tablespaces* and *indexspaces*, respectively. Each space is a collection of "pages" usually 4000 bytes (4K) in length, which represent blocks of physical storage normally read or written with one I/O operation.

A table is contained entirely within a tablespace and its records are more or less contiguous. However, multiple tables can also share the same tablespace in order to place frequently used records that are related in physical proximity. This is illustrated in Figure 7.11, where Quantity records are stored next to the Order to which they apply. As in storage techniques for nonrelational models, free space may be interspersed among records in a stored table.

Each table and index space is assigned to a *storage group*, which is a collection of direct access volumes. Figure 7.12 illustrates the relationship between storage groups, tables, table space, and index space.

In addition to carrying application data, each record in a relational file (table) contains control information prefixed to the record and to each field in the record. Each record prefix identifies the table to which this record belongs. Each field prefix gives field length and indicates if this field is null or contains a genuine value. Figure 7.13 illustrates the relationship between prefixes and fields containing application data (A1, A2, B1, B2, etc.).

Indexes

In order to make data access more efficient, one or more indexes can be defined for attributes in a table. This provides us with a variety of logical sequences by which we can access data.

An index is a flat file containing the addresses of records with specific values in the field we have selected to index on. Thus, an index on Order Date enables us to find all the Order records for, say, March 1, 1986 without the need to perform extensive sequential searching.

Figure 7.14 is a simplified picture of how we can retrieve records from the Order table by indexing on Customer Number and Salesperson—neither of which are primary keys and would not provide convenient access without indexing. The entries in the index point us to the location of records with the desired values. As records are added, modified and deleted, the indexes are updated to reflect the new placement of records.

Indexes in DB2 are of a special variety known as *B-trees*, or balanced trees, as illustrated in Figure 7.15. A pre-set number of levels in the index enables us to get to the desired page in our tablespace in an efficient manner. The maximum number of children each node is allowed to carry is also pre-defined. This is usually an odd number and, for ease of updating, remains small (3 is the most common maximum).

Note that "balanced" simply means that each leaf—remember our terminology—is exactly the same number of levels from the root. As new entries are added and old entries are deleted, the distance between the leaves and the root remains the same. Although a detailed explanation of how this occurs is not germane to the present topic,

A Page in One Tablespace

Order Table

Invoice number	Order date	Customer number	Sales person	Terms	Total amount
1246	04-14-85	0127	122	C	22,575.00
0761	06-17-85	0254	003	N30	1,200.00
1002	05-21-85	0127	122	C	95.00
0845	01-13-86	0307	400	N30	12,640.00
0998	12-12-86	5652	400	C	50.00
1001	12-12-86	0914	921	C	2,850.00
0004	03-01-86	5652	003	N60	1,070.00

Quantity Table

Invoice number	Part number	Order qty.	Ship qty.	Amount
1246	1300	1000	1000	950.00
1246	0122	150	150	225.00
1246	0950	10000	10000	21,400.00
0761	0715	500	200	1,200.00
1002	1240	100	0	0.00
1002	1300	100	100	95.00
0845	0274	1000	500	50.00
0845	0800	900	900	90.00

Order 1246	Quantity for part 1300	Quantity for part 122	Quantity for part 950	Order 761	Quantity for part 715	etc.

Figure 7.11 Storing Multiple Tables in One Tablespace

suffice it to say it results in a widening or narrowing of the tree—that is, the number of nodes on each level increases or shrinks.

Note that this phenomena does not imply a balance of field values: In Figure 7.15 invoice number value ranges are greater or smaller in each part of the tree depending on the actual data. Thus, we may have 900 records in the Invoice Number range of 8000 to 9999 and 900 records in the 4000 to 5000 range—even though the former represents a range that is twice as large as the latter.

The use of a B-Tree index provides uniform and predictable performance for data retrieval. However, this may be at the cost of index maintenance, which can be considerable due to the rearrangements that take place whenever records are added or deleted.

DB2 has two types of indexes: *clustering* and *associated*. A clustering index points to a stored table that is physically in the same sequence as the index. A clustering

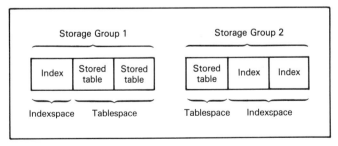

Storage Group 1   Storage Group 2

Index	Stored table	Stored table	Stored table	Index	Index

Indexspace   Tablespace   Tablespace   Indexspace

Application Database

Figure 7.12 Storage Groups

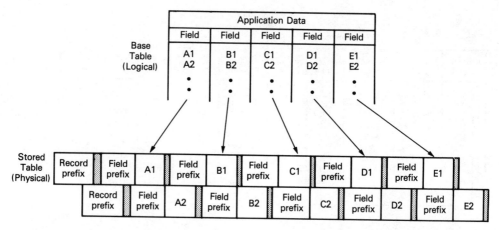

Figure 7.13 Record and Field Prefixes

index is suggested for each table and, ideally, is created prior to the initial table load. Data is then physically loaded and stored in index sequence.

We may, for example, wish to store the Order table in Invoice Number sequence. This approximate physical ordering—approximate because updates to the table will invariably compromise the physical sequence—makes table accessing much faster than if physical ordering were disregarded.

Indexes that are not clustering are called associated indexes. We may, for example, wish to base additional indexes for the Order table on Customer Number and Order Date.

An index may be defined as unique. This eliminates duplicate records. Thus, we could automatically exclude Orders with duplicate Invoice Numbers by specifying our Invoice Number index as unique.

Indexes are not strictly necessary—and, in fact, their use can be counterproductive if there are too many of them (IBM recommends a minimum of one, and a maximum

Figure 7.14 Indexes

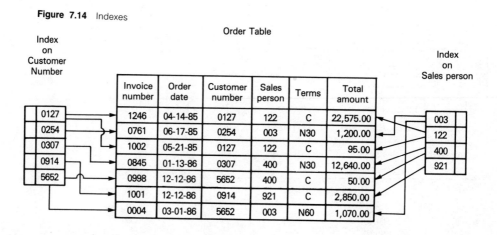

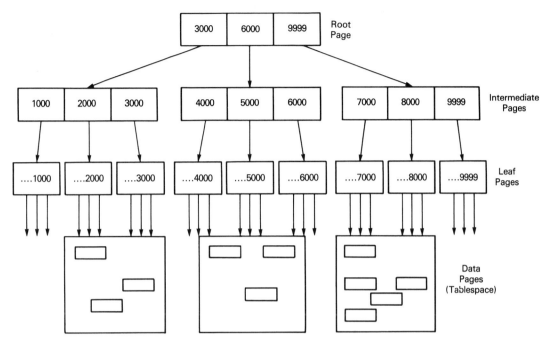

Figure 7.15 A B-Tree Index on Invoice Number

of three, indexes per table). However, it is difficult to envision an effective relational system without some form of indexing or a similar technique that reduces file search time.

The System Catalog

The system catalog is a database consisting of tables that describe application databases. DB2 has about twenty such tables, the most prominent of which are described below.

- Table descriptions. This table contains a row for each table in the application database. It gives the table name, its creator or user, the number of columns in the table and other descriptive information.
- Column descriptions. This table contains a row for every column of every table. It gives column name, the table it belongs to, the type of data carried, and so on.
- Index descriptions. This table contains a row for every index defined in the system. It gives index name, the table for which the index is used, and other index information.

Program views, access rights, security and backup provisions, and other information are also carried in various catalog tables.

The catalog is created by the DBMS software from information keyed in by the database designer. It is subsequently used by the DBMS and represents a kind of "active" data dictionary—that is, one that is actually used at run time, and not just for documentation. It is the mechanism by which the design of the database comes to life.

System catalogs can be queried and updated like any other tables. Thus, we can change data definitions, add new tables and perform other database design work. We can also print out database descriptions for informational purposes.

Additional Comments

Tables, indexes, views and other components can usually be created as needed. Therefore, we are not locked in to a specific design as we are with hierarchical and network models. This can be an important advantage if we do a substantial amount of ad-hoc processing or if our data access needs are not well known at the time the system is developed.

The language used by IBM's relational products is called SQL, which stands for Structured Query Language. It provides the capability for both data definition and data manipulation—a fairly unusual characteristic, since most DBMS products use a different language to define the database and to then use it. SQL terminology and commands have been adopted by about fifteen vendors in their own relational products (e.g., ORACLE). Therefore, SQL may well become a de-facto language standard for relational databases. Specific physical implementations will, of course, continue to be unique.

ADVANTAGES AND DISADVANTAGES

Relational technology, as it is reflected in real products such as DB2, has certain advantages over hierarchical and network systems. It also has some serious disadvantages. Here are the pros and cons of relational systems.

- Programmers don't need to navigate data structures since there *are* no structures—only a series of tables with some common attributes.
- Many systems analysts find two dimensional tables more straightforward than the data cobwebs that result from drawing complex networks or hierarchies.
- Since paths to data are not "hard coded"—a new index can be defined more easily than a new pointer—greater retrieval flexibility exists.
- At the present time, relational systems lack referential integrity. This is known as the "foreign key problem" and goes like this: linkages between records in network and hierarchical databases provide the mechanism for ensuring that a subordinate record or segment isn't added unless a superior exists; conversely, the removal of a superior can be prevented if subordinate records exist.

    The linkage concept has been replaced in relational models by foreign keys. For reasons too complex to explain here, this has made the development of referential integrity for relational products difficult.

- Because of the above, integrity controls must be designed into the application program—an unreliable alternative to the built-in enforcement available in network and hierarchical systems.
- The lack of predefined access paths can be very costly in a relational environment. Joins, in particular, are tremendous computer resource hogs.

- Relational models are not well suited for large-scale transaction processing. Network and hierarchical databases can be designed around the most heavily travelled paths. This results in great speed for some types of processing and, by definition, mediocre performance for others.
- Tables, on the other hand, tend to defy skewing toward a specific access strategy. They are, in this sense, more "neutral" than the structures selected for nonrelational models.
- The relational model is, perhaps, the only one that was deliberately used as the basis for specific products. Hierarchical concepts are, in some ways, an ex post facto explanation of a single product, IMS. CODASYL (i.e., network) standards are fairly complete but still represent theory-by-committee. Relational theory, on the other hand, is the most comprehensive, cohesive and orderly model for a database product.
- The logical and physical aspects of the relational model are more clearly separate than they are in nonrelational products. This may be a consequence of the nonstructural nature of tables.

Relational databases will be more extensively used as ways are found to make them more efficient and to give them more data integrity controls. Given the time and effort lavished on relational systems, this will no doubt come to pass. In the meantime, most bread-and-butter DBMS applications that require a mainframe (e.g., are multiuser, have large files, etc.) will continue to run under products such as IMS and IDMS.

The next chapter describes normalization, a technique for designing tables. Although normalization is usually associated with, and is most directly applicable to, the relational model, it is also useful with hierarchical and network models.

DISCUSSION QUESTIONS

What is the major difference between relational and nonrelational systems? Explain.

Define a table and name three of its components.

Describe the three main relational operators.

What does the system catalog contain? Why is it important?

What is a clustering index and how does it impact the physical arrangement of data?

8

NORMALIZATION

INTRODUCTION

The design of a database is an exercise in problem solving. The problem is to identify data that is important to the applications the database must serve and to make this data reflect the real world in an efficient manner. This is done by collecting all the pieces and arranging them in an optimum fashion.

The process of paring and structuring is called *decomposition*. It is done in one form or another regardless of which data model is chosen. It results in the break-up of an inchoate mass of information into useable records, segments, or tables. In a relational environment, decomposition has been spelled out in formal terms and is called *normalization*.

In a way, normalization is simply common sense. It bolsters our intuition and helps explain why a good analyst does what he does.

Normalization converts a table into tables of progressively smaller degree and cardinality until an optimum level of decomposition is reached—that is, where little or no data redundancy exists. This road to heaven is marked by signposts: First Normal Form, Second Normal Form and Third Normal Form. Each form is governed by the progressively stricter rules described in this section.

If we succeed in our normalization efforts, some positive results will accrue:

- The amount of space needed to store data will be lower.
- The table can be updated with greater efficiency.
- The description of the database will be straightforward.

As we work through the example in this section, it will become clear that these goals can be realized. But first, it is important to become familiar with the dependency concepts that underlie normalization.

DEPENDENCY

Dependency describes the relationship between attributes in terms of how the value of one fixes or determines the value of another. Discovering these relationships can only be done by studying the real-life behavior of the system. Dependency is an important concept because it enables us to decompose data properly into its most efficient form.

Functional Dependency

Functional dependency exists when a unique value of one attribute can always be determined if we know the value of another. For example, Order Date can always be determined by knowing the Invoice Number for that Order. There can only be one Order Date for any invoice. However, since more than one order may have been placed on a single day, the opposite is not true: we cannot infer Invoice Number by knowing the Order Date.

Functional dependency is illustrated by a single-headed arrow going from the *independent variable* (X) to the *dependent variable* (Y). The dependent variable is so called because its value always depends on the value of the independent variable; the value of the independent variable does not depend on the value of the dependent variable. In our example, Invoice Number is the independent variable and Order Date is the dependent variable—or, expressing the relationship another way, Invoice Number *identifies* Order Date.

(Invoice Number) X ⟶ (Order Date)

Total Dependency

Total dependency is a special type of dependency. Suppose that each individual hired by our company must have a valid social security number. For processing and privacy considerations, we also assign employee identifiers. Knowledge of a person's employee number always yields one and only one social security number. Conversely, we can always find a person's employee number by knowing his or her social security number.

Total dependency is illustrated by a double-headed arrow. Thus, attribute X, below, is totally dependent on attribute Y and vice versa.

X ⟵⟶ Y

Full Dependency

Full dependency occurs when one attribute is always dependent on at least two other attributes. If an attribute is ''fully dependent'' on only one other attribute the concept of full dependency has no meaning—we simply have a state of garden variety functional dependency.

The relationship between Invoice Number, Part Number and Order Quantity in a Customer Order database illustrates full dependency. Knowing the Invoice Number alone cannot yield Order Quantity—we must know what the Part Number is. (After all, an Order may consist of multiple parts, each of which may be ordered in different quantities.)

Similarly, we cannot deduce Order Quantity from Part Number alone. The Order Quantity for a Part depends on which Order we are discussing. We can determine Order Quantity only by knowing both Part Number and Invoice Number.

Our full dependency example is illustrated below. X and Y are independent variables; Z is the dependent variable.

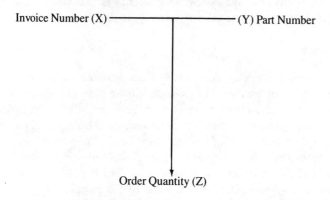

Full dependency does not necessarily imply unique values: 23 washers can be ordered on one invoice and 23 widgets can be ordered on another invoice. The quantity "23" is meaningless if taken out of context.

In addition, Invoice Number and Part Number in our example are always the independent variables. Order Quantity is always the dependent variable. That means that we cannot determine Part Number by knowing the Invoice Number and the Order Quantity (e.g., Order 2001 is for 15 hammers and 15 saws—which Part Number do we want?). Likewise, we cannot determine the Invoice Number by knowing only the Part Number and Order Quantity (e.g., which specific Order for 15 hammers are we interested in?).

Transitive Dependency

Transitive dependency occurs when Y depends on X, and Z depends on Y. Therefore, Z also depends on X.

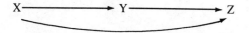

Here is an example of transitive dependency in our Customer Order database:

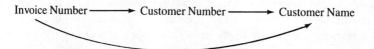

Invoice Number always identifies Customer Number which, in turn, gives us the customer's name. Customer Name can also be derived from the Invoice Number (for simplicity, we are going to assume that each customer has a unique name).

In a university database, there is a hierarchy between Course, Department and College. For example:

- All English literature courses are taught by the English Department.
- The English Department is part of the College of Arts and Sciences.

This is illustrated as follows:

If we sign up for 18th-Century English Poetry, we know which department and College the course is in. We also know that a part-time job in the English Department means that we will be working for the College of Arts and Sciences.

The other direction cannot yield unique results: If someone at a party tells us he works for the College of Arts and Sciences, we cannot determine the Department in which he is employed. Nor can we know which courses a professor teaches by the knowledge that he or she is on the English faculty.

Note that in our university example, Department is functionally dependent on Course, and College is functionally dependent on Department. In the Customer Order example we had one functional dependency (Customer Number to Invoice Number) and one total dependency (Customer Name to Customer Number).

GETTING STARTED

We can begin either with the big picture or at the most detailed level. The former is sometimes called the "top-down" approach and involves identifying objects, documents, people and other "entities" of interest to our application. The creation of a customer order database may start by identifying:

- Customers
- Products
- Orders
- Salespeople

Our identification may not be complete, but, since analysis is an iterative process, it is likely that we will find the missing pieces before the design phase is completed.

The detailed level, or "bottom-up" approach, consists of listing all the small units of data we can think of and grouping them together. We know, for example, that the database must carry customer names and addresses, order numbers, part numbers and unit prices, etc.

Most people think in terms of both entities and smaller units. This iterative give-and-take permits us to jump between different levels of detail: identifying an entity and breaking it into attributes, defining a needed attribute and then finding a home for it in an entity, and so on.

Once we have arrived at a fair amount of detail we can begin the normalization process. In our case, we have done this by studying the customer invoice, illustrated in Figure 8.1. This happens to be an extremely important document that reflects many needs our database must fulfill. We have decided to use it as the basis of our first-cut customer order table.

Notice that our examples contain actual data gleaned from representative invoices, as shown in Figure 8.2. Database design should *never* be conducted without examining a substantial amount of real data. Some characteristics of data simply cannot be deduced through the exercise of logic alone; they can only be discovered through observa-

Figure 8.1 Sample Invoice

TRIANGLE SYSTEMS CORP • 340 W. DIVERSITY
CHICAGO • IL • 60657

INVOICE NUMBER 1246
ORDER DATE 4/14/85

CUSTOMER NUMBER 127
CUSTOMER NAME/ADDRESS

Jones Mfg.
New York, NY

SALESPERSON 122   TERMS Cash

PART NUM.	PART NAME	UNIT COST	ORDER QTY.	SHIP QTY.	$ AMT.
1300	Small clip	.95	1000	1000	950.00
122	⅛" nut	1.50	150	150	225.00
950	1" bolt	2.14	10,000	10,000	21,400.00

TOTAL $22,575.00

Invoice 1 (top):

TRIANGLE SYSTEMS CORP • 340 W. DIVERSITY
CHICAGO • IL • 60657

INVOICE NUMBER 1246
ORDER DATE 4/14/85

CUSTOMER NUMBER 127
CUSTOMER NAME/ADDRESS

Jones Mfg.

New York, NY

SALESPERSON 122   TERMS Cash

PART NUM.	PART NAME	UNIT COST	ORDER QTY.	SHIP QTY.	$ AMT.
1300	Small clip	.95	1000	1000	950.00
122	1″ bolt	1.50	150	150	225.00
950		2.14	10,000	10,000	

TOTAL $22,575.00

Invoice 2 (middle):

TRIANGLE SYSTEMS CORP • 340 W. DIVERSITY
CHICAGO • IL • 60657

INVOICE NUMBER 0761
ORDER DATE 6/17/85

CUSTOMER NUMBER 254
CUSTOMER NAME/ADDRESS

ABC, Inc.

Concord, NH

SALESPERSON ____   TERMS N30

PART NUM.	PART NAME	UNIT COST	ORDER QTY.	SHIP QTY.	$ AMT.
0715	No. 5 bracket	6.00	500	200	1,200.00

TOTAL $1,200.00

Invoice 3 (bottom):

TRIANGLE SYSTEMS CORP • 340 W. DIVERSITY
CHICAGO • IL • 60657

INVOICE NUMBER 1002
ORDER DATE 5/21/85

CUSTOMER NUMBER 127
CUSTOMER NAME/ADDRESS

Jones, Mfg.

New York, NY

SALESPERSON 122   TERMS C

PART NUM.	PART NAME	UNIT COST	ORDER QTY.	SHIP QTY.	$ AMT.
1240	No. 15 screw	.52	100	0	0.00
1300	Sm. clip	.95	100	100	95.00

TOTAL $95.00

Figure 8.2 Invoices with Data

tion. Once we have built a first-cut table resembling our invoice, we can begin normalization.

FIRST NORMAL FORM (1NF)

A table is in First Normal Form if:

- It is a valid table. That is:
  - each column represents one attribute
  - the sequence of attributes is identical
  - each row is unique
  - values for each key are present
  - there are no repeating groups
  - the sequence of rows is unimportant
- A unique key has been identified for each row.
- All attributes are functionally dependent on all or part of the key.

Our first-cut Customer Order table, illustrated in Figure 8.3, is already in first normal form:

- It meets the requirements of being a table (unique tuples, attributes in the same relative place throughout, etc.).
- A key identifies each tuple. In our case, we have determined that it is a composite consisting of Invoice Number and Part Number. As we shall see in the discussion of Second Normal Form, if the key were *not* a composite but, rather, a simple key, the table would already be in at least 2NF.
- All attributes are functionally dependent on part or all of the key. That is, each of the attributes can be determined by our knowledge of either the Invoice Number, the Part Number or both.

However, even a cursory examination indicates that our table is using up a lot of space with redundant data. Of perhaps greater importance, we must *update* all that redundant data—a potentially error-prone procedure!

Our next challenge is to get rid of some of that redundancy by transforming our 1NF table into a higher Normal Form.

SECOND NORMAL FORM (2NF)

Every attribute in a table should be dependent on the entire key (remember, a key can consist of several attributes). This is what Second Normal Form provides. A table is in Second Normal Form if it is in 1NF and *all* nonkey attributes are *fully dependent* on the key. This means that they cannot be dependent on only *part* of the key (i.e., one of its attributes) but must be dependent on the *entire* key.

In order to achieve Second Normal Form, we must examine the relationships in our table and selectively move attributes to other tables as appropriate. A good way to figure out what must be moved is to create and use a dependency graph such as the one illustrated in Figure 8.4.

Customer Order Table

Invoice number	Order date	Customer number	Customer name	Customer address	Sales person	Terms	Part number	Part name	Unit cost	Order qty.	Ship qty.	Amount	Total amount
1246	4-14-85	0127	Jones Mfg.	New York, NY	122	C	1300	Small clip	.95	1000	1000	950.00	22,575.00
1246	4-14-85	0127	Jones Mfg.	New York, NY	122	C	0122	⅛" nut	1.50	150	150	225.00	22,575.00
1246	4-14-85	0127	Jones Mfg.	New York, NY	122	C	0950	1" bolt	2.14	10000	10000	21,400.00	22,575.00
0761	6-17-85	0254	ABC, Inc.	Concord, NH	003	N30	0715	No. 5 bracket	6.00	500	200	1,200.00	1,200.00
1002	5-21-85	0127	Jones Mfg.	New York, NY	122	C	1240	No. 15 screw	.52	100	000	000.00	95.00
1002	5-21-85	0127	Jones Mfg.	New York, NY	122	C	1300	Small clip	.95	100	100	95.00	95.00

Figure 8.3 Customer Order Table—First Normal Form (1NF)

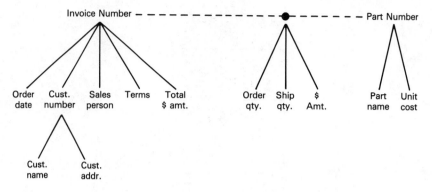

Figure 8.4 Customer Order Dependency Graph

Place each element of the composite key—in our case, Invoice Number and Part Number—at the top of the diagram and connect them with a dotted line. Then, identify the attributes that are dependent on Customer Number, those that are dependent on Part Number, and those that are dependent on both. Also identify and illustrate transitive dependencies such as those between Invoice Number, Customer Number, and Customer Name. The graph will now resemble a large family of trapeze artists performing a high-wire act.

Here are some of the business requirements reflected in this graph:

Figure 8.5 Customer Order Tables—Second and Third Normal Form (2NF and 3NF)

Order Table (2NF)

Primary Key							
Invoice number	Order date	Customer number	Customer name	Customer address	Sales person	Terms	Total amt.
1246	4-14-85	0127	Jones Mfg.	New York, NY	122	C	22,575.00
0761	6-17-85	0254	ABC, Inc.	Concord, NH	003	N30	1,200.00
1002	5-21-85	0127	Jones Mfg.	New York, NY	122	C	95.00

Part Table (3NF)

Primary Key		
Part number	Part name	Unit cost
1300	Small clip	.95
0122	⅛″ nut	1.50
0950	1″ bolt	2.14
0715	No. 5 bracket	6.00
1240	No. 15 screw	.52

Quantity Table (3NF)

Primary Key				
Invoice number	Part number	Order qty.	Ship qty.	Amount
1246	1300	1000	1000	950.00
1246	0122	150	150	225.00
1246	0950	10000	10000	21,400.00
0761	0715	500	200	1,200.00
1002	1240	100	0	0.00
1002	1300	100	100	95.00

- Order Date, customer and salesperson information, Order Terms and Total Amount of the invoice are always recorded at the invoice level.
- Part Name and Unit Cost are dependent on Part Number. They do not vary from invoice to invoice.
- Quantity Ordered, Quantity Shipped and the line dollar amount of each transaction depend on both Invoice and Part Number. (We obviously cannot know part quantities and dollar amounts unless we are familiar with the specific order).
- Customer Name and Address are dependent on Customer Number.

We are now ready to decompose the Customer Order table into three smaller tables (Figure 8.5) based on the information in the graph. The nodes at the top of the graph serve as keys in our new tables. Note that the original composite key survives but is now in a new table we have called the Quantity table, which contains only attributes dependent on *both* parts of the key. All attributes are now fully dependent on the key.

The tables in Figure 8.5 are now in at least Second Normal Form.

THIRD NORMAL FORM (3NF)

A table is in Third Normal Form if it is in 2NF and all transitive dependencies between nonkey attributes have been removed.

As the transitive graph in Figure 8.4 and the Customer Order table in Figure 8.5 show, we have three transitive dependencies in our 2NF tables:

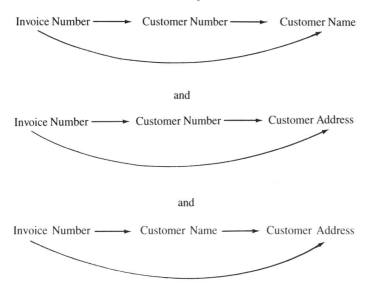

Customer information must be repeated for each Order. Let us remove these transitive dependencies by creating a Customer table. Figure 8.6 now represents a set of tables in Third Normal Form. Customer data appears only once for each customer.

Order Table

Invoice number	Order date	Customer number	Sales person	Terms	Total amount
1246	04-14-85	0127	122	C	22,575.00
0761	06-17-85	0254	003	N30	1,200.00
1002	05-21-85	0127	122	C	95.00
0845	01-13-86	0307	400	N30	12,640.00
0998	12-12-86	5652	400	C	50.00
1001	12-12-86	0914	921	C	2,850.00
0004	03-01-86	5652	003	N60	1,070.00

Customer Table

Customer number	Customer name	Customer address
0127	Jones Mfg.	New York, NY
0254	ABC, Inc.	Concord, NH
0307	Nilges Systems	Seattle, WA
5652	Air-Temp	Chicago, IL
0914	Pollack Corp.	Peoria, IL

Part Table

Part number	Part name	Unit cost
0120	¾" nut	1.50
0122	⅛" nut	1.50
0950	1" bolt	2.14
0715	No. 5 bracket	6.00
1240	No. 15 screw	.52
1300	Small clip	.95
0245	No. 14 screw	.50
0800	No. 3 nail	.10
0274	No. 6 nail	.10
0901	½" nut	1.25

Quantity Table

Invoice number	Part number	Order qty.	Ship qty.	Amount
1246	1300	1000	1000	950.00
1246	0122	150	150	225.00
1246	0950	10000	10000	21,400.00
0761	0715	500	200	1,200.00
1002	1240	100	0	0.00
1002	1300	100	100	95.00
0845	0274	1000	500	50.00
0845	0800	900	900	90.00
0845	0901	10000	10000	12,500.00
0845	1300	100	0	0.00
0998	0245	100	100	50.00
1001	0120	1000	900	1,350.00
1001	0122	2000	1000	1,500.00
0004	0950	500	500	1,070.00

Figure 8.6 Customer Order Tables—Third Normal Form (3NF)

THE ADVANTAGES OF NORMALIZATION

Let us now compare the original, nonnormalized table to our final product. The process we went through to get from first to second to third normal form is summarized in Figure 8.7. What advantages have we gained?

Minimization of Redundancy

Figure 8.8 illustrates our 1NF table with all the information for seven complete invoices. Notice that fourteen rows are needed to carry all the information.

Now look back at Figure 8.6, which shows the same information in Third Normal Form. A substantial amount of redundancy has been eliminated—about 40 percent of the table if we assume realistic lengths for Customer Address and other attributes that were abbreviated in our example.

The actual amount of redundancy that can be eliminated in a large customer order table will, of course, depend on the average number of parts per invoice, the average number of orders per customer, and other factors.

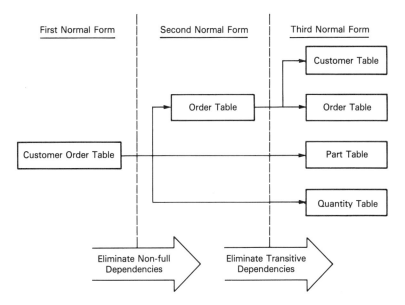

Figure 8.7 Summary of Customer Order Normalization

The only case in which normalization would *not* reduce redundancy is if all of our customers *never* had more than one outstanding order at any given time, *always* ordered only one part, and *never* ordered a part that someone else had already ordered—a highly unlikely situation!

The Elimination of Update Anomalies

Update anomalies are difficulties in adding, deleting and modifying desired information. An *insert* anomaly in the Customer Order database occurs when we try to add customer information before an order is placed. (We may, after all, wish to add a customer to our file before he has placed an order!) In the First and Second Normal Forms this is impossible to do because all customer attributes (Number, Name, Address) are part of a table that requires an Invoice Number. (See Figures 8.3 and 8.5.) Conversely, once all Invoices for a Customer are deleted, information about him is irrevocably lost. This is called a *delete* anomaly.

A problem also occurs when we attempt to <u>change</u> Customer information. In order to maintain consistency, we must find and modify each Order record for that Customer. In the 1NF table, a change of address for a Customer with ten invoices requires the update of ten records—a wasteful, error-prone procedure. In contrast, our 3NF Customer table requires the update of only one record.

Although normalization up to and including 3NF is generally recommended, a table can be in 2NF or even in 1NF and still provide reasonable service. In fact, tables that are not volatile and are used extensively for ad hoc queries may actually suffer from "over-normalization."

Customer Order Table

Invoice number	Order date	Customer number	Customer name	Customer address	Sales person	Terms	Part number	Part name	Unit cost	Order qty.	Ship qty.	Amount	Total amount
1246	4-14-85	0127	Jones Mfg.	New York, NY	122	C	1300	Small clip	.95	1000	1000	950.00	22,575.00
1246	4-14-85	0127	Jones Mfg.	New York, NY	122	C	0122	1/8" nut	1.50	150	150	225.00	22,575.00
1246	4-14-85	0127	Jones Mfg.	New York, NY	122	C	0950	1" bolt	2.14	10000	10000	21,400.00	22,575.00
0761	6-17-85	0254	ABC, Inc.	Concord, NH	003	N30	0715	No. 5 bracket	6.00	500	200	1,200.00	1,200.00
1002	5-21-85	0127	Jones Mfg.	New York, NY	122	C	1240	No. 15 screw	.52	100	000	000.00	95.00
1002	5-21-85	0127	Jones Mfg.	New York, NY	122	C	1300	Small clip	.95	100	100	95.00	95.00
0845	1-13-85	0307	Nilges Systems	Seattle, WA	400	N30	0274	No. 6 nail	.10	1000	500	50.00	12,640.00
0845	1-13-85	0307	Nilges Systems	Seattle, WA	400	N30	0800	No. 3 nail	.10	900	900	90.00	12,640.00
0845	1-13-85	0307	Nilges Systems	Seattle, WA	400	N30	0901	1/2" nut	1.25	10000	10000	12,500.00	12,640.00
0998	12-12-86	5652	Air-Temp	Chicago, IL	400	C	1300	Small clip	.95	100	000	000.00	50.00
0998	12-12-86	5652	Air-Temp	Chicago, IL	400	C	0245	No. 14 screw	.50	100	100	50.00	50.00
1001	2-15-86	0914	Pollack Corp.	Peoria, IL	921	C	0120	3/4" nut	1.50	1000	900	1,350.00	2,850.00
1001	12-12-86	0914	Pollack Corp.	Peoria, IL	921	C	0122	1/8" nut	1.50	2000	1000	1,500.00	2,850.00
0004	3-01-86	5652	Air-Temp	Chicago, IL	003	N60	0950	1" bolt	2.14	500	500	1,070.00	1,070.00

Figure 8.8 Customer Order Table—First Normal Form (1NF) with Data for Seven Invoices

This can happen because several rows with redundant information in a large table are often faster to access than selected rows from a number of smaller tables. The dispersion of data across multiple tables requires joins and other expensive operations to combine. A good rule of thumb is that 3NF is good for updating but may not be good for queries.

Remember, the limitations of hardware and software make compromise with theory a frequent necessity. Furthermore, normalization relies on the accuracy of data analysis and a keen awareness of business needs. For example, if any of the following conditions had been present, our tables could be substantially different:

- The need to assign more than one saleperson to a customer.
- The ability to store multiple customer addresses (e.g., ''ship to'' and ''bill to'').
- A provision for price discounting large orders.
- The need to create back orders when part of an order cannot be filled because of an out-of-stock condition.

The identification of needs such as the above cannot be accomplished simply by looking at current paperwork or at the way things are presently done (in our example, the Invoice form in Figure 8.1 cannot accommodate these needs). Therefore, an experienced analyst considers the future as well as the present.

DISCUSSION QUESTIONS

Define functional dependency.

Describe the difference between functional, full and transitive dependency. Why are dependency concepts important?

What is the difference between First and Second Normal Form?

Between Second and Third Normal Form?

Describe update anomalies and how they justify normalization.

Can normalization ever be inappropriate? Comment.

9

INTRODUCTION TO DATABASE DEVELOPMENT

INTRODUCTION

This chapter provides guidelines for selecting and building the first database application, explains the differences between developing systems in a traditional environment and in a DBMS environment, and introduces a methodology that can be used to develop databases.

SELECTING THE FIRST DATABASE APPLICATION

The first DBMS system is different from subsequent applications in several important respects. Its initial data structure is often defined before specific DBMS software is selected—and, conversely, the DBMS selection is then based largely on the needs of the first application. In a sense, this makes the design somewhat more independent of the DBMS than subsequent applications, which are heavily influenced by the features and capabilities of the chosen product.

Also, the company is unfamiliar with DBMS technology and must rely on the vendor and, perhaps, outside consultants. This lack of experience will make the first application cost two to three times as much as similar systems built after users and data processing people learn the technology.

These differences between the first and subsequent systems suggest differences in selection criteria, design guidelines and cost estimates. Although some of the factors

152

discussed are also applicable to later implementations, they are of particular importance for the first system.

A DBMS is usually selected because an organization needs it for a specific application or applications—and certain applications are better suited for a first-time user than others. Applications meeting the following criteria should be the first candidates.

Identifiable, Tangible Benefits

Applications with a questionable payoff potential are not good candidates for the first database system. The selected application must have clear, concrete, significant benefits. Ideally, it should be something that all levels of management agree is important to the company.

Obviously, a calculation of benefits is important when investing in any project; it is doubly important in the case of the first DBMS system, which will be disproportionately expensive in comparison to later systems. A better-than-average expected payoff makes the expense of the first application—and, often, the DBMS itself—more acceptable to management.

An Important (but Not Critical) Addition to the Company

It is axiomatic that acquisition of a DBMS will be based on the expectation of using it for important applications. What is not so obvious is that a company shouldn't put all its chips on a technology new to the firm. A product may have been installed successfully in hundreds of other firms, but if it is unfamiliar to a given organization, reliance on it to support an absolutely critical application courts disaster.

If the chosen application is, in fact, central to the business, it is important to define its scope in such a way as to minimize the risk of failure.

An Eager, Capable User

The success or failure of the first database application—or, indeed, any application—depends largely on the enthusiasm, intelligence, and participation of the client. The first implementation will be technically difficult, expensive and time consuming. Therefore, it is absolutely the wrong situation for a lukewarm or disorganized client.

Small but Part of Something Larger

The ideal first application is part of a bigger system. This can occur naturally—for example, an order entry component may be an integral part of an inventory control system. Or, a system that appears at first glance to be one undifferentiated mass may, in fact, be divisible into several smaller applications.

In either case, developing a portion of a large system is preferable to implementing a stand-alone system that does not integrate with anything else.

Manageable Proportions

No true DBMS is easy to learn or to use the first time. Its storage technology, access methods, concurrent update provisions and myriad other complexities can present serious obstacles for first-time users. Therefore, an effort must be made to select an application or a portion of an application that uses data which does not require an excessively complex database.

Experience has shown that applications with more than twenty to twenty-five identifiable record types (or tables, in a relational DBMS) should be left for later development. Initial database structures can be (and usually will be) rearranged, redefined and expanded in the future, *if the original installation was successful*—and this is what we are trying to ensure.

Reasonable Transaction Volumes

Don't select an exceptionally high-volume application for your first database system. The ability to coax maximum performance out of a high-volume system requires substantial experience.

A Mix of MIS and Transaction Processing Characteristics

Management Information Systems, or Decision Support Systems, known generically by their acronyms "MIS" and "DSS," are designed to provide information with which decision makers, usually management, make day-to-day and strategic decisions. MIS provides after-the-fact information (e.g., daily sales volumes by region) on which management can base future decisions.

DSS also provides data but, in addition, provides "what if" and other modelling capabilities. The interaction between human and machine occurs more or less *as decisions are made*. For example, a manager wishing to determine what the product mix should be in a given geographic area can project the results of potential product combinations based on historical sales data. The computer is helping this manager make decisions in a very direct way.

Transaction processing systems, on the other hand, are the infantry of the data processing world. They produce paychecks, customer bills, reorder notices and other tangible products whose usefulness is not dependent on the intelligence and skills of the recipient.

If the first DBMS application is oriented exclusively toward providing information for decision makers, the people who "do the work" can legitimately ask "what's in it for me?" Also, the pay-off from MIS/DSS is rarely as clear-cut as from a system with a significant transaction processing component—something people can see, touch and feel.

Conversely, a database system that does nothing but crank out invoices does not appear any different than any other system developed over the past fifteen years. The production of management information, particularly of the ad hoc variety, should be an important part of the first application. It is a palpable demonstration of the difference between this and nondatabase systems.

In addition to providing something for everyone, a "mixed" system helps exercise the entire spectrum of DBMS features. This gives programmers, analysts and end-users good experience, and validates (or invalidates) the claims of the vendor. Incidentally, it is usually advantageous to develop systems with both MIS and transaction processing characteristics in subsequent systems as well as for the first DBMS application.

Replaces a Nonexistent or Poorly Functioning Application

"If it ain't broke don't fix it" is often good advice. A new system should only be used to replace something that doesn't work well. The new application will thus provide a dramatic contrast to its predecessor. The cold reality of many software advances is that benefits are not always immediately apparent. It is clear that an improvement has been made when a new product can be favorably compared to the previous system.

In summary, the ideal first application is:

- Profitable in a tangible way
- Part of a larger system
- Important, but not absolutely critical to the company's future
- Not too small, not too large, not too complex, not excessively high volume
- Enthusiastically supported by a capable user
- Useful to both management (decision makers) and line people (those who actually do the work)
- A dramatic improvement over its predecessor system or process

DEVELOPING THE FIRST SYSTEM

Following are some procedural and design suggestions that can help make your first DBMS application a success. In most cases these suggestions are also applicable to subsequent applications.

Develop a Realistic System Scope

Don't try to be all things to all people. This is dangerous under the best of circumstances. It can spell disaster when combined with the use of an unfamiliar product. A realistic system scope is one in which system deliverables are no more than nine months apart. This is not to say that the whole application must be done in nine months, but *something* tangible should be accomplished. One or more of the following are suggested:

- A database loaded with actual applications data
- Programs capable of updating that database
- Some very basic inquiry capabilities
- Some very basic reports

Don't Try to Satisfy All User Needs on the First Attempt

People have a tendency to overestimate the capabilities of the DBMS and to underestimate its complexity. They try to do too much at once. It is far wiser to reduce initial user expectations than to explain later failures.

A good DBMS with comprehensive supporting products will enable you to change reports, screens, system processing characteristics, and even some data structures without trauma. This flexibility is a very good reason to add low priority features only after the user has gained experience with the system.

Beware of "Paralysis through Analysis"

Spend an adequate amount of time defining the data requirements for your first database but don't assume that you will get it right the first time. You probably won't.

The "80/20" rule applies in spades to your first application: you will spend 20 percent of your time defining most of your data needs. The other 80 percent will be spent on thorny details and on resolving imprecise or cumbersome data relationships. Don't drive that figure up to 90 or 95 percent. Learn when to stop; know when to say "Let's go with it and see if it works." Remember, no matter how much time you spend, some of your solutions will be wrong anyway.

Prototype

Prototyping is a method of developing screens, reports and processes on an iterative basis—preferably with a user-friendly, nonprocedural, "fourth-generation" language. This provides the client with easy-to-change working models of selected system components. Design changes can be easily implemented, allowing experimentation with various alternatives *before* system specifications are finalized.

Prototype as much of your first (and subsequent) applications as possible. This not only reduces the chances of a misdesigned system—one that doesn't do what the user wants—it also reduces development time. It is especially valuable for performing *path analysis*, a method of helping validate data relationships by *navigating* the database in search of desired records (failure to find the correct records can signify a faulty database design). Path analysis is described in detail in the next chapter.

Some high-volume or complex prototype programs may need to be converted to a "traditional" data processing language before the system is actually implemented. The reason for this is the lack of extensive logic capabilities and the poor performance of many prototyping languages. However, many of the simpler programs can be used in the final system.

Opt for Simple Structures

Don't attempt to take full advantage of all the theoretical benefits of a DBMS. Some data redundancy, for example, is unavoidable even under the best of circumstances—usually for performance reasons.

It is more important to have the first application in operation, warts and all, than to exploit the full range of structural features the DBMS offers.

Get Help from the Vendor

If you are selecting a DBMS with a specific application in mind—the most common situation—ask each competing vendor to help you prepare some sort of data construct that illustrates your logical data relationships. Then ask the vendors to produce a prototype database loaded with sample data provided by you. This will have several beneficial effects:

■ You will see how suitable each potential DBMS is for handling your specific data requirements.

■ You will be able to form an opinion about vendor competence (or incompetence).

■ You will have a head start on developing your first application —no matter which product you select.

In addition to working with the vendor *before* acquisition, it frequently pays to retain the services of that vendor for specific activities *after* you buy the product.

Although vendor rates can be substantial—$100 per hour plus expenses is not uncommon—the vendor knows things about the product that can save you hundreds of hours, missed deadlines and a lot of headaches.

The following services are specifically recommended:

■ Help in creating the first logical and physical design

■ Validation that your logical design reflects the data relationships needed for your first application

■ Validation that the physical design accurately reflects the logical design and will, in fact, work

■ Suggestions on optimizing performance

■ Help in performing complex conversions of data from your present files to the new databases

■ Help in correctly using DBMS components such as the report writer

■ Help in tuning the database for optimum performance after the system is in production

Incidentally, consultants not connected with the vendor can also be used. However, this may not be feasible if you have acquired a DBMS with a small customer base or one that has only recently been introduced. Pioneering customers will rely heavily on vendor support.

Don't "Overintegrate"

Build provisions into your first database that anticipate obvious future applications. However, don't spend too much time speculating. It is very difficult to predict if and how future systems will be integrated into your first database.

Try a Wide Variety of DBMS Features—but Be Cautious!

Make an attempt to exercise the following features of the DBMS as part of the first application:

- The report writer
- The query language
- The host language interface
- Backup, recovery and security provisions

Avoid relying on features that are not essential to the application. For example, the performance capabilities of DBMS query languages vary substantially. You may discover that yours is not suitable for high-volume inquiries or updates. Therefore, don't base your schedules on the optimistic assumption that all of your on-line programs can be written in the user-friendly, fast-to-develop but slow-running query language. Your report writer may have similar problems. Complex data manipulation and formatting features may not be available and performance may prove inadequate.

THE COST OF THE FIRST APPLICATION

The cost of developing the first database application is usually two or three times higher than the cost of subsequent applications of like scope and complexity. The reason for this is the enormous overhead of learning the technology and preparing the foundation for future systems.

Consider the total costs incurred over the useful life of the DBMS as falling into fixed and variable categories. Fixed costs are those that must be incurred whether one, three or ten DBMS applications are developed. Variable costs are those that are incurred only as applications are built.

When developing the first application, much of the cost is a down payment for future benefits. This is the fixed cost component. Fixed cost consists of training, the initial implementation of DBMS software, the learning curve reflected in slower-than-normal progress toward completing the first application, and the rework needed because of mistakes made through inexperience. It can also represent that part of the database development effort that results in data structures usable by future systems.

Fixed cost is what is needed to get in the game. Once implementation, education, experience (i.e., mistakes), and part of the initial data structure is paid for, fixed costs are not repeated in any significant way until another major new technology is adopted.

Variable costs are the "real" costs of the first application—that is, costs that cannot be amortized over the life of the DBMS; costs that are applicable specifically and exclusively to this application.

Variable costs of building DBMS applications are no higher and, in fact, may be lower than the costs of developing traditional file systems. They are dependent only on considerations such as system complexity, size, technical features, and other factors typically accounted for when estimating a development project.

There is no accurate way of determining how much of the total cost of the first application is fixed and how much is variable—nor is there a compelling reason to do so. But be prepared for an expensive first application. Fifty to 75 percent of its total cost may be a fixed cost investment for the future.

THE SYSTEM DEVELOPMENT LIFE CYCLE IN A DBMS ENVIRONMENT

The purpose and major steps of each phase of the traditional System Development Life Cycle remain essentially unchanged with the introduction of a DBMS. However, there are some differences in tasks and emphasis. Life Cycle steps and their companion database design checkpoints are illustrated in Figure 9.1 and are briefly described in the following sections.

The Preliminary Investigation and Feasibility Study

The purpose of this phase or phases is to supply adequate information to management to enable an informed go/no-go decision. It also provides the groundwork and common understanding of system scope, major functions and overall technology.

In a well-managed data processing environment—DBMS or otherwise—an EDP plan that supports corporate objectives will play a role in suggesting development priorities and the kinds of systems that should be developed.

The potential for system integration that a DBMS provides makes serious adher-

Figure 9.1 The System Development Life Cycle in a DBMS Environment

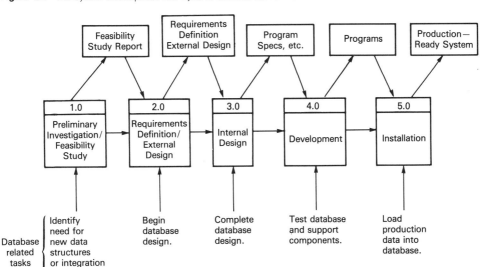

ence to the plan important. This requires accommodation to the corporate data model as well as rational selection of application priorities.

Of course, slavish adherence to any plan is misguided. The plan may have been wrong in the first place or the passage of time may have changed the needs that data processing must address. A flexible, open-minded approach is needed.

In a DBMS environment, a database or databases may already exist that, with little or no modification, can provide data to a new system. If we already have such databases, we may still wish to develop some new data structures that will be redundant with parts of existing databases. This may provide better performance. If a new data structure must be developed for the proposed application, its use for future applications must be assessed and development costs should reflect this future potential use.

The trade-offs between using existing structures and building new ones are rarely simple and must be dealt with early in the development life cycle. Otherwise, accurate predictions of costs, schedules, etc., cannot be made.

The active involvement of both the DBA and the DRM function begins during the Feasibility Study phase and continues through the entire development cycle.

Business Requirements Definition/External Design

This phase, or phases, of the development cycle is also known as General Design, Functional Design, etc. The purpose here is to define the system from a functional, business perspective and to outline its technical shape and characteristics. This includes major data inputs, screens, reports, and files.

All file and database design begins here. In DBMS-based systems, the emphasis is on the logical rather than physical aspects of data—that is, how the ultimate user perceives data, not how it is stored in the computer.

The logical data constructs are compared with existing database structures and with the corporate data model. An attempt is then made to integrate the new data requirements with existing structures. Inconsistencies between the corporate data model and the proposed structure are examined and appropriate changes made—either in the corporate data model (likely) or in the design of the new database (less likely, because it represents "real life" rather than a theoretical model).

Internal Design

The purpose of this phase is to define all portions of the system to the point where computer programs can be written. Although Internal Design activities are begun in previous phases they do not result in their ultimate level of detail until this phase. Key tasks are the preparation of detailed input and output specifications, program-to-program flows, program specifications, and backup/recovery procedures.

All file and database design—or redesign, if new requirements are being grafted onto existing structures—is completed during this phase. Many of the database development steps described in the next chapter's methodology are also considered part of Internal Design.

Performance, data integrity and definitional consistency factors loom large in this phase. This is especially true when new data is redundant with data in existing databases, or when new data must be added to existing databases. Specifically:

- The addition of new data elements, records, and relationships to an existing database to accommodate a new application may cause across-the-board performance degradation. This may be sufficient reason to create an additional application-specific database—even though this may compromise the notion of data integration and may cause some redundancy.
- The same data elements, records and relationships, should generally not be updated by more than one update component. For example, a customer's last payment amount is normally updated in the accounts receivable system. The billing system should not be allowed to update the same field.
- The definitions of seemingly identical data elements and relationships used in more than one system may, in fact, differ. Care must therefore be taken to ensure that existing structures really meet the needs of the new application.

We should also decide on the technical facilities that will provide the balance we seek between performance, ease of development, and maintainability. This includes choosing the appropriate programming languages, deciding whether or not to use native DBMS inquiry and report writing components, and selecting backup and recovery techniques.

An important aspect of Internal Design for a DBMS application, as well as for a flat file system, is data conversion. This can consume as much as 25 percent of total development costs.

Since database structures tend to be more complex than conventional files, more attention must be paid to how existing data will be gathered, rearranged and loaded. Frequently, the meaning of individual data elements and the relationships between records are dissimilar between old and new systems.

Therefore, automated and manual means must be developed to ensure accurate representation of data in its new home. This can entail a significant design and programming effort and should begin during External Design and end with Internal Design.

Development

The purpose of this phase is to complete all programming, program testing, system or integration testing, and all support components such as documentation and manual procedures. After the completion of this phase, the system should be ready for installation.

Aside from the usual development activities in any data processing environment, DBMS-based systems present special problems. Database load, unload, backup, recovery and other ancillary DBMS components must be tested. This is absolutely essential for a new DBMS user. It not only verifies that the components actually work, but validates our understanding of product features. Given the poor documentation that accompanies some DBMS products, a clear understanding of how features work is more difficult than it should be.

The testing of ancillary components is also recommended for more experienced users. Subtle differences between applications can cause widely different results when the same DBMS feature is used.

Installation

The purpose of this phase of system development is to convert files from the old (or manual) system to the new, complete all necessary parallel testing, and place the new system into production. Installation-related activities that must be performed for a DBMS application prior to, or during, this last phase are similar to those needed for conventional systems. They include:

- Preparation of data to be loaded into the new database
- Execution of programs that will perform data conversion
- Completion of training for clerks, computer operators and others who use or operate the new system
- The loading of new data
- Parallel operations, if the old system is being emulated
- Production cutover

INTRODUCTION TO A DATABASE DESIGN METHODOLOGY

The remainder of this chapter will introduce the reader to a database development methodology described in detail in Chapter 10. It is largely based on the Entity-Relationship (E-R) approach espoused by Professor Peter Chen of the MIT Sloan School of Management.*

This is only one of many design techniques that are taught and promulgated by academics, training organizations and DBMS vendors. The E-R approach is oriented toward network databases and is, in fact, used by Cullinet, the creator of the most popular network system, IDMS.

The E-R approach can also be used to design hierarchical, relational and hybrid databases. The terminology may differ, but most of the concepts remain the same. Mastery of any good design technique will enable an analyst to apply his or her knowledge to other kinds of databases.

The development of databases differs in some important respects from the development of conventional files. Some of these differences are described below.

- A more distinct separation exists between logical and physical design.
  As explained later in the chapter, logical design refers to the definition of data elements, records, and the relationships between them needed to satisfy the functional or business requirements of the system. Physical design refers to the way records are actually

---

* Peter Chen, *The Entity-Relationship Approach to Logical Data-base Design* (Wellesley, MA: QED Information Sciences, 1977).

stored on a disk (e.g., record dispersion, access techniques, the physical proximity of logically related records, etc.).

■ Although logical and physical design influence each other, DBMS software allows us to concentrate on logical relationships without immediate concern about physical storage.

■ A greater amount of "tuning" takes place to ensure adequate performance.

Because most flat file storage and access methods offer fewer design options for the average analyst, less tuning can be done to improve system performance. Expect to spend more time tuning and testing a database than conventional files.

■ There is greater potential for system integration. When designing a new system using a DBMS, special attention must be given to the corporate data model (if it exists) and databases that are already in production. Duplication of data should generally be limited in order to benefit from the greater system integration potential offered by DBMS applications.

The essential steps of database development—or data modelling, a more exotic term—are identified below. They are also illustrated and described in detail in Chapter 10. They are:

1. Identify Entities
2. Define Relationships
3. Prepare an Entity-Relationship (E-R) Diagram
4. Identify and Define Entity Attributes
5. Translate the E-R Diagram into a Bachman Diagram**
6. Analyze Volumes
7. Perform Path Analysis
8. Design Records
9. Define Sets
10. Test and Implement the Database

The first nine steps consist of defining data requirements, translating them into database terms, and validating the correctness of the result. The last step consists of actually building and prototyping the database.

Database development can begin once the Requirements Definition phase of system development is under way. It then proceeds in parallel with subsequent development steps, continues into External Design and culminates in System Installation, when "live" production data is loaded into the finished product.

Incidentally, only the first four or five of the above steps should be completed if a specific DBMS has not yet been selected—and even these will probably be repeated when designing the database "for real."

After initial design is completed, the database is built using the appropriate DBMS utility routines. Representative data is put into the database, tested and refined. When we are satisfied that the database meets our requirements, live application data is converted as appropriate and loaded. We now have a production database.

** The Bachman diagram is named for Charles W. Bachman, an early DBMS pioneer who helped develop General Electric's (later Honeywell's) Information Data Store (IDS) system in the early 1960's. That product contains many of the features that comprise the network DBMS model.

LOGICAL AND PHYSICAL DESIGN

Database development involves *logical design* and *physical design*. Although there is some argument about where one leaves off and the other begins, the logical/physical dichotomy is useful as an aid to understanding the development process.

In a sense, logical design is akin to the architecture and decoration of a house: its height, the color of its walls, the quality of the bathroom fixtures, the positioning of windows, and all the other things that make it pleasant, practical and livable.

Physical design represents the technological, financial, and site factors. There is only so much you can do with a 50 × 50-foot lot, a $100,000 construction budget, reliance on standard components, the need for children's bedrooms, etc. Although the architectural and decorative elements are visible, obvious, and seemingly all-powerful, they are, in fact, severely limited. So it is with database design. The lion's share of development activities are "logical." Nevertheless, physical design is crucially important.

Logical Design

Logical design is the definition of data and the identification of relationships between data from a business or functional perspective.

As we shall see in the next chapter, steps 1-4 (Identify Entities, Define Relationships, Prepare an E-R Diagram, and Identify and Define Entity Attributes) are entirely logical. Steps 5–7 (Translate the E-R diagram into a Bachman Diagram, and Perform Volume and Path Analysis) are partly logical. The last three steps, Design Records, Define Sets, and Test and Implement the Database, are primarily physical.

The logical design approach described here is essentially "top down." Entities, which are broader and more encompassing than data elements, are identified and defined first. However, the correctness of entity identification and definition is later verified by compiling a list of data elements needed to support desired reports and screens. Each element must find a home in an entity; otherwise, the entity definitions are incomplete.

Although logical design tasks are performed in sequence, the process is iterative. Each iteration provides greater levels of detail and certainty. Each step is influenced by the results of the previous step and, in turn, influences the succeeding steps. For example, the selection of entities implies the presence of certain data elements. Conversely, the identification of needed data elements may trigger the creation of a new entity.

Physical Design

The purpose of physical design is to prescribe how records are stored, accessed and manipulated by the DBMS and its host systems. It is the process of developing a physical data structure for a logical data structure—the two are not the same—and using the computing environment in a manner congenial to good performance and storage utilization.

Physical factors exert a pervasive, albeit subterranean, influence on the design process. Because we are ultimately obliged to make a database conform to the limitations imposed on us by the DBMS, our computer hardware and our system software, almost every decision we make will have physical ramifications.

For example, the need to find a specific customer record quickly mandates the use of a nonsequential searching technique. Although we really don't care how the computer finds the desired record, we know, a priori, that sequentially searching one million records will not work! Thus, a ''logical'' need (e.g., customer information) has a ''physical'' ramification (e.g., the need to use customer identifiers in order to perform a nonsequential search for specific customer records).

Here are some examples of activities that are entirely, or primarily, in the realm of physical design. They are not necessarily available with all DBMS products.

- Selection of record addressing and storage techniques
- Selection of techniques for linking related records
- The definition of free space and overflow
- Data compression, which reduces the physical space taken up by data on a mass storage device
- Identification of database areas

In addition, some physical factors are normally independent of a specific database and are established for the entire environment. Here are two examples:

- Page or block size. This is the amount of data physically transferred between memory and a mass storage device with one read/write operation.
- Buffer pool management. A buffer pool is a section of memory containing records that have already been read in. With each input operation, some (but not all) records must be released to make room for new ones. On what basis should they be kicked out? Should the oldest record in the buffer be the first to go? How about the least-used record? etc.

Now that we have established the context within which database development takes place, and have outlined the major steps of development, we can flesh out this process. Chapter 10 gives us the details.

DISCUSSION QUESTIONS

Name and describe four important criteria for selecting the first DBMS application.

Why are limited system scope and simple data structures important for the first application?

Explain ''paralysis through analysis'' in the context of developing a database application.

Name some differences in emphasis between application development in a DBMS and non-DBMS environment.

What is the difference in emphasis between logical and physical database design?

10

THE STEPS OF DATABASE DEVELOPMENT

INTRODUCTION

This chapter contains a detailed description of the database development methodology introduced in Chapter 9.

Although the methodology was developed specifically for network-based models and the terminology tends to be network oriented,* most of the development steps apply to the design of relational as well as more structurally oriented models. With the exception of some design choices, diagramming techniques and tuning options, the major principles remain valid—no matter which DBMS we use.

The methodology consists of ten steps. The first nine are predominantly design oriented and the tenth consists of the actual creation, testing and implementation of the database. The entire approach is highly iterative. It consists of:

1. Identifying entities
2. Defining relationships
3. Preparing an Entity-Relationship (E-R) diagram
4. Identifying and defining entity attributes
5. Translating the E-R diagram into a Bachman, or Data Structure, diagram
6. Analyzing volumes

*Some of the information in this chapter is covered in greater detail in Chapter 6, which describes the network model. The reader may wish to refer back to that chapter, particularly when the discussion turns physical, as it does when sets, chains, pointers, record insertion techniques and membership options are discussed.

166

7. Performing path analysis
8. Designing records
9. Defining sets
10. Testing and implementing the database

Figures 10.1 and 10.2 illustrate the steps of the development process and the resultant products. Examples of the two major constructs discussed in this chapter, the Entity-Relationship diagram and the Bachman diagram, are illustrated at the end of the chapter in Figures 10.14–10.17. These figures show E-R diagrams for Personnel and Customer Order databases and their respective Bachman diagrams. The chapter concludes with a detailed checklist of deliverables.

IDENTIFY ENTITIES

The first step in the design process is to identify entities. An entity is a person, place, or thing of interest to the user community, about which the system is expected to maintain, correlate and display information. An entity may be a customer, a product, an invoice, an employee or anything else that is important to the application. The sample E-R diagrams (Figures 10.14 & 10.15) contain nine and eight entities respectively, which are shown as rectangular boxes. Please examine these figures carefully before continuing.

Initially, very little may be known about each entity. However, as logical design progresses, our knowledge will increase.

It is important to note that, strictly speaking, entities are *not* records in the computer sense of the term. Though the terms "entity" and "record" are used interchangeably in all chapters except the present one, entities represent a conceptual view of data—records have a more physical orientation.

As we shall see in the following sections, entities must be translated into logical records and then into physical records before we can construct the database. The difference in terminology is important only when we distinguish between a purely *logical* structure, such as an Entity-Relationship diagram, and its *physical* counterpart, the Bachman (or Data Structure) diagram.

DEFINE RELATIONSHIPS

A *relationship*, or *association* in relational terminology, is a description of how two or more entities relate to each other on a logical level. Examples of relationships are Customer/Order, Employee/Job, and Part/Component. These logical relationships can be:

- *One-to-many*
- *Many-to-many*
- *One-to-one*
- *Iterative*

A description of each follows.

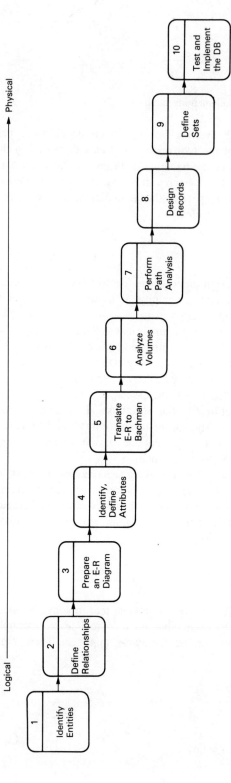

Figure 10.1 The Steps of Database Development

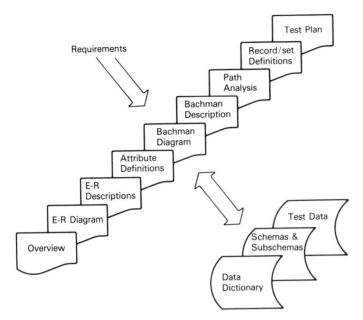

Figure 10.2 Major Database Design Deliverables

One-to-Many

A one-to-many relationship occurs when an entity is related to zero, one, or more occurrences of another entity. This is indicated on the E-R diagram by placing a ''1'' and an ''M'' next to the appropriate entity boxes. Note that we normally read the E-R diagram from top to bottom and from left to right. The name of each entity is always referred to in the singular.

An example of a one-to-many relationship in the Personnel database is the relationship between a Department and an Employee. Departments contain many employees but an employee cannot work for more than one department.

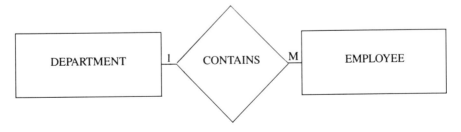

In the Customer Order database, a customer may have many orders but one order is never split between customers.

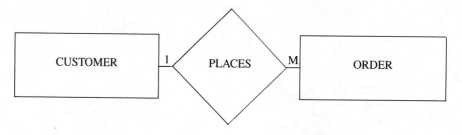

Note that a one-to-many relationship does not require each Customer to have multiple Orders or each Department to have multiple Employees. It simply allows such a condition to occur.

Many-to-Many

A many-to-many relationship occurs when each of two entities can be related to more than one occurrence of the other. This is indicated on the E-R diagram by placing ''Ms'' next to the appropriate entity boxes.

A many-to-many example from our Personnel database is illustrated below. The relationship is between an employee and a skill. An employee may have many skills useful to the organization. At the same time, a skill can be (and usually is) possessed by more than one employee.

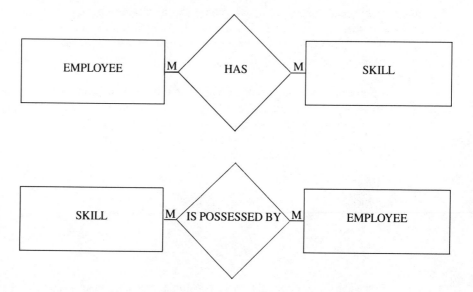

In a Customer Order database, one Order may represent one Part or several Parts:

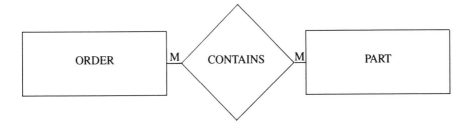

Conversely, a specific Part can appear on many Orders.

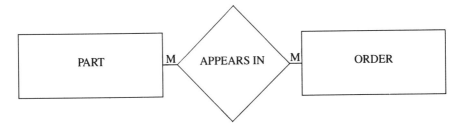

Incidentally, to keep E-R diagrams as simple as possible, relationships are illustrated and interpreted in only one direction: from top to bottom and from left to right. Thus, we would illustrate Order-to-Part or Part-to-Order but not both.

The many-to-many form does not require an Order to have multiple Parts; nor does it require a Part to appear on multiple Orders. Most Orders may, in fact, be for only one Part. The many-to-many form allows a many-to-many condition to occur.

A many-to-many relationship is not limited to two entities. For example, the product database of a software vendor must depict different versions of the product, depending on the computer model and operating system under which it was designed to run. This relationship is illustrated as follows.

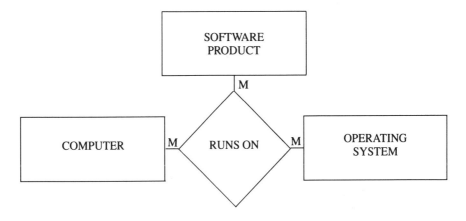

One-to-One

A one-to-one relationship exists when one occurrence of an entity is related to one and only one occurrence of another entity. This relationship is represented by placing a "1" next to each of the entity boxes. This is also called a *total dependency* relationship and is described in Chapter 8, Normalization.

A one-to-one relationship in the Personnel database is illustrated by the relationship between an employee and his or her current address. If we assume that a person must always have an address and we keep only one address on file, the Employee/Address relationship is one-to-one.

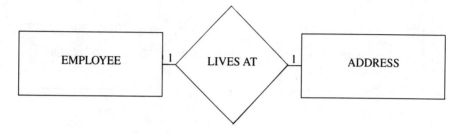

Iterative

An iterative relationship, sometimes called a *loop*, exists when there is a relationship between two or more occurrences of the same entity. Iterative relationships can be one-to-many, many-to-many or one-to-one.

In project management, one person may be designated a project leader while others are team members. Representing this with two entities, "team leader" and "team member," is a redundancy since both entities will carry the same information. If we assume that each person belongs to one and only one project team, we can define a one-to-many loop as illustrated below.

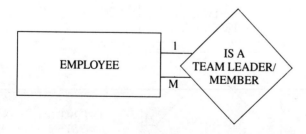

If we allow project teams to overlap, and people to be project leaders on some projects and subordinates on others, the loop becomes a many-to-many iterative relationship. That is, one person can be a member of one or more project teams and, at the same time, be a project leader for one or more projects. Thus:

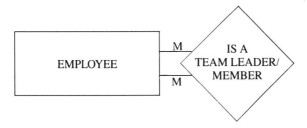

Another example of a many-to-many binary relationship occurs between components in a Manufacturing database. An automobile consists of assemblies that contain individual parts and subassemblies. Thus, a door handle is part of a door; but it also contains screws, springs, and a lock. These screws, springs, and locks are also used in other components.

Since the information carried about each component is the same regardless of its role, the definition of two separate entities is redundant. Here is how the parts database can be illustrated:

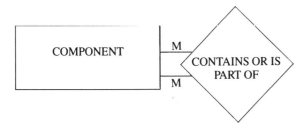

What about a one-to-one loop? A "couples" database provides an example of such a relationship: exactly the same information is kept on both husbands and wives and there can be only one of each in a family at a given time.

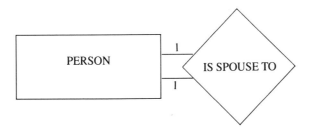

PREPARE AN ENTITY-RELATIONSHIP (E-R) DIAGRAM

The purpose of an E-R diagram is to illustrate clearly the logical relationships in a database. It is used from the inception of logical design and is modified as the logical design and physical design progress.

An E-R diagram contains the following elements:

- Entity boxes in the shape of rectangles, lozenges or similar symbols (we will use rectangles). Each box represents the entity named within (Customer, Order, Part, etc.).
- Diamonds, which explain relationships between entities (e.g., an Order "contains" Parts).
- Straight lines with optional arrowheads, which connect entity boxes and diamonds.
- The number "1" and the letter "M," which indicate relationship types.

Here are some guidelines for preparing an E-R diagram:

- Continue identifying entities and relating them to each other until you are satisfied that they cover all (or most) of your application data needs. This is an absolutely critical part of the design process and should not be shortchanged.
- Weed out irrevelant relationships and unneeded entities. The E-R diagram should be as simple as possible, while still representing the data needs of the system.
- Whenever possible, make your E-R diagram move from top to bottom and from left to right.
- Prepare a short description of each entity, including the types of attributes it contains and which attributes (or combinations of attributes) makes it unique.

IDENTIFY AND DEFINE ENTITY ATTRIBUTES

Data elements, fields, or attributes, depending on your terminological preferences, are the smallest usable pieces of data in a database. They must now be identified, defined, and placed in the data dictionary. The attributes that make each entity unique must also be identified.

Initially, we are interested in external definitions. That is, we want to know what a data element looks like and what it means to the end-user. However, we must eventually have internal definitions as well. We must provide the DBMS and the application programmer with detailed physical characteristics.

Some of the information outlined below will not be available on the "first pass." In fact, we may be filling in the blanks well into the final stages of design.

The definition of attributes is not only a necessary part of the design process but, as a side benefit, enables us to test the correctness of entities and relationships. For example, we may discover attributes for which we have failed to identify an entity. Conversely, we may find entities that are redundant; they may have attributes that are already part of another entity.

Data element definitions must contain:

- The "official" name of the data element. This should follow the specific naming rules at your installation.
- A narrative definition.
- Whether or not this attribute is a key—that is, does its value make the entity unique?
- Synonyms and acronyms by which the data element is also known.
- Size and characteristics of the data element, including:
  — Length

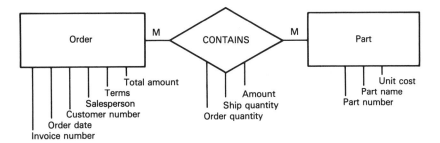

Figure 10.3 Data Attributes

— Number of decimal places
— Whether this is a group or elementary item. For example, a Date field may be a group item that is further subdivided into Year, Month and Day
— Denominating factor (e.g., dollars, pounds, inches, etc.)
■ Validation rules, including:
— Values (e.g., employee code must be 1,2 or 6)
— Value ranges (e.g., month must be 1 to 12)
— Edits (e.g., alpha vs. numeric)
— Cross-validation for values (e.g., net pay + deductions = gross pay)
— Cross-validation (e.g., gross pay must be present in order to have net pay)

In addition to defining attributes, we must connect them with the appropriate entities or relationships. The visual technique illustrated in Figure 10.3 may be used. It illustrates the data elements belonging to the Order and Part entities and the relationship between them.

As we shall see in the next section, the data that belongs to the combination of the Order and Part entities will find a home when entities are resolved into records. The rationalization of data element into entities, the identification of keys, the removal of redundant elements, and the creation of needed entities can be helped through the use of normalization techniques described in Chapter 8.

TRANSLATE THE E-R DIAGRAM INTO A BACHMAN DIAGRAM

We have now identified entities, determined the relationships that exist between them, and defined attributes. The next step is to translate our entities and relationships into records.

This is, in fact, the last step in which we refer to "entities." Our translation will result in the identification of "records," the tangible pieces from which we will generate a database using DBMS software. Although these records do not necessarily resemble the physical records ultimately manipulated by DBMS software, they are close enough to justify the new term.

The translation analysis results in the creation of a Data Structure, or Bachman diagram (we will use the latter term), named for its inventor (see the previous chapter).

A Bachman differs from an E-R diagram in the following ways:

- All relationships between entities have been translated into records, which are represented by rectangular boxes.
- The diamonds that were used to explain relationships between entities on the E-R diagram are no longer needed and have therefore been removed.
- Volume statistics and ratios are (optionally) included.
- Set and record descriptions in coded, highly abbreviated form may be placed inside the record boxes and on the connecting lines. Some DBMS vendors (e.g., Cullinet) suggest this representation, but for clarity our Bachmans do not show such data.

A Bachman diagram consists of *sets* of records. A set consists of one (and only one) *owner* record and one or more related *member* records (see Chapter 6). An arrow always points from the owner to the member. A set is illustrated below.

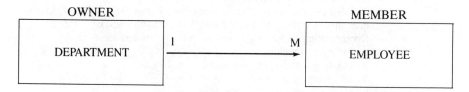

The rules for resolving an E-R diagram into a Bachman diagram—that is, converting entities and relationships into sets of records—are described below. Note that the diamonds containing relationship descriptions disappear as soon as each translation is accomplished. They were used only as an aid to understanding.

Resolving One-to-Many Relationships

One-to-many relationships are resolved by making the ''1'' side the owner and the ''M'' side the member. One record is defined for each entity box, as in Figure 10.4. An *instance* of this set is illustrated in Figure 10.5: the Sales Department has three employees, Smith, Jones and Thomas.

Figure 10.4 Resolution of a One-to-Many Relationship

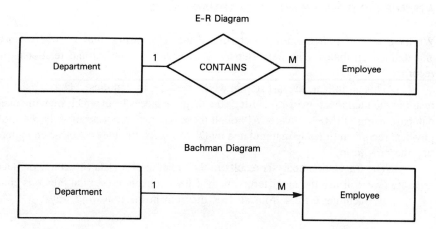

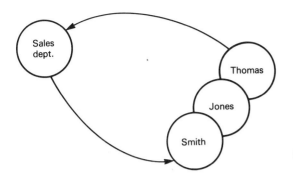

Figure 10.5 An Instance of the Department/Employee Set

One-to-many relationships in which there are two or more members for one owner are translated the same way as one owner/one member sets. One record is defined for each entity.

Resolving Many-to-Many Relationships

Many-to-many relationship are resolved by making both sides owners and creating an intersection record between them. This is illustrated in Figure 10.6.

Note that we have transformed a many-to-many relationship into two one-to-

Figure 10.6 Resolution of a Many-to-Many Relationship

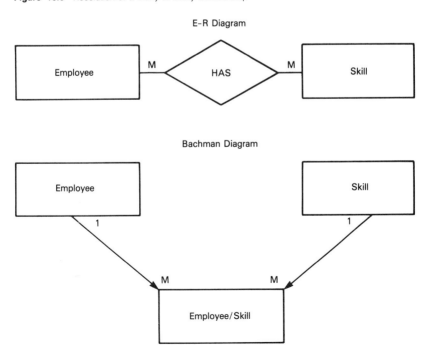

many relationships. An additional record type, which we will call an Employee/Skill record, now exists for each combination of employee and skill. Based on this design, we can list every employee who is proficient in French. We can also list each person's job-related skills.

A simplified instance of the Employee, Skill and Employee/Skill set is illustrated in Figure 10.7.

Incidentally, the Employee/Skill record may or may not have data in it. In this case, we may wish to carry the date on which the employee became qualified in the skill. Information that is an inherent and exclusive part of a relationship becomes visible when we construct a Data Attributes Chart, part of which is illustrated in Figure 10.3.

In some DBMS products, a member is not really allowed to have more than one owner except in a "logical" sense. Physical storage and access is built around one, but not both, pairs of records. The choice of which set should have the "real" owner is up to the designer and is largely dependent on which pair of records is most commonly used together.

Resolving Many-to-Many Relationships with More than Two Entities

More than two entities connected by a common relationship represent a special case of the many-to-many construct. An example is the product database of a software vendor. It must accommodate multiple versions of a product designed to run on a variety of computers and operating systems. Figure 10.8 illustrates how these relationships are converted to a Bachman diagram.

The Configuration record that results may or may not have application data attached to it. If it represents a specific version of the Computer/Operating System/Software Product combination, it may contain a version ID, release date, price and other such information.

Figure 10.9 illustrates an instance of the Computer/Software Product/Operating System/Configuration set. In this example, Release 3.10 of the Statistical Analyzer is

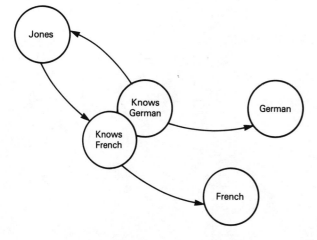

Figure 10.7 An Instance of the Employee, Skill, and Employee/Skill Set

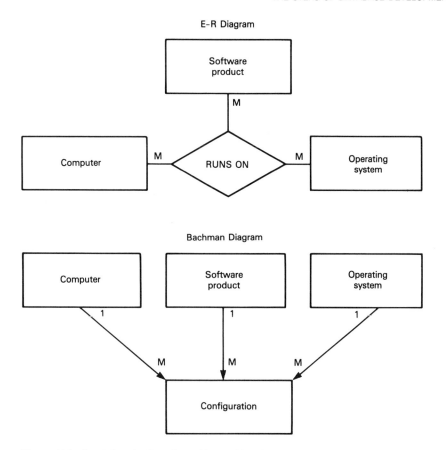

Figure 10.8 Resolution of a Three-Entity, Many-to-Many Relationship

specifically intended for use with the IBM 4341 running under the DOS/VSE operating system.

Resolving One-to-One Relationships

In a one-to-one relationship, either record can be the owner or the member. One record is created for each entity box as in Figure 10.10.

Resolving Iterative Relationships

In a loop, or iterative, relationship, two record types are defined from one entity but only one record is actually used by the DBMS. The translation of a one-to-many binary relationship is illustrated at the top of Figure 10.11. Figure 10.12 shows Jones managing a team that consists of Smith, Thomas and Brooks.

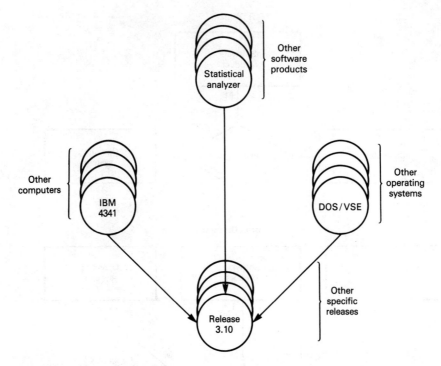

Figure 10.9   An Instance of a Computer, Software Product, Operating System and Configuration Set

Things get more complicated if the loop relationship is many-to-many. An intersection record is now needed and is shown at the bottom of Figure 10.11. A simplified version of two overlapping project teams is illustrated in Figure 10.13. Team ''A'' is led by Jones and consists of Brooks, Thomas and Smith. The Project Leader for Team ''B'' is

Figure 10.10   Resolution of a One-to-One Relationship

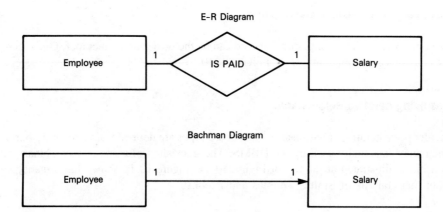

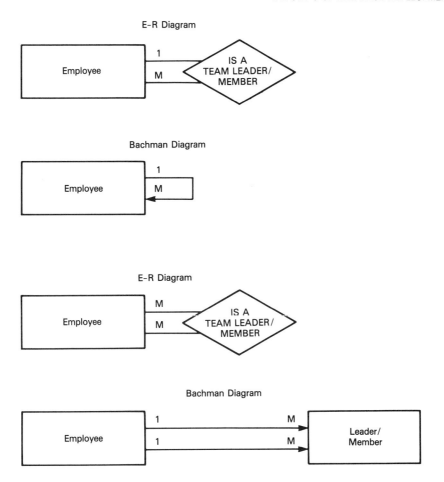

Figure 10.11   Resolution of an Iterative (loop) Relationship

Smith. He manages Jones, Edwards and Thomas (notice that Jones participates in both Team A and Team B, as a Team Leader and a team member, respectively).

ANALYZE VOLUMES

Volumes are needed in order to determine database storage requirements. They are also important because of their great impact on database performance. Now that we have a first-cut Bachman diagram, as well as a good notion of the information the database must contain, we must pause and examine our design in the light of application volumes.

Absolute Volumes

Absolute volumes give us a sense of magnitude and direct our attention to potential bottle-necks. The storage and accessing of ten thousand Employee records requires a far more painstaking design than the accommodation of twenty Benefit records.

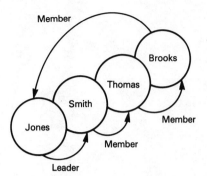

Figure 10.12 An Instance of a One-to-Many Employee, Project Leader/ Member Set

Incidentally, volumes for database entities (number of customers, number of orders, number of warehouses, etc.) should have been determined during Requirements Definition. In this step we attach those volumes to specific records and, in case of intersection records that were created during the E-R/Bachman translation, we calculate poten-

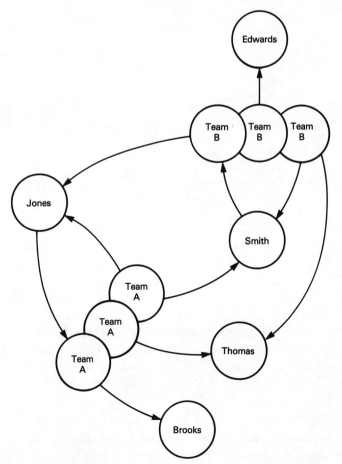

Figure 10.13 An Instance of a Many-to-Many Employee, Project Leader/Member Set

tial combinations of many-to-many relationships—e.g., the average number of skills per employee.

This process will provide a valuable check on the validity of our database design, will help us estimate needed overflow and free space requirements, and will enable us to define database area sizes when we construct and compile the database schema.

Relative Volumes

Relative volumes are an important factor in storage and accessing arrangements. For example, a 1:100 relationship between Departments and Employees requires a different storage strategy than a 1:2 Customer/Order ratio. In one case, we may wish to store all employees adjacent to the department record to minimize disk reads. In the other case the number of related records is too small to cause a problem. Therefore, member records can be spread over a wider area.

Relative volumes should be researched from several different perspectives in order to provide us with the most complete understanding of the database. The first perspective is a simple average. This is the ratio between the actual number of owner records and the actual number of member records in each set. In our Personnel database, this yields a 1:.6 ratio between the Employee record and the Employee/Project intersection record.

We determined this ratio by finding out that about one hundred fifty projects are active at any given time and each project is manned by an average of forty people. Thus, six thousand Employee/Project records are divided by ten thousand Employee records giving the 1:.6 ratio. However, this information is incomplete. If we dig a little deeper, we discover that there is a substantial crossover of people between projects. In fact, each employee usually works on three projects. Furthermore, only 20 percent of the workforce participates in project activities. The other eight thousand perform support tasks that are not project oriented.

Taking this information into account, our ratio now becomes 1:3, which was calculated by dividing the six thousand Employee/Project records by two thousand, the number of Employees who actually work on projects. What are the practical implications of this?

If we wish to minimize overflow processing, which can significantly degrade performance, we should use the 1:3 ratio in reserving space for Employee/Project records. This will give us room for thirty thousand Employee/Project records—far more than we need—but will virtually eliminate overflow processing. The price we pay is poor space utilization. The 1:3 ratio will have the following result:

- Three free space "slots" will be wasted for each of the 8000 employees who do not work on project teams.
- However, the only overflow that will be required is for employees who work on more than the average three projects.

If, on the other hand, we are short of space and are not concerned with performance—at least for this set of records—we should use the 1:.6 ratio. This requires a lot of overflow but only one contiguous space following each Employee record. Here is the result:

- Only one free space slot will be wasted for each employee who does not work in a project environment.
- However, one slot (.6 rounded up) will usually not be enough for each of the 2000 people who work on projects—after all, they work on an average of three projects. This will cause extensive use of overflow.

Incidentally, we may wish to avoid the above problem altogether by creating two separate Employee record types, one project-oriented, the other for support staff. This increases database complexity but provides more efficiency.

Another way of looking at relative volume ratios is by examining the difference between *mean* (average) and *median* (most occurrences) values.

An average order in a customer order database may be fifty items. But this may mask the fact that our one dozen biggest customers order thousands of items per invoice while our other ten thousand customers order two or three items! In such a case, we may wish to plan our database around two or three orders per customer and make special arrangements for our few high-volume buyers.

Volumes should be included in the narrative accompanying the Bachman diagram. In addition, absolute volumes may be noted on the inside of each record box and relative volumes may be placed on the relationship lines that connect records as illustrated below. If the Bachman becomes too messy, you may restrict volume information to the narratives.

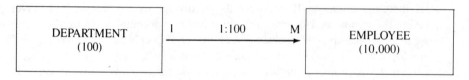

In addition to determining application volumes at the time the database is placed into production, we must attempt to predict its growth and the pattern of record updating.

Growth Volatility

Growth volatility is a prediction of the growth (or shrinkage) in the number of records over time. For example, the number of customers (i.e., occurrences of the Customer record) may grow 5 percent per year; but the number of orders per customer may increase by 15 percent. This helps us define the size of free space and overflow areas and plan database reorganization and reload strategies.

Update Volatility

Update volatility is an approximation of update activity against records. For example, 75 percent of all Invoice records may turn over each year. However, customer demographic and credit information may remain relatively stable (e.g., 10 percent volatility). Update volatility is an important consideration in deciding the sequence in which new records are inserted and the sequence in which records are accessed.

PERFORM PATH ANALYSIS

Path analysis helps us verify the correctness of our database design in light of reporting and on-line access requirements. Although we have, of course, taken those needs into account during the design process, we have not yet attempted actually to retrieve desired records based on our design.

The identification, definition and prioritization of data access requirements via path analysis are very important for both logical and physical design. These steps are important for logical design because the correctness of relationships is tested. They are important for physical design because tortuous paths to frequently used data may severely degrade system performance.

Path analysis is done as follows:

- Translate the access needs identified during the Requirements Definition into specifics, including:
  — An English language description (e.g., "find all management level employees who speak French and have been at their present job at least five years")
  — Records to be accessed (e.g., Employee, Skill, Employee/Skill, Start Date, Job)
  — Keys needed (e.g., Employee ID, Skill ID)
  — Type of access needed (on-line for query purposes only, on-line for updating, batch for reporting purposes, etc.)
  — Frequency and intensity of use (used in daily update processing, used to produce monthly reports, used ten times per day for ad hoc management queries, etc.)
  — Currency of record access (Are the newest or the oldest record occurrences accessed most frequently?)
- Establish access request priorities. A suggested order of importance is:
  — High-volume on-line update transactions
  — High-volume on-line queries
  — Low-volume and ad hoc on-line queries and high-volume batch update transactions
  — High-volume report generation
  — Low-volume and ad hoc report generation
- Determine if the desired data can be accessed. If it cannot:
  — Review the access request to see if it is really needed
  — Review the path used to see if a different path can be constructed
  — Redesign the database to accommodate the request if the request is important.

DESIGN RECORDS

This step consists of the following tasks.

Group Data Elements into Records

All attributes associated with an entity on the E-R diagram are placed into the resulting Bachman diagram record. If a record is created from a relationship between entities, fields associated with the relationship are placed into the intersection record. In the Employee/ Skill example, the date a specific skill was acquired would be placed into the Employee/ Skill intersection record.

Assign a Unique Name and ID to Each Record Type

A record name should be a short, unique, descriptive word, abbreviated if appropriate. An intersection record may be named by combining the names of the records it links and separating them by a slash (e.g., Employee and Project records are linked by the Emp/ Proj record). Avoid the use of special characters and numbers. A record ID can be any meaningful alphanumeric code.

Select Access Methods and Keys

Database records can be accessed randomly through the use of a key. Or they can be accessed sequentially. This is usually accomplished by first getting to the owner record randomly and then reading each member sequentially until the desired record is found. Finally, an index can be used. An index is a table or file used to determine the location of a record with a specific value. Combinations of these techniques are also used.

The selection of access methods depends on:

- The presence of a unique "natural" identifier, such as an invoice number for orders, or a student ID for students.
- The need to access a record directly. Many records, such as Job Start Date, are rarely used without first referring to the owner record—in this case, the Employee record.
- The number of similar records that must be read during a specific query or update operation. Sequentially accessed records are often clustered together in physical proximity to their owners. Hence, more records can be picked up faster in one read operation than if each record had to be accessed randomly.
- The need to access records by nonunique, nonkey attributes such as Order Date. An index that helps us locate all the records with the desired values may thus be very useful.

For a more complete description of access methods, see the chapters covering specific data models.

Decide on Duplicate Records

Many DBMS's provide the option of accepting or not accepting duplicates. If duplicate records are accepted, they can be inserted either before or after the original record.

The determination of how to treat duplicates depends on their validity from a business perspective. Obviously, we cannot have two customers with the same customer identifier. On the other hand, we may wish to tolerate duplicate part numbers. This can be a reasonable way to carry temporarily both a new and an old version of a part after an engineering, price or other change has occurred.

Assign Each Record to an Area

An area is a portion of the disk reserved for the storage of specific record types. A database is often divided into multiple areas for greater storage efficiency and performance. The selection of areas is based on the anticipated number of occurrences of various record types and the degree to which related records are usually accessed together.

Place Record Definitions in Data Dictionary

All entity, attribute and record definitions that we have developed should go into the data dictionary. If our dictionary is "active" we need this data in order to compile the schemas and subschemas required for system operation. If the dictionary is "passive," the information is still useful for documentation.

DEFINE SETS

Set definition consists of deciding how the relationships between records in each set are to be handled and how sets are to be traversed. The physical positioning of records in each set is also decided. Here are the major set definition tasks.

Assign a Meaningful Name to Each Set

Potential sets were identified earlier in the design process when the E-R diagram was translated into a Bachman diagram. They must now be named. A suggested approach is to use owner and member names separated by a dash (e.g., Employee-Proj/Emp and Dept-Employee).

Define Pointers and Other Navigation Mechanisms

Pointers are fields in a record that contain addresses of related records. They are maintained automatically by the DBMS and are "transparent" to the application. Pointers are described in detail in the chapters on network and hierarchical models. Here are the pointers generally available in network and hierarchical databases:

- A pointer which contains the address of the owner record occurrence
- A pointer which contains the address of the next occurrence of the same record type
- A pointer which contains the address of the first member record occurrence for this record

A selection of pointers that accurately represents the most commonly needed paths can have a significant impact on system performance.

Select Record Insertion Technique

Many DBMS's allow a choice of where new records are to appear in the chain: at the beginning, the end, or in a specified sort sequence. The latter is usually very expensive in terms of machine resources and system performance (imagine rearranging the pointers of hundreds or even thousands of records each time a new record is added!).

The choice of insertion techniques depends on the frequency of record retrieval. If the newest record is usually in the highest demand, it may be appropriate to place it in the front of the chain. If, on the other hand, the oldest record is in high demand, the best alternative may be to place each new record at the end of the chain.

Select Membership Options

Some DBMS's maintain the integrity of set relationships by controlling the addition and deletion of records based on the presence (or absence) of related records. This is called *referential integrity*.

For example, an invoice record should not be added to the database without also adding a customer record or making sure one already exists. Conversely, we may wish to prevent the deletion of a customer record until all invoices for that customer have been removed.

Although we can program referential integrity into our application, it is usually safer—and more efficient—to let the DBMS software do it for us.

The major consideration in selecting membership options is, of course, the degree of automatic (i.e., DBMS) control vs. program control that is desired. If we need to enforce referential integrity on a selective rather than constant basis, we must do it ourselves. For example:

- In the Personnel database, we may have a Union/Employee set which must reflect the fact that not all employees belong to a union. Therefore, some member records (i.e., employees) will not have an owner record (i.e., a union) to which they are attached.
- In a customer order database, we may wish to enable the processing of invoices for a major new customer before that customer has been officially cleared for credit and, therefore, placed on the file. The update program must be smart enough to find the Order record and connect it to the right customer when the customer record is finally added.

TEST AND IMPLEMENT THE DATABASE

The last step in the creation of a database brings to life the concepts and ideas developed during the design phase. We will test the validity of our design through prototyping. We hope to end up with a database that meets our functional and performance requirements. Conversion programs (if any) will then be written and production data loaded. Here are the tasks that must be performed.

Compile Database Definitions (Schemas and Subschemas)

A schema is the definition of the database given to the DBMS for compilation. A subschema is the "view" an individual program has of the database. It usually represents only that slice of the data structure needed by the program to do its job.

The compilation process checks for contradictory or invalid options and syntactical and definitional errors. It provides the DBMS with information on how to access, store and control data for this database.

Initialize the Database and Load With Sample Data

The disk space that will be used by the database is allocated by an operating system utility and initialized by DBMS software. This results in the creation of directories and other control information on the disk in anticipation of data loading.

Sample data is then prepared. This can be done by creating make-believe information via a line editor or other file creation utility. It can also be accomplished by stripping ''live'' data from an existing file and reformatting it to suit the database design. A DBMS utility or a custom program can be used to reformat and load the data. If complex rearrangements such as combining or splitting existing records must be performed, conversion programs may be necessary.

It is important to understand that the data initially loaded into the database is used for testing purposes only. Therefore, care must be taken to create a variety of conditions that will enable you to ''exercise'' the database design. Be sure your data meets the following criteria:

- Provides several occurrences for each record type
- Represents every set and record definition (e.g., duplicates for record types that allow duplicates)
- Represents every relationship
- Is realistic and comprehensive

Test the Database

Database testing helps verify that the database meets business needs and appears to provide adequate performance.

Business needs are tested first. This is done by repeating the path analysis done earlier in the design process. This time, however, it is done against a real database rather than a conceptual model. The quickest way to do this is through the use of the native DBMS query language. It provides an accurate indicator of what to expect without the need for extensive programming. Thus, we can verify the functional soundness of our design regardless of which programming technique is ultimately selected.

An important part of testing is to verify user data requirements. Test results should be shared with users and functional changes given due consideration. Earlier misunderstandings and changes in business requirements may require modification of the original access specifications.

Several iterations of testing and refinement should result in a database that appears to meet functional requirements. At this point, volume testing can be performed. Volume testing should be done prior to system implementation if one or more of the following conditions exist:

- Large transaction or database volumes
- Critical timing requirements (e.g., a very small ''window'' of time during which it is possible to update a database that is utilized during business hours by cities that are widely scattered over the globe)
- Concurrent use by many people
- Complex access paths
- A single update process that encompasses many record types

Testing that approximates production volumes can indicate potentially serious bottlenecks that are best resolved before system installation. Even a relatively small database can give us important performance clues: five-second access time in a thousand-record test database does not bode well for the one-hundred-thousand-record production version!

Refine the Database

The database is redefined, reinitialized, reloaded and retested in response to test results. Test data becomes progressively more complex and voluminous. The refinement process may include major redesign as well as minor tuning. It continues until the database accurately reflects user needs and performs according to expectations—at least with the test data that is available.

Load Production Data

This step appears deceptively simple but may, in fact, be very complex and time consuming.

If existing data is to be loaded, some form of data cleaning may be needed to ensure that our application begins life with accurate, relevant information. This may require considerable clerical effort as well as sophisticated programming.

We may also need to perform complex data conversions in order to facilitate the loading process. For example, customer records from our old system may need to be split into multiple components corresponding to our database record and set definitions. Other records may need to be dissected and their data elements redefined and/or recombined.

If we are creating a database from nonmachine-readable sources such as paper records, a substantial data entry process may be required. This, as well as any conversion and data cleaning programs, should be started early on—despite the fact that the load step is the last task on our agenda.

After the database is loaded, we may begin to execute our application.

DATABASE DESIGN DELIVERABLES CHECKLIST

Database Overview Narrative

- Purpose, scope and applications for which it is used
- Type of data
- Record volumes
- Approximation of growth
- Update volatility

E-R Diagram With Supporting Narratives

- Entity name/identifier
- Entity description
- Relationship type
- Relationship description

Attribute Definitions

- External name (i.e., English, free-form name)
- Internal name (e.g., Cobol acronym)
- Type (e.g, numeric)
- Description
- Length
- Number of decimal places
- Group or elementary item
- Denominating factor (dollars, pounds, etc.)
- Possible values
- Validation rules
- Synonyms (''also known as'')

Bachman Diagram With Supporting Narratives

- Record name/identifier
- Record description
- Relationship type
- Absolute and relative volumes (optional)

Path Analysis (for Each Function)

- Purpose of access
- Description
- Records to be accessed
- Keys needed
- Type of access (on-line, batch, query only, update only)
- Frequency and intensity of use
- Currency of records accessed (e.g., the newest records, oldest records, etc.)
- Priority

Record and Set Definitions (Schemas and Subschemas)

- Data elements in each record
- Record names, IDs, etc., from Bachman
- Set names and definitions
- Area identification
- Access methods
- Keys
- Treatment of duplicates
- Membership options
- Pointers
- Insertion techniques

Test Plan and Test Data, Covering:

- Path testing
- Volume testing
- Data loads and unloads

Other

- Free space definitions
- Overflow definitions
- Area definitions
- Other physical arrangements per specific DBMS

SAMPLE ENTITY-RELATION (E-R) AND BACHMAN DIAGRAMS

Figure 10.14   Sample Entity-Relationship Diagram for a Personnel Database

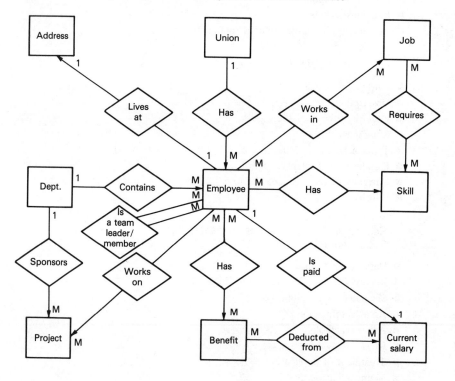

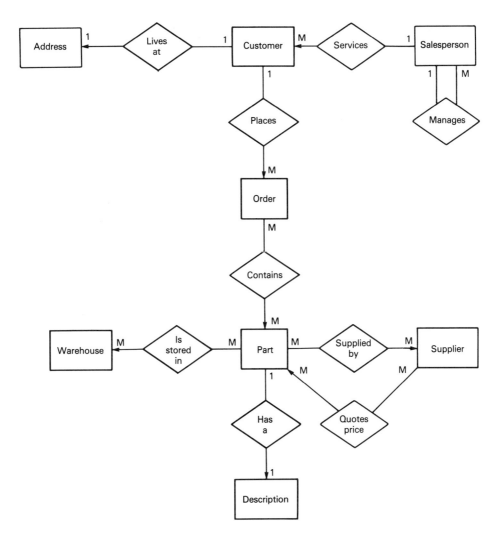

Figure 10.15 Sample Entity-Relationship Diagram for a Customer Order Database

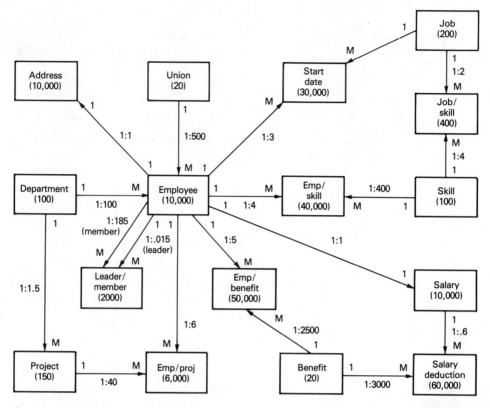

Figure 10.16 Sample Bachman Diagram for a Personnel Database

Figure 10.17 Sample Bachman Diagram for a Customer Order Database

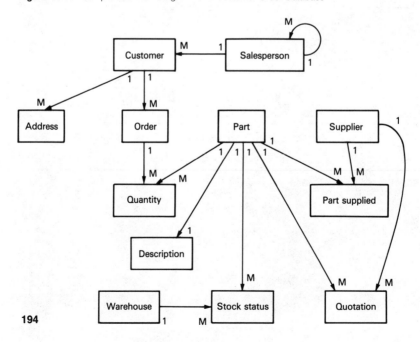

DISCUSSION QUESTIONS

What is an entity?

Describe the first three steps of database development.

How are one-to-many and many-to-many relationships translated from an E-R diagram into a Bachman diagram?

What is an iterative relationship and why is it used?

Identify the two types of volumes that must be examined when designing a database. Explain the importance of each type.

What is path analysis? Why is it important?

Describe three activities that are part of set definition.

11

CURRENT TRENDS AND NEW DIRECTIONS

INTRODUCTION

Four trends are having or are beginning to have a major impact on the DBMS world. They are:

- Microcomputer-based DBMS
- Distributed databases
- Relational DBMS
- Database machines

Following is a description of how developments in these areas are affecting traditional flat file environments, as well as DBMS installations.

DBMSs FOR PERSONAL COMPUTERS (PC)

Fifteen years ago, anybody predicting the development of complex DBMS products for computers no bigger than a television set would have been considered a lunatic. Yet, today, the microcomputer, or PC, DBMS is a reality. A number of very good products are available; some were designed specifically for personal computers and others are microcomputer versions of mainframe products.

What are these products? Do they meet our definition of a ''real'' DBMS? How do they compare to the complex mainframe products described in this book? Will IMS, IDMS, etc., become obsolete?

First, a comment on terminology. The first deviation from large scale mainframe technology was the minicomputer. When minis first gained a foothold in the late 1960's and early 1970's, they were distinguished from mainframe computers by their relatively low price, small physical size, limited capacity, and (sometimes) a greater degree of user-friendliness. As technology developed, minis became more and more powerful.

But mainframes also became more powerful and offered better-than-ever price/performance ratios. Today's minicomputer is as powerful as yesterday's mainframe—and tomorrow's mini will be as powerful as today's mainframe.

Something similar is happening with personal computers. Although they started life as single-user, low-capacity machines, we now have PCs that can accommodate multiple users and a wider variety of peripheral devices. It is, therefore, difficult to provide a definition of what micro-based DBMS products can—and cannot—do at a given time. This is a field in which technology changes very rapidly.

Differences between Mainframe and Micro-Based DBMSs

At the present time, micro-DBMS products differ from their mainframe and mini cousins in the following respects:

- They are designed *primarily* for single-user operation. Although some PC-based DBMS products allow more than one person at a time on an application, the big systems with dozens, hundreds or even thousands of users accessing the same database at the same time must use a mainframe product. Some lockout and other simultaneous access features are available on micro DBMSs. However, they are not as extensive, complete or sophisticated as those for products that are specifically designed to accommodate a large number of interactive users. Even when run with a multi-user operating system such as Unix, the DBMS software is inadequate.

- They are designed for smaller businesses. It is interesting to note that virtually all examples used in dBASE, R:base 5000 and other micro-DBMS manuals center around small stores: a liquor store, a video rental shop, an art gallery, etc. One doesn't find examples dealing with insurance policyholders or bank credit card customers.

- Concomitant with their small business orientation, the physical storage, access and control techniques used by micro-based products presuppose relatively small files and transaction volumes. For example, the use of multiple keys in some products can result in the actual duplication of the entire database in several different key sequences. This is an unsatisfactory technique for large databases. Even if adequate storage is attached to a personal computer to accommodate files of one hundred thousand or a million or more records, the system's performance would be untenable given present microcomputer hardware/software capabilities.

- In theory, at least, Micro-DBMSs are designed to be installed, programmed and operated directly by end-users. Therefore, micro-DBMS vendors shy away from offering options that would increase performance at the cost of making the products more difficult to use. Mainframe DBMS vendors have never been sqeamish about this. Their products are frankly intended for computer professionals.

- Micro-DBMS products are much easier to use than their mainframe cousins. Although one is tempted to dismiss this as the natural result of a simpler, more limited product, the fact is that mainframe software vendors could learn a lot about user friendliness from their peers in the micro business. The developers of software for personal computers have done a marvelous job of making their products easy to understand and use.

In summary, the major PC database products provide many of the same functions and capabilities as their mainframe counterparts, except on a smaller scale and for fewer interactive users. For the right application, a micro-DBMS provides a lot of power for very little investment.

Descriptions of Two Popular Models

dBASE III Plus by Ashton-Tate and *R:base 5000* by Microrim are the current versions of the most widely used micro DBMSs. Their lineage is illustrated in Figure 11.1. Notice that several other early products, mentioned as historical curiosities, died an untimely

Figure 11.1 History of Micro-based DBMS

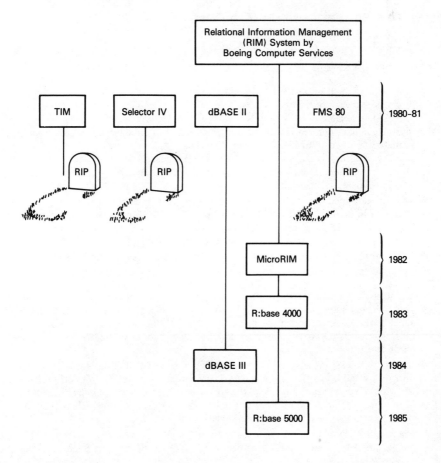

death—partly, one suspects, because their authors failed to foresee the importance of compatibility with the IBM PC.

As the chart shows, dBASE was originally conceived as a microcomputer DBMS. R:base, on the other hand, is a micro version of Relational Information Management (RIM), a DBMS developed by Boeing for the space program. Both products typify the best of the current breed. They are serious, top-of-the line products—not $99 specials that are database systems in name only. Both products follow the relational data model, as do most other micro-DBMSs.

Following is an analysis of how dBASE and R:base (as we will call them for short) meet the criteria for a DBMS.

Data Independence   This is the degree to which the logical aspects of data are isolated from their physical characteristics. Both products successfully meet this criteria.

dBASE enables changes to field definitions, as well as the additions and deletions of fields, through the use of the MODIFY command. The system catalog brings up a screen containing the current definition of all the fields in the desired table and allows the appropriate changes to be made.

Execution of the MODIFY command automatically causes a backup file of the entire database to be made and the backup data to then be loaded back into the new table. Although this is obviously not an effective procedure for very large databases, it isolates the user from the physical aspects of restructuring. Modifications do not affect queries, reports and procedures unless they use the changed data.

R:base utilizes a series of commands to perform the same type of data restructuring.

Complex Data Relationships   As with other relational systems, complex data relationships are accommodated implicitly through the use of tables (called files in dBASE). Both products can pull data together from multiple files or tables. The limit is ten files in dBASE and forty tables in R:base. The theoretical maximum for the number of fields, tables, etc., is adequate in both systems for most applications. In fact, adequate performance almost always ceases before theoretical limits are reached.

Control of Redundancy   Control of redundancy is not the strong suit of *any* relational system, micro or otherwise. dBASE and R:base are probably no worse than mainframe relational products in this regard.

Application Generality   Both dBASE and R:base are designed to accommodate a wide variety of applications.

Ease of Use   Here is where micro-based products really shine. They are far easier to learn and use than any mainframe DBMS. Extensive system development and support tools are available for both products, including a high level report writer, query language, and screen formatter.

In addition, R:base provides a facility for writing macros, which are chunks of code used to perform commonly used functions. A procedural language for programmers is also available. Though not as sophisticated as Cobol, PL1, and other traditional languages, it can be used for fairly complex applications.

Automatic procedures can be built with both systems, but they are compilable in R:base. This can result in a performance edge. Both systems have all the components of their mainframe counterparts, except a host language interface.

Uses of Micro-Based DBMS

Micro-based products can be used in the following environments:

- *In the home.* You have to be a hobbyist to make this use worthwhile. Unlike spreadsheets and personal finance and accounting packages, DBMS applications must be built by the user. This involves use of the DBMS query language, report writer, native programming language (if any) and so on. The effort is not usually justified except as a form of amusement.
- *For a small business.* This can be a very good use for a micro-DBMS. However, one question should be considered first: does the volume and scope of the business justify the effort required to build the system and then to keep the files properly updated? The functional needs of a small business may be better satisfied by a comprehensive spreadsheet, a general accounting system and a good word processor.
- *In a corporation.* This is the use in which we are most interested. It supports small stand-alone applications or it works as part of a larger mainframe system. These two uses are described below.

Stand-alone Applications   In any large company, there are many potential applications that are too small, too parochial or too questionable in terms of costs/benefits to be handled by the central EDP staff. The result is that many tasks that need to be accomplished are continually put off in favor of bigger, more important applications.

Here are a few examples of systems a micro can accommodate quite nicely on a stand-alone basis.

- A documentation and control system for travel and expenses
- A project control tracking and management system for engineers
- A physical examination tickler system for employees
- A menu archive for a food service operation
- A personnel skills inventory system for the personnel department

These are just a few examples of the useful applications that can be developed using a micro-DBMS outside the aegis of a large corporate computing center. The beauty of products such as R:base and dBASE is that an enterprising member of the user department can put together a very useful system *without the help, blessing, or encouragement of the computer department.*

Although this may sometimes raise questions about control and integration (for instance, Is it wise to have twenty different expense tracking systems?), the immediate benefits to individual departments are clear.

The organizational significance of stand-alone micro-based DBMS applications—and this applies to personal computers in general—is the alteration in the relationship between the end-users and the official data processors: end-users become more independent; data processors lose some control over computer applications—specifically the manner in which data is (or is not) integrated; users begin to appreciate the complexity and cost of developing even ''simple'' applications; data processing people learn that they are not quite as indispensible as they may have thought.

Networks of Micro-DBMS Systems   Perhaps the most important corporate use of PC DBMS applications is in a network environment. Figure 11.2 illustrates how personal computers, connected to each other and to a host computer, can provide the best of both worlds. They can supply independent processing that does not rely upon central operations. In addition, they can provide access to subsets of corporate data not normally available to a single user without dependence on the main computer.

A network has several interesting features and components:

■ Each PC is called a *workstation* and represents one *node* on the network. It functions as an independent, stand-alone computer equipped with disk drives, a printer, a modem and other *local* devices as appropriate.
■ A *file server* appears to the user as disk storage that all of the workstations on the network can access. It contains databases of common interest and it controls access to them.

Figure 11.2   A Network of Personal Computers

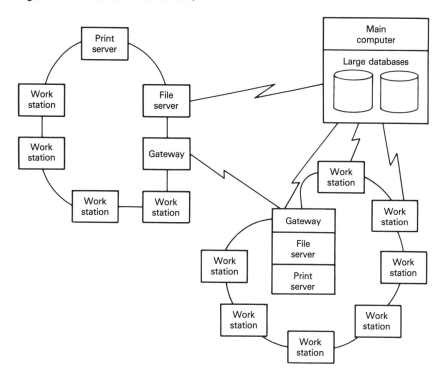

- A *print server* is a shared printer.
- A *gateway* is a component that links this network to other, similarly configured networks.

File servers, print servers and the gateway may be separate computers, as pictured in the upper left hand portion of Figure 11.2 or may be housed in a single computer dedicated to all three tasks, as in the lower right hand portion of the same figure.

The network arrangement allows multiple PCs to share small-to-medium-sized databases and other files without the need constantly to make duplicates. It also saves hardware costs by allowing multiple workstations to share a fast, expensive printer.

Portions of a large database stored on the main computer can be downloaded either to the file server or to individual PCs on the net. This allows access to files that cannot fit on a PC or, more importantly, files that must be centrally controlled.

In order to take advantage of the network concept, the micro-DBMS must be able to operate under a multiuser operating system such as Unix. In addition, some sort of record or file-level lockout procedure must be present—at least if any file updating is to be done.

These lockout provisions must, at minimum, prevent two or more users from updating the same record at the same time. More sophisticated procedures may also be needed to provide control over the update of related records (e.g., User A deleting a customer record while User B adds a new order for that customer).

Here is an example of how a network of PCs might operate in the engineering department of a large company.

- Each PC is used on a stand-alone basis for spreadsheets, mathematical modelling and word processing (memos, reports, etc.). These applications are strictly "personal," in that they help individual engineers to perform their job *without impacting anyone else's data*.
- Each engineer also documents and uses project information on a database that is stored in the file server. Projects are a group activity. Individuals are often assigned to multiple projects and project leadership is temporary—that is, an engineer can be a project leader on one project and a team member on another. Therefore, data must be shared between members of the department, necessitating use of the file server.
- The same project control system is used by Quality Assurance (QA). Since both engineers and QA analysts occasionally work on the same projects, sharing of project data takes place via the gateway facility. When needed, QA can record project hours and other information for projects sponsored by Engineering, and engineers can feed data to QA projects.
- Our hypothetical company manufactures extremely complex industrial equipment. The bill-of-materials database, which contains extensive price, cost and engineering data, is too large, too complex and is used simultaneously by too many people to be an appropriate PC application. The information on this database is very important and is scrupulously maintained and controlled by a central staff of trained update clerks.

  Therefore, information about a component must either be "imported" by copying a portion of the main database to a PC, or the PC must be able to work with the mainframe data interactively. In either case, our PCs, each of which is equipped with a modem, can access this mainframe data. IBM, Unisys and other vendors offer microcomputers that can perform on a stand-alone basis or can function as "dumb" terminals that are almost entirely dependent on the main computer for their capabilities.

The technology for linking together personal computers, mainframes, minicomputers, and various input/output devices is rapidly improving. However, this is useless unless data can be deployed across this wide spectrum of devices with reasonable efficiency and integrity. This is the topic of the next section.

DISTRIBUTED DATABASES

Definition

A distributed database is one that is spread across a network of computers at different geographic sites. Each site is essentially autonomous and performs local as well as global applications (i.e., applications of common interest).

Autonomy means that little control is exercised by a central authority. Thus, each site may have its own data administrator, programmers, operations staff, etc. The relationship between sites is a partnership in which individual sites cooperate with each other but are not subject to heavy-handed central control.

A distributed system assumes that there are multiple computers at different locations. A single database spread over more than one CPU at the same site is not really a distributed database. To qualify, computers must be tied together with a communications network such as the one illustrated in Figure 11.3.

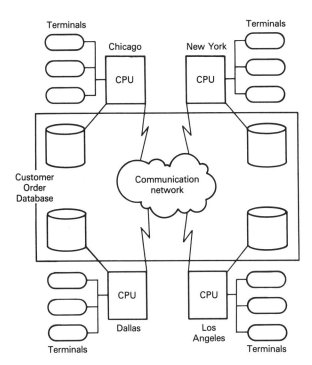

Figure 11.3 A Distributed Database System

We also assume that the same DBMS product is running at each site. Eventually, a technology may be developed that enables, say, IDMS, IMS, and DB2 databases to harmonize across a distributed network. For now, however, we cannot reasonably expect a shared system to support multiple DBMS products.

Although distributed databases vary in their physical implementation, they attempt to meet the following ideal criteria:

- *Location transparency.* Users behave as if the entire database resides at one location. They do not need to know the specific site at which any given piece of data is stored. How and where data is distributed is thus transparent to end-users.
- *Data fragmentation.* A logically related set of data (e.g., a table, a record, a segment) can be divided up for physical storage purposes. Thus, data for all Chicago customers can be stored in Chicago, data for all Los Angeles customers can be stored in Los Angeles, etc. Alternately, if we wish, we can store billing and payment information in Dallas and buying history in New York. There are two types of data fragmentation:
  - — *Horizontal fragmentation* takes place when the table or file is split in such a way that each record remains whole but specific attributes, such as customer location, dictate where the record will be stored (Chicago, Los Angeles, etc.).
  - — *Vertical fragmentation* takes place when certain attributes (e.g., account balances) are stored in one location while others (e.g., buying history) are stored in another. Each record is thus split between locations.
- *Fragmentation transparency.* This is the flip side of data fragmentation. It is the ability to pull together logically related pieces of data, no matter where they are stored. Again, the end-user is unaware of the physical source of the information.
- *Data replication.* This is the ability to support multiple copies of the same data. For example, records for national customers can be stored at all sites while data for local customers are stored at their site of origin.
- *Replication transparency.* This enables the system to select the copy of the data asked for by the user, thus providing the most efficient link. For example, national accounts accessed by Chicago should be pulled from the Chicago database—not from the New York database. The selection is done by the system and not by the user.

As of mid-1986, no commercially available distributed DBMS met all of the above criteria.

Advantages

Why are distributed systems important? What advantages do they have over a single, centrally controlled database? When should they be used?

Organizational Factors Many organizations are decentralized and/or geographically dispersed. A distributed DBMS fits more naturally into the structure of such organizations. This is probably the most important justification for a distributed system.

Incremental Growth If a company expands by adding new organizational units that are functionally or geographically different from existing units, a distributed approach provides the most promising growth path. A centralized system cannot accommodate this type of expansion as easily.

Reduced Communications Overhead Accessing local data is cheaper and more efficient than accessing a database one thousand miles away. This, of course, assumes a preponderance of data that is of local, rather than national, interest. If all or most data is national, extensive replication would probably be necessary.

CPU Performance As with any multiprocessor system, a distributed approach enables parallel processing. This reduces bottlenecks and minimizes contention between common system services (see Figure 11.4).

Incidentally, the traditional economies-of-scale argument favoring a giant CPU, as against multiple, smaller CPUs, is largely obsolete. Today's hardware prices often turn that argument around: it may actually be cheaper to provide a series of dedicated machines than to run a very large mainframe. (Of course, staffing and other nonhardware factors must also be taken into account.)

Reliability

Although *total* system reliability is no better in a distributed environment—it may, in fact be worse due to more complex interface requirements—the reliability of *individual* nodes is higher. Suppose, for example, that Chicago's CPU goes down. Los Angeles, Dallas and New York can still process. In a centralized system, all four sites would be knocked out.

The same advantage may hold true for system degradation. If Chicago's transaction volume becomes exceptionally heavy, only that location will suffer performance problems. If, however, the database is centralized, the entire operation is penalized.

Disadvantages

Although distributed databases have some powerful advantages, they also have serious drawbacks.

Slow Transmission Speeds If a lot of data must go back and forth between the nodes of the system, processing will be agonizingly slow. Long-haul line transmission speed, 50K–100K bits per second at most, is *always* slower than local data transfer (e.g., disk transfer is one to two *million* bytes per second). Replication of data for use at local sites will reduce this problem.

Update Propogation The control problems associated with keeping replicated data synchronized can be tremendous: timing the transmission of updated files to remote sites; local malfunctions that prevent a site from being able to use latest data; failure to coordinate updates that are not performed centrally; all of these issues can reduce the value of a distributed DBMS.

Concurrency Update time can be considerably higher in a distributed system. Lockout procedures—the normal way of enforcing update integrity in both distributed and nondistributed systems—require the transmission of messages in distributed systems but

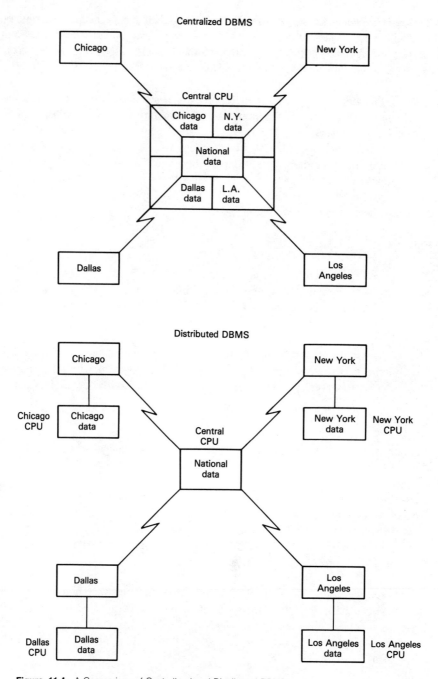

Figure 11.4 A Comparison of Centralized and Distributed DBMS

are done at CPU speed in nondistributed systems. Thus, requests to test, set, and release locks can easily take twenty or thirty times longer in a distributed environment.

Recovery   Database systems use a *commit* concept to ensure that a *logical unit of work*—the addition of a new customer with its biographic, address, credit and other records, for example—is properly applied to the database.

The function of the commit is to trigger the physical updating of the database after it is determined that the desired action should take place (e.g., no duplicate customer record exists). If a problem occurs, a rollback is issued. This aborts the update and restores the database to the way it was before the update.

As with concurrency, the transmission of commit/rollback messages between sites takes much longer than processing on one machine.

Catalog management   In a distributed system, the catalog or data dictionary must contain information about the present location and "birth site" of each piece of data. This is in addition to the usual database information carried on a catalog for a nondistributed system. Furthermore, catalog information must be accessible by multiple sites. How, then, to distribute this data?

The catalog can be *centralized*—that is, stored exactly once, at the central site, and accessed as-needed by each site. This reduces autonomy but is perhaps the least complicated and most manageable alternative.

The catalog can be *fully replicated*—that is, stored in its entirety at each site. This provides maximum autonomy but presents formidable control problems.

The catalog can be *partitioned*, each site having only data that relates to it. This alternative is fine as long as the need to look at other people's data is infrequent. Otherwise, a time-consuming search of each site on the node may need to be made before we find the right data.

Finally, we can have a combination of all of the above. This may be a good compromise between the extremes of autonomy and centralization.

A number of distributed DBMS products are currently available or will be available in the near future. Some of these DBMSs are based on current nondistributed models; others are brand new. Figure 11.5 shows some of the distributed products that are available or in prototype.

Following are brief descriptions of three distributed DBMS products. Two are prototypes and the third—ENCOMPASS—is commercially available. We will begin with a description of ENCOMPASS.

ENCOMPASS

This is an interesting product because it was developed by Tandem, Inc., to run on its multi-CPU NonStop computer system. ENCOMPASS therefore has the advantage of being part of an architecture congenial to distributed processing. Unlike other DBMSs, which must accommodate themselves to environments originally designed for single-CPU processing, Tandem's ENCOMPASS runs on hardware, a communications network, and an operating system that is, in a way, already distributed.

Product	Based on	Type	Vendor
Distributed INGRES	INGRES	R	University of California
R*	DB2	R	IBM
IDMS-DDS	IDMS	N	Cullinet
D-NET	DATAcom/DB	IL	ADR
VDN	—	N/R	Nixdorf Computer Co.
IDMS-DDB50	IDMS	N	ICL
UDS-D	UDS	N	Siemens, A.G.
NET-WORK	ADABAS	IL	Software, A.G.
ENCOMPASS	—	R	Tandem Computer
SDD-1	—	R	CCA

Key: R = Relational
         N = Network (CODASYL)
         IL = Inverted list

Figure 11.5 A Survey of Distributed DBMS Products

A Tandem computer consists of two-to-sixteen independent CPUs sharing disk drives and other peripherals. Each CPU has independent memory, which distinguishes NonStop from "multiprocessor" systems such as those available from IBM. The CPU and other components are thus replicated, providing a very high degree of reliability that gives Tandem computers their main sales appeal.

The CPUs in a Tandem communicate via messages—the same principle that underlies communication between computers in a distributed network. The message system makes communication between CPUs transparent to the user. Location transparency is, in effect, a built-in part of the architecture.

Although a NonStop system does not, as it stands, meet our definition of a distributed system—the Tandem CPUs are all in one box, in one site—the guiding principles are the same. A truly distributed system can be built on the foundation provided by the hardware and its operating system, GUARDIAN.

Here are the salient features of ENCOMPASS:

- Location transparency is, of course, supported. Users are not asked to know the source of information.
- Horizontal fragmentation is supported. We can store all Chicago data at one site and all New York data at another—and get at either without explicitly knowing the storage site.
- Vertical fragmentation is not supported. Hence, we cannot store, say, customer addresses in Chicago and buying history in Los Angeles *if address and buying history are part of the same record.*
- Data replication is also not supported. Each site containing replicated data must be explicitly (and redundantly) updated by the user. Replication is not performed automatically.
- Major system components are illustrated in Figure 11.6. They are:
  - *The requester.* This component receives information from the terminals under its jurisdiction, performs rudimentary data validation (e.g., customer number is numeric), calls the servers needed to complete the transaction, and displays the results on the terminal.
  - *The server.* This component performs database access and returns the required data to the requester. The relationship between servers and requesters is dynamic: Requester 1 may go to Server 1 for one query and go to Server 2 for another one.

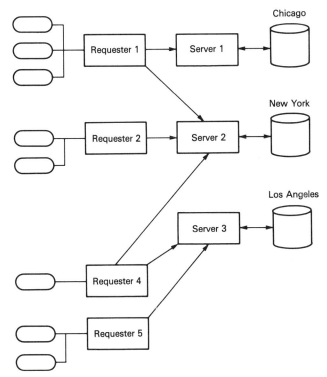

Figure 11.6 Components of ENCOMPASS

ENCOMPASS is commercially available. Following are descriptions of two prototype systems.

R∗

This is IBM's major foray into the world of distributed DBMS. R∗ (pronounced ''R star'') was derived from ''System R'' (the ''R'' stands for ''Relational''), IBM's relational prototype. R∗ shares its paternity with, and provides most of the functionality for, its sister products, DB2 and SQL/DS, but in a distributed environment. R∗ is, of course, relational.

Figure 11.7 illustrates the three major components of R∗: a local DBMS, a data communications component, and a transaction manager—all of which operate under IBM's Customer Information Control System (CICS).

The local DBMS consists of a storage system, which is concerned with the storage and retrieval of data; and the language processor, which translates SQL statements into terms the storage system can understand. The job of the data communications component is to communicate with other sites through the Inter System Communications (ISC) facility (see Figure 11.8). The transaction manager coordinates and controls all the activity against the database.

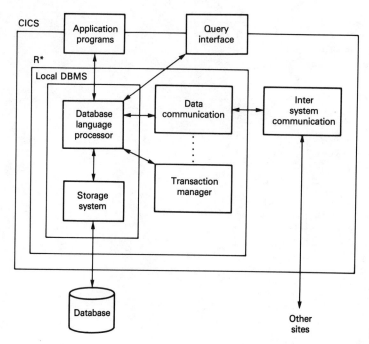

Figure 11.7 Components of R*

R* does not currently support fragmentation, replication or the transparency aspects of same. However, it does support location transparency.

SDD-1 (System for Distributed Databases-1)

SDD-1 was developed by Computer Corporation of America (CCA) in the late 1970's and is likely to remain a prototype forever.* Like R*, it is relational. It was designed for a network of Digital Equipment Corporation (DEC) computers hooked together by an ARPANET communications network.

The architecture of SDD-1 consists of the three components illustrated in Figure 11.9: the Data Module (DM), the Transaction Module (TM) and the Reliable Network (RelNet).

The function of the DM is to manage data. It reads, manipulates and writes data from and to the local database.

The TM plans and controls the execution of transactions; each command is considered a separate transaction. Query translation and execution, as well as access planning and concurrency control, are the TM's main jobs.

*An entirely different implementation of SDD-1—but containing most of its functionality—is scheduled for release during 1988. This system, transportable between machines of various vendors, is called ADAPLEX, for the language in which it is written (ADA). ADAPLEX will have an SQL front-end, making it conform to the de facto standard for relational data languages that followed in the wake of IBM's SQL.

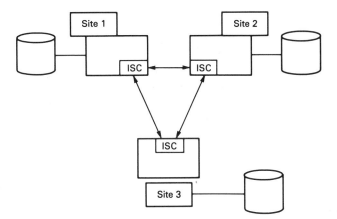

Figure 11.8 R∗ Site Interconnection

RelNet delivers messages from site to site and coordinates intersite activities. Copies of RelNet, as well as the other two components, reside at each site.

Distributcd DBMS products will become more available and more usable in the future than they are today. However, the daunting challenges of inadequate performance and data control must be alleviated before this happens.

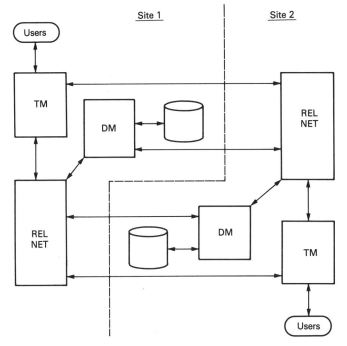

Figure 11.9 Relationship Between SDD-1 Components

RELATIONAL DBMS

Database technology follows the same trends as other software. Cheap, powerful computers have made it possible to develop products that trade complexity and high overhead for increased usability. The "fourth generation" phenomenon is simply the automation of functions that could not previously be automated due to lack of horsepower.

In the DBMS corner of the 4GL world, this manifests itself in relational database technology—an internally complex but externally straightforward data model. The problems associated with relational databases (performance, data integrity, etc.), are solvable given time, experience and—most importantly—continued hardware price/performance improvements.

Where does this leave the older DBMS's? First, there is a tremendous investment in applications based on IMS, IDMS, TOTAL and other nonrelational models. This investment is not likely to be sacrificed as long as these "traditional" products continue to improve and provide more and more features previously associated only with relational technology.

Established vendors such as IBM and Cullinet are meeting the challenge not only by offering new relational products, but by enhancing older products with "relational-like" capabilities. Nonrelational databases can be made to appear relational by applying some clever, but resource-expensive, technical wizardry. Cullinet's IDMS/R, for example, allows use of IDMS databases in either a network or relational mode, depending on the needs of the application.

Second, most applications are still in the business of performing repetitive processes and producing tangible products such as invoices. Unless this primary job is done quickly and accurately, the use of information in an end user environment is fruitless. The "bread-and-butter" jobs will thus continue to be run on the older, more batch-oriented systems.

Based on current experience, relational concepts are easier to master by both end-users and computer analysts than are hierarchical and network concepts. Tuning, and the efficient physical layout of databases, will, of course, continue to remain an esoteric part of the technology. Flexibility of use and the relative ease of application design definitely favors the relational model as the DBMS of the future.

It is interesting to note that some of the newer DBMS technologies, such as distributed DBMS and Database Machines (covered in the next section), are predominantly based on the relational model. In both cases, the reason is the lack of physical linkages needed in other models to connect related records. Thus, tables can more easily be fragmented and distributed over geographically dispersed machines.

For a more detailed analysis of relational technology, see Chapter 7, The Relational Model.

DATABASE MACHINES

A database machine, or backend processor—there is no definitive term—is a special purpose hardware component dedicated to performing data manipulation normally done by DBMS software (see Figure 11.10).

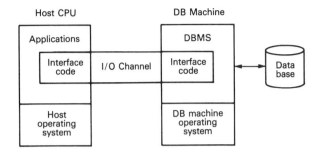

Figure 11.10   Typical Database Machine Configuration

The concept is partly analogous to the programmable functions modern communications terminals and control units perform—functions that, in earlier days, could only be done through interaction with the host computer. Computer peripherals are now "smart" rather than "dumb."

A database machine lives between the disk drives that store application databases and the computer. In theory, if not always in practice, the search for data is done more efficiently by the specialized hardware and software in the database machine. The host computer also becomes more efficient because it is now freed to do other tasks.

Britton Lee's IDM 600 system is probably the best known backend DBMS. It consists of the database machine running a full-blown relational DBMS. The IDM 600 was designed for DEC VAX and PDP-11 machines.

Database machines have been commercially disappointing. This is probably due to some serious performance and other problems. However, much more progress can be expected in the next few years.

DISCUSSION QUESTIONS

What is the primary difference between a mainframe and micro-based DBMS?

Give an example of how a micro-DBMS can be used in a large organization as a stand-alone system. Explain how it can be used as part of a network of personal computers.

What is a file server? A print server? A gateway? What role do they play in a network of PCs?

What is location transparency?

Name and define the two kinds of data fragmentation capabilities that distributed DBMSs attempt to achieve.

List two advantages of distributed systems. List two disadvantages.

What is the function of a database machine?

12

A POSTSCRIPT: COMMON MISCONCEPTIONS ABOUT DATABASE MANAGEMENT SYSTEMS

A LOOK AT THE MYTHS

This chapter is devoted to a discussion of popular myths, misunderstandings and illusions about databases. They have been introduced in previous chapters but will be brought together here for a comparative discussion.

Like other major data processing innovations, DBMS's have been subject to hype, oversell and bloated expectations. The result, predictably, is a certain amount of cynicism on the part of people who have used them—and continued naïveté on the part of those who have not.

The truth is this: DBMS is a powerful, useful technology that is quickly becoming the prevailing approach to the organization and extraction of data. But it is not an easy technology to master and is not universally appropriate. Just as a small tractor with a lawnmower engine may be better suited than a large John Deere to farming in some parts of the world, flat files remain a more practical technology for many applications. Here are some common misconceptions.

Database Applications Are Always Faster.

Two factors mitigate against this. First, a DBMS adds extra layers of software to an already large operating system overhead. In addition, a DBMS is hostage to the need for generality—it must, by definition, support a wide variety of applications.

DBMS overhead is unavoidable. However, a skilled implementation, and appropriate use of DBMS features, can minimize it. The generality of the DBMS is also unavoidable. Tasks are performed by the software that are not always needed for a specific application. For example, some DBMS products automatically maintain extensive logging facilities that degrade performance. Although the majority of users may be better off with this feature, it may not be needed for a specific application.

The performance issue is not an argument against acquisition of a DBMS unless unusually large volumes of data are to be processed in a limited time period. As Chapter 2 points out, there are ample reasons for acquisition (improved data access, data independence, etc.). The point here is, simply, that performance should not be the *reason* for acquisition. People should not expect a DBMS to cure performance problems.

Database Systems Are User Friendly.

Not necessarily. Three factors determine user friendliness: the design of the application, technological limitations, and system performance.

Quality application design is largely in the hands of the designer. All the sophisticated technology in the world cannot prevent clumsy screen layouts, unreadable reports, poor data validation programs, and difficult operating procedures. User friendliness is still determined to a large extent by the skills of the designer and his ability accurately to gauge user needs.

However, good technology can significantly increase the potential for good system design. Applications are more user friendly today than they were fifteen years ago, not because system developers are smarter, but because technology is better. Faster, cheaper machines and telecommunications products have spurred the development of software that can result in more user-friendly systems. *But it is still up to programmers and analysts to do their job right*!

Performance—that is, the speed with which a user can access the information needed—is also a significant part of user friendliness. A three-week wait to get a desperately needed report kills a system's effectiveness. DBMS technology, with its unique ability to bring data together, helps eliminate or reduce those delays. However, poor response time at a terminal does not always go away.

Database Applications Are Easy to Implement.

Applications that do not require complex logic or extensive data controls are, indeed, easy to implement under a DBMS. On the other hand, they are not particularly difficult to implement using conventional file systems. High-level query and report languages, available for almost every environment, can do the job.

It's the big, complex systems that cause so many problems. They may, in some cases, be implemented more quickly with the development tools, such as data dictionaries, that accompany DBMS products. But it is a gross exaggeration to think that they are "easy."

It is true that some complex applications are virtually impossible to develop without DBMS technology. From that standpoint, a DBMS may be "easier" than a conventional file system.

All Significant Corporate Data Can Be Maintained in One Large Database.

This was an arrogant assumption put forth by gurus who had little experience in day-to-day computer work and by DBMS vendors who had nothing to lose by exaggerating the virtues of their products. Two things are wrong with this theory—one is organizational, the other technical.

The organizational reason is that people and systems work best when directed toward limited, specific goals. A "corporate database" is, by definition, all things to all people. Everyone is responsible for providing it with accurate information, but no one is really accountable. To be really effective, data must be tied to a specific organizational unit and must be used for specific purposes *that are important to that unit.*

The technical reason is our present inability to make a single, large database provide satisfactory across-the-board performance. We need databases that are designed for specific applications. Although we are slowly replacing the terribly fragmented data environment of old with a more integrated approach, we still have a long way to travel.

A Well-Designed Database Will Contain No Redundancy.

A well-designed database is one that meets users' needs, has adequate performance, and is relatively easy to maintain—in that order of importance.

The amount of data redundancy is important only to the extent that it detracts from these three goals. It is not an end in itself and, as pointed out in earlier chapters, some redundancy may actually be needed to enhance performance and maintainability.

The DBMS "Model" (Hierarchical, Network, or Relational) Is a Key Selection Criterion.

Not so. This notion emphasizes theory over concrete user needs. It also neglects the fact that today's DBMS technology is almost always a blend of all three models.

Making an assumption about the type of database that is needed prejudices the selection process. It confuses *what* we are trying to accomplish with *how* we are going to do it. This is a particularly common sin with respect to relational databases, which are sometimes acquired because they are relational and not because they will solve a concrete user problem.

Avoid worrying about the theoretical foundation of a DBMS. Concentrate on how well it meets your specific requirements.

Logical and Physical Design Are Completely Independent.

Some design activities are clearly "logical" (e.g., identifying entities) and others are almost entirely "physical" (e.g., choosing pointers). However, most decisions made during the design process will have both logical and physical implications.

For example, the decision to access invoice information directly without first accessing the customer record, requires the use of an invoice number. This may well lock us into a specific storage and access technique.

Sometimes, a desired "logical" feature can be physically implemented in a number of different ways. For example, there are almost always alternate techniques for achieving a desired set of logical relationships between records. However, there are times when compromise is necessary. This is frequently true when optimizing a database for a specific function. For example, we may need to design a database for fast, efficient updating and this may reduce its effectiveness in satisfying ad hoc queries.

Although we would like to design functionality into a database without worrying at all about its physical dimensions, this is not possible—at least at the present stage of computer technology.

The DBA or DRM Is (or Should Be) the "Czar" of Information Stewardship.

No one has a monopoly on the data that is critical to a company's work and no one can really "control" information. The concept of an all-knowing data administrator is misguided. Knowledge of how data is used and what it means is an integral part of knowing the business or the application. It is not something that can be picked up by attending database seminars.

People who know data best—whether they succesfully verbalize it or not—are the people who use it. Database administration is useful if it helps develop a common terminology (to the extent that this is possible), if it helps the end-user translate his data needs into systems that work, and if it contributes to greater system integration. Anything more ambitious will probably fail.

A Database Reflects All Relationships between Data.

Data relationships may or may not be important, and they may or may not be possible to describe and capture. For example, a customer database used to produce invoices and send sale announcements will not normally contain much customer demographic data. A customer's income may be important for market surveys but it is totally unimportant for mailing invoices. In addition, this information may be impossible (and, in some cases, illegal) to obtain.

This gets us back to the notion that a database, if it is to be useful, must be a "subject" database. It must describe data and relationships that are specific to at least one application.

"Data-Driven Design" Will Make the Analysis of Processes Almost Trivial.

Data-Driven Design is the conviction that, when building a system, the study of data is more important than the study of processes. Proponents of Data-Driven Design claim that data structures should precede the definition of processes and should be independent of them. In contrast, traditional development methodology emphasizes the determination of what a system must do *before*, rather than *after*, defining data.

The rationale behind Data Driven Design is that the type and structure of information needed to run a company changes little, but processes change constantly: they must reflect new markets, product line additions, new technology, etc. Therefore, once data is designed, the development of processes becomes almost trivial.

This is an appealing concept but is somewhat misleading. The advent of database and other technologies has certainly enabled us to provide mounds of data quickly—and this has focused everyone's attention on data.

However, computing does not occur in a vacuum. Information is useful only when we do something with it—produce paychecks, make decisions, and so on. This is where the critical importance of processes comes in. Unless we know *what* we wish to do, we cannot know *what data* is needed.

Data-Driven Design will influence, but not revolutionize, our thinking. It will provide a much needed emphasis on data but will not eliminate the need for disciplined and extensive analysis of processes.

DBMS and "Fourth-Generation" (4GL) Technology Will Make Application Programmers Extinct.

It is tempting to think that "user-friendly" software will enable end-users to develop their own systems with little or no help from the traditional data processing department. Alas, this is not the case. Two reasons mitigate against it: *specialization* and *underlying complexity*.

Specialization is what makes the modern industrial state. Instead of growing our own food, weaving our own cloth and building our own houses, we let others do it. Even when something is relatively simple and we are perfectly capable of doing it, the specialists take over. How many of us change the oil in our automobiles? Bake our own bread? Paint our own house? None of these things are particularly difficult and yet we let others do them.

For the same reason, an accountant, an architect, or a lawyer normally prefers to practice his own profession rather than play with computers. He wants to use the computer but he doesn't want to spend a great deal of time becoming a computer expert. Hence, the need for programmers.

The second reason programmers won't soon be out of work is complexity. The point at which an end user has the ability to access and manipulate data without help is often reached only after a mighty struggle by systems analysts and programmers to establish the baseline system.

Even modestly complex applications using the most user-friendly tools cannot be done entirely by end-users. For the most part, end-users are not experienced in the systematic analysis needed to build computer systems; nor do they possess the technical skills to design and generate databases, develop file conversion strategies, tune the system for optimum performance, etc. It is interesting to note that some of the most popular languages used by programmers today—Cobol, RPG, Mark 4—were originally created for end-users!

DISCUSSION QUESTIONS

Why are DBMS systems not necessarily faster than conventional systems?

Can all significant data in a corporation reside on a single database? Why or why not?

Is the presence of redundancy in a database necessarily bad? Explain.

Will programmers become extinct? Why or why not?

Will the emphasis on "Data Driven Design" render the analysis of processes trivial? Explain.

G

GLOSSARY

Access Method: Any technique for moving data between the computer's memory and input/output devices, enabling the retrieval and updating of data. The most commonly used access methods are sequential, random and various index-related methods such as IBM's popular Virtual Sequential Access Method (VSAM).

Addressing: A generic term that covers all the physical aspects of storing and retrieving data. Also see Access Method.

Ad Hoc: A Latin term meaning "to this"—for a specific purpose, case or situation. Refers to a query, report or other data manipulation that was not specifically defined when the system was built. The ability to perform ad hoc data manipulation is important because it is virtually impossible to predict all (or even most) user needs at the time an application system is developed.

Application: Used to describe data and computer programs oriented toward a business process such as preparing customer invoices, managing inventory or paying employees. This is in contrast to the operating system, utilities, the DBMS, and other support components.

Application System: A set of application programs oriented towards a specific business process, such as preparing a payroll.

Area: A contiguous portion of direct access storage that comprises all or part of a database. Each area contains a collection of records that are usually related in some fashion.

Assembler Language: A low-level (i.e., highly symbolic) computer language once widely used but now restricted to software and applications requiring high speed and complex manipulation of data. Also known as Assembler.

Association: The relational database term for Relationship. Also see Relationship.

Attribute: The relational term for Data Element.

Bachman Diagram: Graphic notation for illustrating data structures. Named for Charles Bachman, who invented the technique. Also called a Data Structure Diagram.

Back-end DBMS: See Database Machine.

Back-end Processor: See Database Machine.

Batch Processing: Refers to an application or process with one or more of the following characteristics: makes little or no use of teleprocessing facilities; sorts transactions into a convenient sequence before processing; and processes each group or batch of transactions through the entire system before processing the next group.

Before-and-After Images: Data logged to a journal file prior to the application of a change against a database and subsequent to a change. This is done in order to enable recovery in case of hardware or software failure.

Benchmark: This is a comparison test between two candidate software packages or between a proposed system and the one that is currently in use. Data access and updating speed are typically the characteristics that are benchmarked.

Block: An area of computer storage, temporarily reserved for use in performing an input/output operation, into which data is read or from which data is written.

Cell: A relational database term for the specific data value found at the intersection of a column and a row in a table. It is a single value of an attribute.

Chain: A series of records in a set relationship connected by pointers embedded in each record. The owner record points to the first occurrence of the member record. The first member points to the next occurrence of the member, etc., until the last occurrence of the member record is reached. It, in turn, points back to the owner, thus completing the chain.

Checkpoint: A snapshot of the current database and/or transaction record taken every one hundred, two hundred or other specified number of records during an update. In case of failure, the update can be restarted at the last checkpoint.

Child: The subordinate entity in a relationship between records or entities in a hierarchical database. Known as a member record in network terminology. Also see Parent.

Cobol: A high-level programming language characterized by English-like statements. It is very widely used for business applications. Originally, Cobol was an acronym for *CO*mmon *BU*siness *O*riented *L*anguage.

CODASYL: This is an acronym for the *C*onference on *D*ata *S*ystem *L*anguages, an organization composed of vendor and user representatives devoted to the creation of standards for data management languages and DBMS products. The so-called CODASYL standard reflects the network data model.

Column: A relational database term that refers to the vertical dimension of a table. It represents a single attribute.

Concurrency: The ability of multiple users to update a database simultaneously without damaging database integrity. An example of potential damage occurs when two people update related records at the same time without coordinating their changes. Concurrency is an extremely important consideration in selecting a DBMS.

Corporate Data Model: A conceptual representation of the major entities in a company and the relationships between them. The corporate data model is a theoretical construct, not a real database.

Cross Validation: The validation of data fields or records by checking against other fields or records, rather than against predetermined values. For example, the Net Pay field in a payroll record should not exist unless Gross Pay is present.

Database (DB): A collection of data that is logically organized to reflect the functional requirements and data interdependencies of one or more application systems. In the context of this book, a database is always accessed and updated by a Database Management System (DBMS).

Database Administration (DBA): The function that coordinates and technically supports DBMS-related activities in an organization.

Database Call: A Data Manipulation Language statement embedded in a host language program that enables database records to be read and written. The Call results in the creation of specific DBMS subroutines and/or macros for the needed task.

Database Machine: A specialized or dedicated hardware component that performs all, or most, DBMS functions traditionally performed by software. This may be a minicomputer connected wuth a mainframe system. Also called a Backend Processor or a Back-end DBMS.

Database Management System (DBMS): Software that provides the mechanism for defining, loading, storing, updating, and accessing application data on a database. It differs from conventional data access software in that it handles complex data structures, provides for independence of data from programs, enables control of redundancy, and usually includes a high-level data access language.

Data Compression: A technique that saves storage space in a database by eliminating blanks or shortening long values through codification.

Data Definition Language: The DBMS language that allows us to define the database to the DBMS through the creation of a schema and subschemas.

Data Dictionary (DD): A software product that maintains information about the database and may provide the ability to create schemas automatically. A Data Dictionary is usually integrated into a DBMS but can also be freestanding—that is, it may be useable with multiple DBMS's or even with conventional file systems.

Data-Driven Design: A concept that postulates the overwhelming importance of data in the development of an application. Processes are said to be less important because they change more frequently and are less stable than data definitions. This concept challenges the implied dominance of processes over data in traditional development methodologies.

Data Element: The smallest unit of data that, in and of itself, has meaning in describing information. Also known as a field or data item and, in relational terminology, an attribute.

Data Independence: The ability to change logical data definitions and relationships, as well as physical structures, without massive changes in application programs. An important DBMS characteristic.

Data Item: See Data Element.

Data Management System (DMS): A software product primarily designed to facilitate easy access to data via reports or on-line queries. It typically works with existing files or creates its own. It does not usually have the extensive data structuring and other capabilities provided by a DBMS.

Data Manipulation Language (DML): These are the instructions provided by the Host Language Interface for use in Cobol, Assembler, PL1 and other standard programming languages to access the database.

Data Redundancy: The repetition of the same data element or elements across different records or files. This may be needed in order to tie related records together or because incompatible applications need the same data. Redundancy tends to be reduced with a DBMS.

Data Resource Management (DRM): The concept of data as an important corporate asset that needs to be managed—the way cash, capital equipment and other corporate resources are managed. This requires common definitions of terms across organizational boundaries, the coordination of data collection and use, and the constant improvement of access capabilities. Also refers to the function or organizational unit that performs these tasks.

Data Structure Diagram: See Bachman Diagram.

DBMS Application: An application system that utilizes a Database Management System.

DBMS Software: All program products associated with a Database Management System.

Decision Support System (DSS): An application designed primarily to produce information for decisionmaking. This is in contrast to Transaction processing systems, which are designed to produce tangible products such as payroll checks or customer invoices. An example of DSS is a sales forecasting system that provides data for market planning. Also see Management Information System.

Dependency: The description of a relationship between data attributes or records in terms of how the value of one fixes, or determines, the value of the other. Dependency is an important tool in normalization.

Detail Design: The systems development step that brings the design of an application to its ultimate level of detail, allowing programs to be written and processing steps implemented. Also see Internal Design.

Direct Access: An access method that permits a record to be found by deriving its physical location from its key. This obviates the need to read the file sequentially. Also refers to peripheral storage devices, usually disk drives, that permit direct accessing.

Director of MIS: The top data processing officer in an organization.

Distributed Database: A database that is spread across a network of computers at geographically dispersed sites. Each site is essentially autonomous and performs functions of local interest as well as global functions that impact the system as a whole.

Domain: The set of all possible values for an attribute in a table in a relational database.

Electronic Data Processing (EDP): Generic term that refers to work done by computers or the organizational unit where such work is performed.

End-User: The individual or organizational unit that is the ultimate beneficiary of an application system. This term always refers to a business or functional area. Also see User.

Entity: A person, place, thing or event of interest to the enterprise about which data will be maintained on the database.

Entity-Relationship (E-R) Diagram: A database diagram illustrating logical relationships between entities. It is the precursor to a Bachman diagram, which represents actual records and their relationships. Although used extensively in designing network databases, an E-R Diagram can also be used for other data models.

Field: See Data Element.

File: A generic term that describes a set of similarly constructed records occupying a common space on tape or a mass storage device. Files usually represent one or a very limited number of record types—customer records, for example.

First Normal Form (1NF): Describes the state of a relational table or group of attributes in the beginning stages of Normalization. A table is in 1NF if each row is uniquely identified by a key and all attributes are functionally dependent on all or part of that key.

Flat File: A two-dimensional array of data items. All records in a flat file are of the same record type (e.g., A Customer file containing Customer records). Although relational databases consist of tables that are flat files, common usage has made the term synonomous with nondatabase systems.

Flat File System: An application based on traditional, non-DBMS technology.

Foreign Key: A relational database term that refers to an attribute which is repeated in another table and is that table's primary key. Foreign keys serve to link tables through common application data.

Fortran: A highly symbolic programming language with powerful mathematical capabilities. Used widely by the scientific community. Fortran was originally an acronym for *FOR*mula *TRAN*slator.

Fourth Generation: Software and hardware—but primarily the former—developed in the late 1970's and the 1980's to increase the productivity of computer programmers and end-users. It consists of products such as easy-to-use, English language-like query and report languages; screen development aids; prototyping facilities; code generators; flowcharting software; and DBMS's.

Fourth-Generation Language (4GL): Any high-level, easy-to-use, English-like computer language that can be used by people with little or no experience with computers.

Free Space: Empty space distributed throughout the area of a mass storage device reserved for a specific record type in a database. Free Space is used to accommodate new records.

Gantt Chart: A horizontal bar chart used to depict a plan for, and progress toward, the completion of a project. The Gantt chart was invented during World War II by the redoubtable Colonel Gantt.

Hierarchical: Refers to a DBMS in which some records are subordinate to others in a parent-child relationship where a child cannot have more than one parent. The most prominent example of a hierarchical DBMS is IBM's IMS.

Host Language: A standard programming language such as Cobol that is used to develop a database application. In order to access the database, a Host Language Interface is needed.

Host Language Interface: A component of the DBMS that makes it possible for application programs written in standard languages such as Cobol and Assembler to access data in the database. Access is accomplished by database "calls" embedded in the program and translated by the Host Language Interface into macros or subroutines understandable to the DBMS. The calls comprise the DBMS Data Manipulation Language (DML).

Integrated Database Management System (IDMS): Cullinet's IDMS is one of the earliest and most popular network DBMS's that substantially follows CODASYL standards.

Integrated Database Management System/Relational (IDMS/R): The new name for IDMS. It reflects the addition of some relational capabilities in Release 10, the latest version of the product.

Information Management System (IMS): IBM's IMS is one of the earliest and most popular DBMS products. Although it has evolved considerably over the years, it is still considered the most important example of a hierarchical model.

Index: A table or other file used to determine the location of a record containing a specific value.

Instance: Real data contained in one or more records spanning different but related record types. An example of an Instance is all the Parts for one Order for one Customer in a Customer Order database.

Internal Design: The design of the technical, as opposed to the functional or business-oriented, aspects of an application system. Internal Design is essentially synonomous with Detail Design, an older term. Also see Detail Design.

Intersection Data: Data that is found only at the intersection (or junction) of two or more records of different types that are related in a many-to-many relationship. For example, Quantity is Intersection Data for a Part and an Order record—that is, a specific Quantity is relevant only in the context of a specific Order and a specific Part.

Iterative Relationship: A relationship that exists between two or more occurrences of a single record type. An example is the relationship between a Project Team Member and a Project Team

Leader. Both are represented by the Employee record type but also have a Project Leader/Project Member relationship.

Join: A relational operator that pulls together rows from two or more tables based on a common value, such as a common Order Date.

Journal File: A record of changes to the database, often kept on a tape file. It may also include time-and-date, user identification, attempted security breaches and similar information.

Junction Record: A record created either to accommodate intersection data or to resolve a many-to-many relationship into several one-to-many relationships. This term is normally used in network terminology. Also see Intersection Data.

Key: A data element or attribute that identifies a record or, in relational parlance, the row of a table.

Logical: Refers to the way data and data relationships are perceived by an application program, programmer or user. This implies a functional or business orientation and may differ from the physical form data assumes on the database. For example, data that appears to be one logical record to an end-user may, in fact, consist of multiple physical records brought together from different parts of the database.

Macro: A set of program instructions used to perform data validation and other commonly used functions. Macros are always embedded in a host program, usually in assembler language. They differ from subroutines in that they are usually shorter and are assembled with the host program, rather than being called from the program library at execution time.

Management Information System (MIS): An application system that provides management with information used primarily to support strategic planning and policy making. MIS is often used as an umbrella term to describe *any* application that provides management with information. The term has also come to represent the organizational unit that performs the data processing function. Also see Decision Support System.

Member: The subordinate record in a set relationship that consists of one owner and one or more members. This is the network equivalent of the child segment in hierarchical terminology.

Microcomputer-Based DBMS: A DBMS designed specifically for personal computers or converted from a mainframe/mini version to run on a personal computer. Although these products are extremely useful, they are often limited in their ability to process large amounts of data, to support concurrent access by many users, or to provide adequate backup and recovery.

Modeling: In a database context, this is the process of building a logical data structure that can be converted into a working database.

Navigation: The process a program follows in order to find the desired record in a database. With most DBMS products, a series of records may need to be read and interrogated before the DBMS locates the desired record.

Network: A set of relationships between record types whereby any record type can be connected to any other record type. Record types are related to each other in an Owner/Member relationship. In contrast to a hierarchical structure in which a Member may have only one Owner, each Member in a Network may have more than one owner. Networks are based on Plex Structures. Also see Plex Structure.

Node: Each intersection point in a Tree or Plex structure.

Normalization: A formal process of organizing data into records in such a way as to minimize data redundancy and avoid update anomalies. Although usually associated with the design of relational databases, Normalization can also be used to advantage with other data models.

Occurrence: Real data for one record of a specific record type (e.g., Jones Manufacturing Company is an Occurrence of the Customer record).

On-Line Refers to computer programs or systems that provide immediate access to information through the use of teleprocessing facilities.

Operating System: The complex computer programs, usually provided by the hardware vendor, used to control execution of application programs and other software. Operating Systems allocate resources, monitor error conditions, select the next program for execution and perform many other control activities.

Overflow: A contiguous part of disk storage, usually at the end of each cylinder, reserved for record additions that have exceeded the allocation of free space. Also see Free Space.

Owner: The superior record in a set relationship that consists of one owner and one or more members. This is the network equivalent of the parent segment in hierarchical terminology.

Page: A physical division of data, often 4K bytes, transferred to and from storage when records are accessed or written. Often equivalent to a block.

Parent: The superior, or higher level, entity in a relationship between two records or segments in a hierarchical database. The parent is equivalent to an owner record in a network database.

Patch Program: A DBMS utility used to identify and, if possible, mend severed or damaged physical relationships, such as pointers, between records.

Path Analysis: The process of determining if a proposed database structure will allow desired data to be accessed and if such access is reasonably straightforward and efficient. This is done by navigating the database on paper or by running a prototype access program against a small test database.

Personal Computer (PC): A small, usually self-contained, usually single-user computer based on microprocessor technology. Examples of commonly used personal computers are Apple's Macintosh and IBM's XT and AT.

Physical: Refers to the way data is stored on the database, as opposed to the way it is presented to users.

Plex Structure: A data structure in which any record can be linked to any other record. The Plex structure forms the theoretical basis of a network database architecture. It stands in contrast to a tree structure, which is strictly hierarchical (i.e., a record can be linked to many other records in a downward direction but to only one record in an upward direction).

Pointer: The address of a record embedded in a related record. Used to navigate a database by going from one record to another.

Primary Key: A relational database term that refers to one or more attributes which, taken together, ensure the uniqueness of each row within a table. Sometimes used to describe the same phenomenon in non-relational databases.

Projection: A relational operator that extracts selected columns from a single table based on desired attribute values. Rows with redundant attribute values are usually not presented.

Prototype: A program that simulates or models key features of the final product. Usually written in a high-level language, a prototype enables users to experiment prior to the development of a production system. Sometimes the prototype code becomes the end product.

Purge: A DBMS utility program that recaptures the disk space used by records that have been deleted. Normally, space that was so occupied cannot be used to store new records until a purge has been run.

Query Language: A high-level, end-user oriented, interactive language that enables database access without a host language program.

Random Access: See Direct Access.

Real-Time: The concept of returning the results of a computer process quickly enough to enable the user to take action. For example, the ability to update a customer database with orders as they are called in enables customer service personnel to provide the latest product availability information.

Record: A group of related data elements or fields treated as one unit by an application program.

Record Type: Indicates the kind of record—from a functional perspective—that is being referenced (e.g., a Customer Record).

Recovery: Any procedure that corrects the effects of a software or machine failure on a flat file or database.

Redundancy: See Data Redundancy.

Referential Integrity: The state of owner/member occurrences whereby a member record cannot be added without the presence of an owner and, conversely, an owner cannot be deleted while members still exist. Some DBMS products can automatically ensure such a relationship, while others cannot, requiring application program code to perform the same function.

Relation: See Table.

Relational: Refers to a database consisting of a series of two-dimensional arrays, called tables, which store application data. A relational database has the ability to recombine data into many different relationships without the need for physical linkages.

Relationship: A property or characteristic shared by two or more data attributes or entities that makes them relate to each other in a specific way (e.g., Customer to Invoice). Called an Association in relational database terminology.

Reorganization: An operation required periodically for databases in order to improve performance and storage efficiency. New additions to a database eventually fill existing space and result in slow updating because available space is increasingly hard to find. Reorganizations are typically done by unloading data, reallocating available space and reloading data into the newly emptied database.

Replicated Database: A distributed database that is fully or partially recreated for multiple locations. For example, an inventory system running on distributed warehouse minicomputers may include complete copies of the customer database at each warehouse for inquiry purposes.

Report Language: A high-level language designed to assist programmers and, sometimes, end-users, in producing reports without the need for complex and time-consuming conventional programming languages. Also called a Report Writer.

Report Writer: See Report Language.

Request For Proposal (RFP): A document given to prospective bidders of DBMS and other computer products. It contains the requirements that the desired product is expected to fulfill, instructions on how and when the vendor is to reply, and the basis on which the vendor's products will be judged. The RFP is an orderly way to procure bids and review competing products.

Requirements Definition: The systems development step, during which the application is defined from a functional, business perspective. This includes major data inputs, screens, reports and files. Major technical characteristics may also be identified here.

Restart: Reinitiation of a job either from a prior checkpoint, the last record that was succesfully processed, or from the beginning. This takes place after a software or hardware failure.

Ring Structure: See Chain.

Root: The top node in a hierarchical structure or Tree. This term is specifically associated with IMS.

Row: A relational database term for one complete, horizontal entry in a table. A row is composed of one or more columns and is the equivalent of a record or segment in nonrelational databases. Also called a Tuple.

Schema: A complete description of all fields, records, data relationships and other components of a database. A schema is compiled by DBMS software.

Screen Formatter: A software product that helps programmers develop screens or "maps." This is done in lieu of specifying the multitude of control characters and other information required to define screens to a program.

Second Normal Form (2NF): Describes the state of a table when all attributes are fully dependent on the entire key.

Segment: The IMS term for a record type.

Selection: A relational operator that extracts rows from a table based on desired attribute values. The entire row is normally presented to the user.

Sequential: Access to, or storage of, records in sequence, usually by some key value.

Set: A collection of related records in a database. In a "physical" sense, this consists of one occurrence of an owner record and zero, one, or more occurrences of its member records. In a "logical" sense, a set consists of an owner record type and the member record types we choose to attach to it.

Simulation: The process of approximating run times or other characteristics for an application. In a DBMS context, simulation attempts to predict the performance of a specific database design for a specific application.

Software: Generic term used to describe all computer programs. Frequently refers to operating systems, utilities and other support programs, as opposed to application programs.

Subject Database: A database specifically designed either for one or for a limited number of applications. This is in contrast to a "corporate" database, which contains important data for the entire organization. Most databases are subject databases.

Subroutine: A single-function computer program that performs a task commonly needed throughout an installation. Subroutines are always used in conjunction with regular, multifunction programs. They are called by those programs at execution time but assembled or compiled apart from those programs. An example of a subroutine is a program that calculates future dates based on a start date plus a desired number of days.

Subschema: The description of that part of a database specifically needed by an application program. Subschemas enable access to appropriate information without violating security restrictions (e.g., a personnel clerk cannot examine employee medical histories; a nurse using a medical inquiry program can). Subschemas are compiled by DBMS software.

System Development Life Cycle (SDLC): The steps normally required to develop and implement an application system. These steps are identified by different names and subdivided in various ways depending on the life cycle methodology that is used. The SDLC usually consists of a feasibility study, the definition of functional requirements, technical design, program development, and installation.

Table: A two-dimensional data array consisting of columns and rows containing application data.

Third Normal Form (3NF): Describes the state of a relational table in the stage of Normalization that is sufficient to satisfy normal data structure requirements. A table is in 3NF when it is in 2NF and all transitive dependencies between nonkey attributes have been removed. Also see Second Normal Form.

Throwaway: A prototype that is not used as the ultimate production version.

Transaction: The record of an external event, usually of a temporary, repeating nature (e.g., a withdrawal from inventory).

Transaction Processing System: An application system designed primarily to produce tangible products such as payroll checks or customer bills. This is in contrast to systems used primarily for decision-making purposes.

Tree Structure: A structure that the hierarchical data model follows. It describes record relationships whereby each record can have many records in a subordinate position but can have only one record that is superior to it. Also see Parent and Child.

Tuning: The process of improving the performance of a DBMS by modifying the physical arrangements used to store and access data.

Tuple: See Row.

Update Anomaly: A condition whereby data cannot be added, is inadvertently deleted, or requires redundant updating because of poor record design. Usually associated with tables or records which have not been normalized to Third Normal Form.

User: The ultimate or intermediary recipient of data from a database. The former is usually part of the business function and is usually called an end-user. The latter is a programmer or systems analyst who uses the data and the facilities of the DBMS to provide the end-user with a workable product.

User Friendly: Software that is easy to use by either an end-user or an intermediate user such as a programmer.

Utility: A computer program that supports the development, operation, or maintenance of application systems. Examples are sorts, reorganization programs (in a DBMS environment), and performance monitors.

ACR

ACRONYM CROSS REFERENCE

CODASYL	Conference on Data System Languages
DB	Database
DBA	Database Administration
DBMS	Database Management System
DD	Data Dictionary
DDL	Data Definition Language
DMS	Data Management System
DML	Data Manipulation Language
DRM	Data Resource Management
DSS	Decision Support System
E-R	Entity-Relationship
1NF	First Normal Form
4GL	Fourth-Generation Language
IDMS	Integrated Data Management System
IDMS/R	Integrated Data Management System/Relational
IMS	Information Management System
MIS	Management Information System
PC	Personal Computer
RFP	Request For Proposal
2NF	Second Normal Form
SDLC*	Systems Development Life Cycle
3NF	Third Normal Form

*In this context, this is not IBM's Synchronous Data Link Control communications protocol.

B

BIBLIOGRAPHY

BYERS, ROBERT A. *Everyman's Database Primer, Featuring dBase III Plus.* Torrance, CA: Ashton-Tate Publishing Group, 1986.

CERI, STEFANO, AND GIUSEPPE PELAGATTI. *Distributed Databases.* New York: McGraw-Hill Book Company, 1984.

CHEN, PETER. *Data Base Management Monograph No. 6: The Entity-Relationship Approach to Logical Data Base Design.* Wellesley, MA: Q.E.D. Information Sciences, Inc., 1977.

DATE, C. J. *A Guide to DB2.* Reading, MA: Addison-Wesley Publishing Company, 1985.

DATE, C. J. *An Introduction to Database Systems, Volume 1,* 4th ed. Reading, MA: Addison-Wesley Publishing Company, 1985.

DATE, C. J. *Relational Database.* Reading, MA: Addison-Wesley Publishing Company, 1986.

FLORES, IVAN. *Data Base Architecture.* New York: Van Nostrand Reinhold Company, 1981.

GAYDASCH, ALEXANDER, JR. *Principles of EDP Management.* Reston, VA: Reston Publishing Company, 1982.

HANNAN, JAMES, ED. *Data Base Management.* Pennsauken, N.J.: Auerbach Publishers, Inc., 1982.

KAPP, DAN, AND JOSEPH F. LEBEN. *IMS Programming Techniques.* New York: Van Nostrand Reinhold Company, 1978.

KING, JUDY M. *Evaluating Data Base Management Systems.* New York: Van Nostrand Reinhold Company, 1981.

MARTIN, JAMES. *Computer Data-Base Organization.* Englewood Cliffs, N.J.: Prentice-Hall, Inc., 1977.

MARTIN, JAMES. *An End-User's Guide to Data Base.* Englewood Cliffs, N.J.: Prentice-Hall, Inc., 1981.

MARTIN, JAMES. *Principles of Data-Base Management.* Englewood Cliffs, N.J.: Prentice-Hall, Inc., 1976.

ROSS, RONALD G. *Data Base Systems.* New York: AMACOM, A Division of the American Management Association, 1981.

ROSS, RONALD G. *Data Dictionaries and Data Administration.* New York: AMACOM, A Division of the American Management Association, 1981.

TAYLOR, ALLEN G. *R:Base 5000 User's Guide.* Indianapolis: Que Corporation, 1986.

WELDON, JAY-LOUISE. *Data Base Administration.* New York: Plenum Press, 1981.

INDEX